Doing Business in Shanghai

2004 Edition

*China*Knowledge Press *Private Limited*

www.chinaknowledge.com

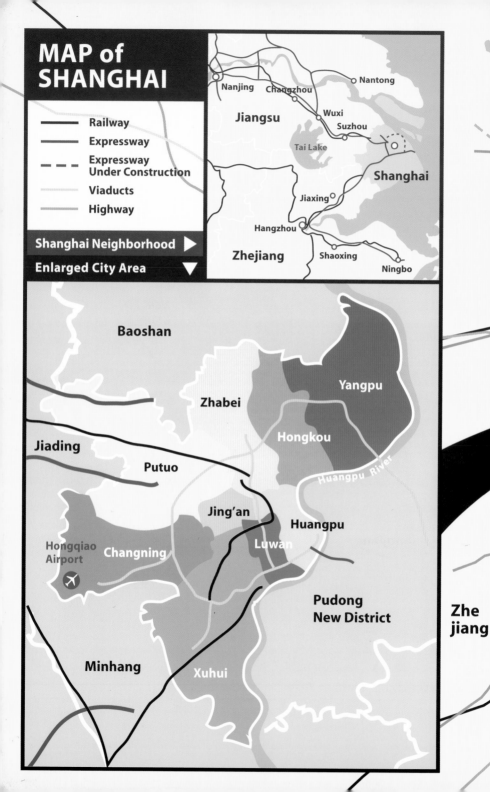

We would appreciate it if readers could alert us as to errors and omissions by writing in to:

China Knowledge Private Limited
Doing Business in Shanghai Editor
8 Temasek Boulevard
#37-01A Suntec Tower Three
Singapore 038988

ISBN 981-4163-01-5

Printed in Singapore

Foreword

I am pleased to bring you the Second Edition of Doing Business in Shanghai. In this edition, we feature some of the most popular investment hotspots in Shanghai, and give you the latest statistics and data to guide your investment decisions in this booming economy.

China has consistently registered healthy growth rates in recent years. Even as economies reeled from the effects of the Sars outbreak and the Iraqi War in 2003, I was confident that China's strong economic resilience would stand her in good stead. At a seminar on the Sars crisis hosted by China Knowledge last year, I had posited 8.5% GDP growth rate for China at year-end – a figure that defied the estimates of every analyst.

My confidence was not misplaced. China surprised the world with a whopping 9.1% growth.

As global interest in China continues unabated, China attracted a total of USD 53.5 billion in Foreign Direct Investment (FDI) last year. Of the various economic regions in China, the Yangtze River Delta, with Shanghai as the "Dragon Head", has been an investor favorite. More than one-third of China's total FDI inflow in 2003 was committed along this Delta region.

Shanghai itself had consistently outperformed the country's overall growth rate. In 2003, its GDP growth rate peaked at 11.8%. With the forthcoming Formula One Powerboat Championships in August, Formula One Grand Prix in September and then EXPO 2010 all held in Shanghai, the mood in the investment market is bullish and exuberant. Shanghai's economy is expected to attain new heights.

The future holds much promise for Shanghai's continued economic prosperity and growth. We invite investors to share in her success.

Charles Chaw C. Loong
Managing Director
China Knowledge Press

July 2004
Singapore

CONTENTS

Doing
Business in

Major Industries

Directory

SOLVING YOUR BUSINESS PUZZLE

With experience, expertise and an extensive research network in China, ***China Knowledge Press*** brings you our series of unique products – **China Market Research Reports**. These high-quality research reports are prepared with the best methodologies and the most rigorous standards of quality control, by our team of experienced professionals. Our clients use CKP's unique China Market Research Reports to assist them in making strategic market decisions and managing risks in China's growing market.

Newly Released Reports

SHANGHAI TODAY

In the first quarter of 2004, Shanghai's economic development had accelerated so rapidly the municipal authorities found it necessary to rein in lending by state-controlled commercial banks. It was a move to prevent the economy from being over-heated.

This prompted many economists to ask: "Is the economy getting too hot to handle?" The answer is both yes and no. Yes, because certain sectors are attracting excessive funds, and the threat of an over-supply situation is looming. The building and construction industry is a case in point. No, because some other sectors are still in dire need of funds to achieve greater pace of development. The agricultural and the energy industries are good examples in this regard.

So the city government has a delicate balancing act to play: how to ensure money flows to the right areas to ensure a more equitable situation. One quick answer would be to improve the quality of investment in the economy and prevent further escalation of bad loans in the banking system.

Brighter Economic Prospects

By all accounts, the outlook of the economy this year is even brighter than in 2003, even though pressure from unemployment and inflation may need closer attention. With the opening up of more sectors to foreign businessmen, particularly the financial and service sectors, an increasing number of investors are waiting in the wings to jump on to the bandwagon. The number of foreign contracts continue to multiply. Foreign investment continues to flow into Shanghai.

Today, Shanghai remains one of the hottest destinations for foreign direct investment (FDI) in China. It is leading many cities in economic performance, foreign trade growth and infrastructural development. This, coupled with a stable political situation and secure investment environment, has made it a hot spot for attracting hot money. So long as the city

FDI Top Ten Countries / Regions 2003

Source: www.sfisc.com

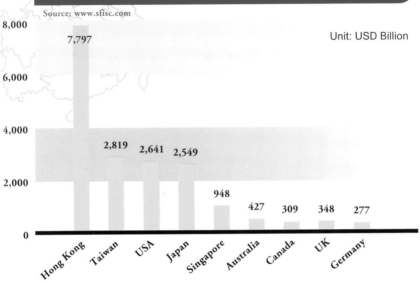

Unit: USD Billion

- Hong Kong: 7,797
- Taiwan: 2,819
- USA: 2,641
- Japan: 2,549
- Singapore: 948
- Australia: 427
- Canada: 309
- UK: 348
- Germany: 277

FDI in Different Industries 2003

Source: www.sfisc.com

Unit: USD Billion

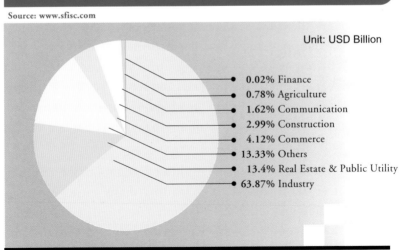

- 0.02% Finance
- 0.78% Agriculture
- 1.62% Communication
- 2.99% Construction
- 4.12% Commerce
- 13.33% Others
- 13.4% Real Estate & Public Utility
- 63.87% Industry

government is able to ensure that inflow of funds is channeled to the most productive areas, an even steadier pace of economic expansion may be realized in the near future.

Last year, it is estimated that the city achieved a record RMB 624 billion (USD 75 billion) in Gross Domestic Product (GDP), up 11.8% year-on-year, the highest growth rate since 1998. For this year, as the favorable domestic and international economic situation looks likely to stay, another 7% growth in GDP can be expected. But, as the city gears up for the World Expo 2010, economists believe that growth rate of more than 10% is not unachievable.

As for industrial output, initial estimates for last year was RMB 285 billion (USD 33 billion) in value added, up 17.5% year-on-year. The high-tech sector accounted for 26.5% of local industrial output. The service sector was estimated to have grown by 8% and agriculture by 2.3%. Information transmission and computer and software services witnessed the fastest growth among local service industries.

The high growth rate of the real estate industry is expected to result in an increase of 12% in fixed assets investment to reach RMB 245 billion (USD 29.5 billion) while local fiscal revenues are expected to report a 10-year high growth rate of 32.5%.

Future Challenges

Shanghai's population had soared to 13.4 million in the past year as more than three million new job seekers flock to the city in search of employment. The rapid shift of workforce from the agricultural sector to the industrial sector is likely to accelerate. Job creation therefore has become one of the top priorities.

But faster industrial growth has brought about soaring demand for electricity, resulting in the current severe shortage in energy supply. Traffic congestion, which may slow down economic development, is another pressing problem the city has to overcome urgently. The greatest threat, however, is still inflation. Its negative effects can be extremely disruptive. Ensuring moderate wage increases is imperative if continued economic growth is to be assured.

In the coming years, the economically progressive and culturally rich metropolitan is certain to attract more foreign businessmen from various parts of the world. Currently, foreign-invested enterprises already make up about one-third of the city's total economy. The impact of entry to the WTO is that many restrictions on trade have been removed, and a more congenial environment is created for the business community.

However, competition is getting keener by the day, and not only between foreign and local businesses; an increasing number of foreign enterprises are descending on the city in search of a share of the economic pie. Newcomers invariably face competition from well-entrenched local companies as well as major Japanese and European corporations already well-established internationally.

Nevertheless, as the number of competitors swells, the market in Shanghai continues to expand at a rapid pace. Under the current Unification Concept, Shanghai, the "Dragon Head", is expected to lead in the further development of the surrounding regions in the Yangtze River Delta Economic Zone, providing investors with greater room for maneuver and more opportunities to explore.

It is said that 2003 was an extraordinary year for Shanghai. For this year, and the years ahead, Shanghai can also be your key to unlock the largely under-explored markets in the hinterland.

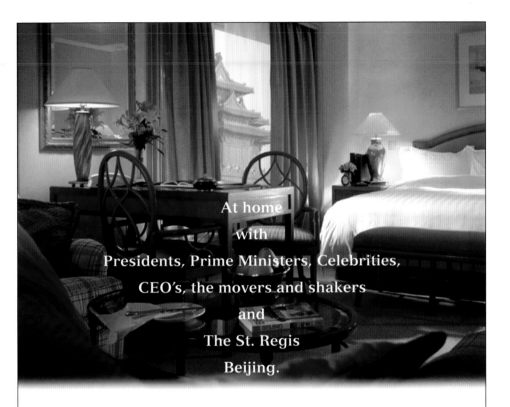

HISTORY

Shanghai – Old and New

Up until the 7th century AD, Shanghai, then known as "Hu" or "Shen" (after the local bamboo fishing traps), was a barely developed marshland. Most of eastern modern Shanghai did not exist until the 17th century, when a complex web of canals was built to drain the region.

Shanghai began as Huating County, an administrative district established in the year 751 AD. In 991 AD, the town of Shanghai was set up. During the period of 1260-1274, the town evolved into an important trading port, and in 1292, the then central government of Yuan Dynasty approved the formal establishment of Shanghai County in the area. This is widely considered as the official beginning of the city of Shanghai.

An ideal port, Shanghai is the gateway to the mighty Yangtze River. With the British opening their first concession in Shanghai in 1842, after the first Opium War, and the French turning up in 1847, it was not long before an International Settlement was established. When the Japanese arrived in 1895, the city was divided into settlements by the foreigners, all autonomous and immune from Chinese law.

The world's greatest institutions of finance and commerce descended upon Shanghai in the 1930s. A period of commercialization and industrialization followed. In the next half century, Shanghai developed a distinctly western character and experienced a period of economic prosperity. It had the tallest buildings in Asia, and more motor vehicles on its streets than the rest of China put together.

End of the Old Era

When the Communists gained control of the country in 1949, they took on the job of eradicating slums, rehabilitating hundreds of thousands of opium addicts, and stamping out child and slave labor.

In spite of political upheavals, the city continued to grow, with new underground stations, highways crisscrossing the city, the most modern stock exchange in the world, a spanking new airport, two gigantic bridges and a whole new city in Pudong. By the mid-1990s more than half the world's high-rise pylons were looming over Shanghai. In the space of a decade, Shanghai had re-emerged as one of the world's great cities.

A Dynamic Cosmopolitan City

In late 1978, after Mr. Deng Xiaoping rose to power, he initiated a program of market liberalization and reforms to promote China's economic development. In 1984, Shanghai was designated among the 14 coastal cities open for foreign investment.

To rebuild its glory in the past and to lead the economic development of the whole Yangtze River Delta, the state government inaugurated Pudong New District, previously a piece of sleeping farmland, in 1990.

In the 1990s, the city grew rigorously as new subways, highways, and expressways crisscrossed its territory. The stock exchange, numerous skyscrapers and luxurious hotels appeared, almost overnight. Foreign influence had once again made Shanghai a Chinese consumer haven.

Although Beijing remains China's capital city, Shanghai is known as the de facto economic, financial, international trade and transportation center of the mainland. It may soon regain its mantle as Asia's most dynamic cosmopolitan city.

GEOGRAPHY

Location

As part of the Yangtze River Delta Plain, Shanghai has low, open terrain about four meters above sea level, crisscrossed by a maze of natural waterways of the Taihu drainage basin. The Huangpu River and its tributaries are the major waterways of the city.

Shanghai is located at 120°29'E and 31°14'N on the Yangtze River estuary in eastern China. To its east lies the East China Sea and to its south Hangzhou Bay. Chongming Island, north of Shanghai, sits in the middle of Yangtze River. Shanghai borders Jiangsu Province and Zhejiang Province in the northwest and southwest respectively.

Shanghai is 1,460 km away from the capital city of China, Beijing, and only an hour's ride from Suzhou, an emerging economic center of Jiangsu, and two hours' drive from Hangzhou, Zhejiang's provincial capital, via train or expressway.

Topography

Shanghai is predominantly made up of flatlands with only a few lowlands and small hills in its southwest. The average altitude of the municipality is about 4 meters. Qingpu, Songjiang and Jinshan were under sea level until 6,000 years ago. The land area east of Jiading-Fengxian line was not formed until the ocean regressed from the mainland 4,000 years ago.

Dianshan Lake, 63 km² in size, lies to Shanghai's west where altitude is below the city's average level. There is a dense waterway network in Shanghai. Two rivers form its trunk – Huangpu River (114 km) and Wusong River, or Suzhou Creek (125 km), with the latter a tributary of the former. Huangpu River runs northwestward through the city's entire territory and pours into Yangtze River at Wusong. It is the busiest river way for Shanghai Port. However, due to gradual river channel sedimentation and frequent shipment of large tonnage vehicles, Shanghai will soon set up a deepwater seaport off its southeast coast.

Chongming Island of Shanghai, with a total land area of 1,083 km², is the third largest island in China, albeit far smaller than Taiwan and Hainan. There are still a few islands set in the north and the south of Shanghai's sea area, such as Changxing island and Dajinshan island. Dajinshan mountain, with a height of 103 m above sea level, is actually the peak in Shanghai.

Land Area

In 1949, the total area of Shanghai was only 636 km². In 1958, 10 counties of Jiangsu joined the city and expanded its territory by almost 10 times. In 2001, Shanghai Municipality measured 6,340.5 km², a mere 0.06% of the country's total. The territory spans over 120 km from north to south and is latitudinally 100 km wide. The total land area is 6,219 km² and water surface 122 km². As two more counties were approved as districts of the municipality in early 2001, Chongming is now the only county left in Shanghai.

Population

Shanghai's population was 13.4 million in 2003. This figure excludes a floating population of more than 3 million.

The official unemployment rate was 4.9% in 2003. This figure does not include many laid-off workers or those not actively seeking work.

When the People's Republic of China was founded in 1949, Shanghai had a population of only 5.2 million, which already made it the largest city in the country. During the period of 1954-1984, Shanghai sent 1.39 million people out of the city for economic construction elsewhere in China. Due to its well-managed system of birth control, Shanghai became the first city with a negative natural population growth rate in 1993.

As Shanghai's economy is taking off, it attracts human influx as well as investment. Statistics show that transitional population in Shanghai is estimated at 3.87 million, or one in four people you meet in Shanghai may probably come from elsewhere.

Climate

Located in northern subtropical oceanic monsoon climate zone, Shanghai has four distinctive seasons and abundant sunshine and rainfall. Spring and autumn are short; summer and winter relatively long. Average annual temperature stands at 15.7°C. July and August are normally the hottest months in the year, with average temperature at 28°C; the lowest average temperature is usually recorded in January, about 4°C. Extreme temperature sometimes reaches 36~37°C in summer and −5~7°C in winter.

Shanghai Climate

Month	Mar	Apr	May	Jun	Jul	Aug	Sep	Oct	Nov	Dec	Jan	Feb
Season	Spring			Summer			Autumn			Winter		
Average Temp.(°c)	8.3	14	18.8	22.3	27.8	27.7	23.6	18	12.3	6.2	3.5	4.6
Average Highest Temp.(°c)	12.6	18.5	23.2	27.3	31.8	31.6	27.4	22.4	16.8	10.7	7.6	8.7
Average Lowest Temp.(°c)	4.9	10.4	15.3	20.1	24.7	24.7	20	14.3	8.6	2.7	0.3	1.4
Rainfall (mm)	78.1	106	122.9	158.9	134.2	126	150.5	50.1	48.8	40.9	44	62.6
Dress Recommended	Woolen Sweater, Coat			Shirt			Long-sleeved Shirt, Woolen Sweater, Coat			Woolen Sweater, Overcoat		

Frost-free period lasts 230 days in Shanghai, approximately, and annual precipitation is around 1,200 mm. However, 60% of the total rainfall is recorded in the high-water season from May to September. There is a so-called "plum rains" period from mid-June to early July when rains are almost incessant. Typhoons often occur during the July-September period.

GOVERNMENT

Political Structure of Shanghai Municipality

COMMUNIST PARTY IN CHINA

Shanghai Municipal Committee
Secretary General: **Mr. Chen Liangyu**

POLITICAL CONSULTATION

Shanghai Committee of
Chinese People's Political
Consultative Conference
Chairman: **Mr. Wang Liping**

LEGISLATURE

Shanghai Municipal People's
Congress & Standing Committee
Chairman: **Mdm. Chen Tiedi**

ADMINISTRATION

Shanghai Municipal People's Government
Governor: **Mr. Chen Liangyu**

People's
Government
of 18 Districts
and 1 County

More than 50
Functional Bureaus,
Commissions,
& Offices

JUDICIARY

Shanghai High People's
Court, 3 Intermediate,
19 Subordinate courts
& Maritime Court

**Shanghai People's
Procuratorate**

CPC Shanghai Municipal Committee

A socialist state, China is led by the Communist Party of China (CPC). In Shanghai, the CPC Municipal Committee is the paramount authority. It exercises great influence and power in the city's political and economic progress, and ensures social stability and security.

In November 2002, Mr. Chen Liangyu succeeded Mr. Huang Ju as secretary-general of the CPC Shanghai Municipal Committee when the latter was placed in the CPC's nine-member Politburo Standing Committee. Chen is also the governor of Shanghai (see also *Administration*).

Political Consultation

Apart from the CPC, there are also eight non-Communist parties, or "participating political parties", which coexist with the CPC, and have participated in important discussions concerning the state's political issues.

The Chinese People's Political Consultative Conference (CPPCC) is the main political platform for the non-Communist parties to communicate with the CPC, to express their political views, exercise democratic supervision, and participate in some policy-making activities related to economic and political reforms. Each of these non-Communist parties has an established committee in Shanghai:

- China Association for the Promotion of Democracy
- China Democratic National Construction Association
- China Democratic League
- Chinese Peasants and Workers' Democratic Party
- China Zhigong Party
- Jiusan Society
- China Kuomintang Revolutionary Committee
- Taiwan Democratic Self-governance League

Within the Shanghai Committee of CPPCC, there are eight specific subcommittees and one administrative department. The current chairman of the Shanghai Committee of CPPCC is Mr. Wang Liping.

Source: shszx.eastday.com

Legislature

Underpinning the political system of China is the nation's legislative body, the People's Congress. In Shanghai, the Shanghai Municipal People's Congress (SMPC) exercises local legislative power. It revises and supervises the implementation of the local regulations; examines, approves and implements Shanghai's economic and social development plans as well as the municipal government's reports and budget. Finally, it also decides and selects the SMPC Standing Committee, the municipal governor, vice-governors, the chief of Shanghai High Court and the chief procurator of Shanghai Procuratorate.

The members of the People's Congress are elected for a term of five years. The current SMPC representatives were elected in 1998. The SMPC typically meets once a year, and when not in session, a Standing Committee assumes its place. The SMPC comprises nine working committees with specific functions, an administrative department, and a research office. The current chairman of the SMPC is Mdm. Chen Tiedi.

Source: www.spcsc.sh.cn

Administration

The Shanghai Municipal People's Government is the administrative organ of the metropolis. The Shanghai governor is Mr. Chen Liangyu, who was elected with his eight deputies in the 5th session of the 11th SMPC in February 2002.

The Shanghai Municipal People's Government exercises administrative functions through its various bureaus and commissions. It also leads subordinate governments at district or county level.

Economic Development

Shanghai Development Planning Commission

Its main duties include:
- creating medium and long-term strategies for urban, economic, and social development;
- setting annual economic and social development targets and forecasts, and monitoring economic growth;
- formulating industrial policy, coordinating sector balance, and developing high-tech industries;

- planning and financing key public projects, and approving and reporting to the State Council on the development of large projects;
- directing Foreign Direct Investment (FDI) inflows;
- setting, adjusting and supervising prices and administrative fees; and,
- analyzing demand-supply conditions, and implementing the State's plans on key exports and imports.

Source: www.jhw.sh.gov.cn

Shanghai Economic Commission

Its main duties include:

- implementing industrial development laws, rules, regulations and policies;
- supervising and analyzing the development tendency of local industries;
- setting development plans for local high-tech, pillar and urban industry; and,
- guiding state-owned enterprises in restructuring.

Source: www.shec.gov.cn

Shanghai Industrial and Commercial Administration

Its main duties include:

- implementing relevant laws, rules, regulations and policies;
- registering industrial and commercial enterprises – checking and verifying registered company names, and issuing certificates upon approval;
- monitoring misdemeanors in the local market, such as monopoly, illegal competition and fraud;
- dealing with customers' complaints and protecting customers' rights;
- monitoring and administering advertisement distribution, and companies' operations; and,
- protecting copyright of registered brands, and supervising the use and printing of brands.

Source: www.sgs.gov.cn

Shanghai Commerce Commission

Its main duties include:

- implementing relevant laws, rules, regulations and policies on commerce;
- studying and preparing development plans for commerce in Shanghai, and adjusting and controlling reserves of strategic commodities;
- promoting innovations in marketing, encouraging development in chain stores, distribution and logistics, brokerage, and direct sales;
- pushing forward technological advancement and development of E-commerce ;
- guiding and monitoring organizations including restaurants, hotels and advertising firms, and supervising alcohol, salt, butchery, auction, and leasing businesses.

Source: syw.sh.gov.cn

Shanghai Foreign Economic Relations and Trade Commission

Its main duties include:

- implementing laws, regulations and policies related to foreign trade, foreign investment and other foreign economic cooperation matters;
- formulating strategies for promoting foreign investment and foreign trade;
- dealing with applications for foreign-funded project and approving the establishment of foreign-invested enterprises (FIEs);
- examining, guiding and monitoring the development of export-processing industries and entrepot trade; and,
- inviting foreign organizations to visit Shanghai and arranging for Shanghai officials to participate in international events.

Source: www.smert.gov.cn

Shanghai Foreign Investment Board

Its main duties include:

- examining and approving the establishment of FIEs;

Shanghai Foreign Investment Board
15/16F, New Hongqiao Plaza, 83 Loushanguan Road, Shanghai 200336
Tel:86 21 6236 8800   Fax:86 21 6236 8024

The board also has representative offices in Los Angeles, Osaka, London and Frankfurt.

• **Los Angeles Representative Office**
#425 World Trade Center, 350 South Figueroa Street, Los Angeles, CA 90071 USA
Tel:1 213 625 1890   Fax:1 213 625 1935

• **Osaka Representative Office**
Tel:81 6 6615 5523   Fax:81 6 6615 5531

• **London Representative Office**
G/F Bank of China Building, 90 Cannon Street, London EC4N 6HA, UK
Tel:44 20 7626 8088   Fax:44 20 7626 8089

• **Frankfurt Representative Office**
Tel:49 160 9114 9540

Source: www.investment.gov.cn

- appraising and redirecting foreign-funded projects with investment amount of more than what the municipal authorities can approve;
- issuing certificates of registered FIEs and Taiwan, Hong Kong, Macau-invested enterprises; and,
- leading subordinate organizations in districts and counties in relevant matters.

Urban Planning and Construction

Shanghai Construction and Administration Committee
- oversees urban and rural construction;
- administers and regulates the construction (including renovation and decoration) industry and construction material industry; and,
- organises the examination and preliminary designs of approved projects.

Source: www.shucm.sh.cn

Shanghai Urban Planning Administration Bureau

- implements laws, regulations and policies pertaining to urban planning;
- organises Shanghai urban master planning and detailed planning;
- examines and approves planning and urban design projects;
- administers and follows up on the issue of permits for construction land and project plans;
- participates in outdoor advertisement examination and approval;
- showcases urban planning, organises and manages urban planning.

Source: www.shghj.gov.cn

Shanghai Housing Development Board

Led by Shanghai Construction and Administration Committee, it undertakes the tasks of urban housing development and construction administration in Shanghai.

Source: www.housing.sh.cn

Shanghai Municipal Engineering Administration Bureau

The bureau is responsible for civil engineering projects in Shanghai, which include the construction and maintenance of city streets, roads, bridges, tunnels and piping works.

Source: www.shsz.gov.cn

Shanghai Urban Transportation Administration Bureau

The bureau is in charge of the planning, construction and maintenance of urban transportation facilities, including public transport interchanges, river ports and routes, stops or stations for passenger and cargo.

Source: www.jt.sh.cn

Shanghai Port Authority

The Authority manages the construction and daily operations of wharves, and transfer of coastal line use.

Source: www.portshanghai.com.cn

Others

Shanghai Finance Administration (Local Tax Bureau)

The bureau is in charge of the local public finance and budget plan, implementation of national fiscal policies, and collection and distribution of fiscal revenues.

Source: www.csj.sh.gov.cn

Shanghai News & Publication Bureau (Copyright Administration)

The bureau generates development plans for the local publishing industry, examines and approves books, newspapers, magazines and electronic publications, and monitors subject selection of local publications.

Source: cbj.sh.gov.cn

Shanghai Statistics Bureau

The bureau collects, analyses and provides statistical information on Shanghai's economic and social development conditions.

Source: www.stats-sh.gov.cn

Judiciary

Courts

The Shanghai municipal judiciary system consists of the Shanghai High People's Court, two intermediate people's courts, subordinate courts in each district or county, and two special courts – a railway intermediate court and Shanghai Maritime Court. Civil and criminal cases can be heard in the normal courts and the party who loses the lawsuit may appeal to the higher courts. Technically, China's Supreme People's Court has the final judgment. However, most cases are settled before they reach the intermediate courts or high courts.

Source: www.hshfy.sh.cn

Procuratorate

Shanghai People's Procuratorate reports to the People's Congress and its Standing Committee. Its main duties are prosecution of government officials guilty of corruption, embezzlement, assault and battery, and misconduct; hearing of criminal cases; and supervision over court's judgments.

Source: www.shjcy.sh.cn

For contact information of other government agencies in Shanghai, please refer to the Directory in Section 4 of this Guide.

INFRASTRUCTURE AND TRANSPORTATION

Introduction

In an all-out effort to build Shanghai into an international metropolis through the utilization of advanced technology, the city is now fully geared towards a three-pronged expansion of its infrastructure, namely land, air and sea. With the forthcoming World Expo 2010, the construction of a world class transportation system has taken a top priority.

Shanghai is one of China's old industrial bases. Since the founding of new China, Shanghai has invested USD 20 billion in urban infrastructure facilities. Important projects include the inner-ring elevated highway, the north-south overhead highway, the No.1 subway route, the multiple tracking of the tunnel in east Yan'an road and the Shanghai section of the Shanghai-Nanjing Expressway.

The city has now taken on an entirely new look. Modernization over the past 20 years has injected the city with new vitality. It is now China's leading industrial and commercial center.

Land Transportation

Metro

The economic boom in Shanghai, which has a population reaching 13.4 million in 2003 (20 million if floating population is included), had created such a surge in traffic by the end of the 1980s that the transportation system was grossly inadequate.

The city's authorities decided to adopt a program, phased over 40 years, that would include 11 metro lines covering over 325 km. The subway, known locally as Metro, is one of the youngest in the world. The first line (Metro Line 1) was opened in 1995 as a north-south axis from Shanghai Railway

Station to the southern suburbs. The first 27.3 km section of Metro Line 2 followed four years later, running from Pudong to Puxi (west of the Huangpu River) and intersecting Line 1 at People's Square.

Line 3, the 19-station Pearl Line, also has the main station as its focal point, but loops northwards from Shanghai South Station to Zhongshan Park and terminates at Jiangwan Zhen. Starting with 25 km and 19 stations, it will eventually be 62 km in length. Since 2002, the number of trains running on the three lines has substantially increased.

The elaborate plan adopted by the Shanghai Metro Corporation for 2025 envisages a comprehensive network of 11 lines, supported by seven light rail routes. Line 1 is being further extended from the current terminal at Shanghai railway station to Baoshan district in the northern part of the city. The Pearl Line will link Minghang District in the southwest and Baoshan District in the north.

Metro Lines 4 and 5 are expected to link the southwest and northeast parts of the city, Pudong New Area and downtown. Line 6 will be a comparatively short line linking the downtown area and Pudong New Area. However, in late 2000 China decided to build a 30 km long magnetic railroad with German technology and design, from Longyang Road Station of Line 2 to the Pudong New Airport. It has been under trial operation since 1st January 2003.

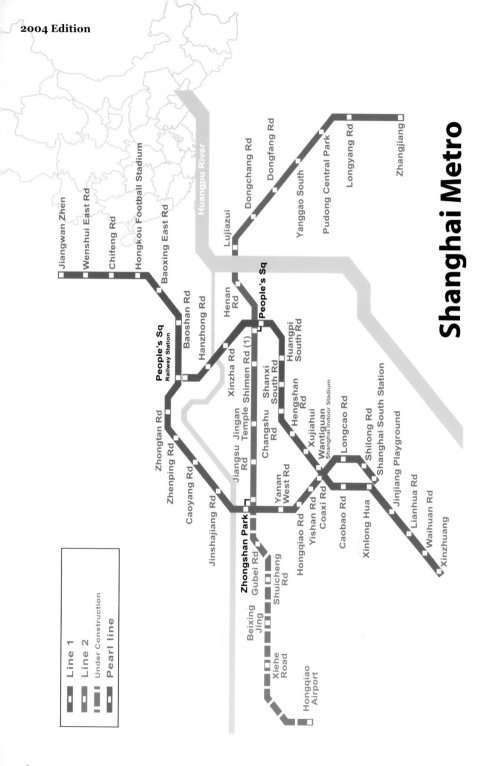

Shanghai Metro

Line 1
Line 2
Under Construction
Pearl line

Interval for each train:

- Metro Line 1 : every 4.5-5 minutes
- Metro Line 2 : every 7 minutes
- Pearl Line   : every 11.5 minutes

The future development of infrastructure is drawn in the 10th Five Year Plan (2001-2005), which includes the construction of a total of 181.5 km of new high capacity transit lines for Shanghai.

Railway

Shanghai Railway Bureau is one of China's largest transportation enterprises. To keep pace with change, it is making full use of information technology to improve operational efficiency in order to meet rising demand. Currently, the railway service moves an average of 1.1 billion passengers and 500 million tons of freight annually.

Its regional service reaches almost every region in the country, while its arterial business extends to a large number of other locations across China. By the year 2005, the Bureau plans to build a 113-km railway line in the booming district of Pudong.

Tips for trips

All Chinese express trains have four different types of seats and sleepers, namely, the soft sleeper, soft seat, hard sleeper and hard seat. The price varies according to the types of tickets you hold. Tickets are normally sold at the ticketing booths outside railway stations and representative offices in town.

Some star hotels may provide the service as well. Reservations, especially for sleepers, should be made two or three days in advance. The most popular routes include Shanghai to Beijing (14 hrs 15 mins) and Shanghai to Nanjing (4 hrs). There is also a route scheduled on alternative days between Shanghai and Hong Kong (24 hrs) with three classes available: hard sleeper, soft sleeper and deluxe soft sleeper. Tickets for these routes can be purchased through the China International Travel Service and China Youth Travel Service.

At the beginning of 2004, the city of Shanghai had nearly 600,000 motor vehicles. To cater to the rapidly growing demand for automobiles in China, the Shanghai Municipal Government plans to establish an International Auto City in Anting Town in the northwest of Shanghai.

With a total area of 68 km², Shanghai International Auto City (SIAC) will strengthen cooperation within the auto industry and fully develop auto trade and auto service in order to integrate the Chinese auto industry into the global auto arena.

SIAC will capitalize on Shanghai's advantages in ports, finance, information, marketing, services, and utilize Internet technology to build an international auto centre. The centre will have multiple functions such as auto trade, auto marketing, auto bonded warehousing, modern logistics, auto exhibitions and expos, auto education,

Under the plan, the railway will cost an estimated RMB 5 billion (USD 600 million) with a handling capacity of one million standard containers each year.

During the 10th Five-Year Plan (2001-2005) period, Shanghai plans to build 10 railway lines. The lines will have a total length of 212 km. Four companies have been set up to undertake the investment, construction, operation, and supervision of the projects. When completed, it will have a daily total traffic capacity of 3 million people, up from the current 700,000.

Shanghai Railway Station

Shanghai Railway Station is a large-scale passenger terminal. The passenger departure hall is on an elevated level with 16 air-conditioned lounges. The station has exits in the north and one in the south. There is a tunnel linked to the subway. Outside the station are terminals for public buses. Luggage claim facilities, ATMs, tourist information center, shops and restaurants can be found within the station premises.

Shanghai Railway West Station

From Shanghai Railway West Station, trains leave for Baotou, Yantai, Changchun, Hengyang, Guangzhou, Ningbo and Nanjing West Station.

information services, auto culture and auto-related sports.

On the premise of enjoying municipal government's support and favorable policies, SIAC will offer a sound investment environment and attract reputable international auto companies.

Within 10 years, the SIAC plans to develop into a core auto trade market and an important distribution centre for complete vehicles and auto spare parts in China and the Asia Pacific region.

Shanghai Railway South Station

It dispatches four trains daily to Hangzhou, taking less than two hours to arrive at Hangzhou East Station. Passengers may get tickets on board. The station is connected to Metro Line 1.

Highways and Expressways

The city of Shanghai is actively stepping up the construction of expressways and highways. Currently, there are 400 km of expressway under construction, and the city is planning to build and improve an additional 710.36 km of highway in the countryside.

The Municipal Road Administration Bureau announced recently that a new master plan for an expressway grid linking Shanghai and the nearby cities had been completed.

According to the plan, the number of expressways between Shanghai and its adjacent two provinces Jiangsu and Zhejiang will be increased to 10 expressways with 60 lanes.

By the end of 2003, the total number of kilometers covered by Shanghai's highways had reached 6,485.61 km, including 240.23 km of expressways.

There will also be 15 other new roads connecting Shanghai and other Yangtze River Delta cities. Currently, the northeastward 1,262 km Beijing-Shanghai Expressway – mainly four lanes but with six lanes on some stretches – runs through Jiangsu, Shandong, Hebei, Tianjin and Beijing, the most developed regions of China. There are 11 major tollgates along its trunk line.

Urban Public Transport

Urban public transport passenger figures for Shanghai overland routes have surged from 15 million in 2001 to 20.5 million in 2002, and this has heightened the urgency to build a transport infrastructure guaranteeing convenient and comfortable trips.

According to Shanghai Urban Transport Bureau, the city currently has 44 long-distance bus stations with routes to 379 counties or cities in 15 provinces in the country. One track stretches for 2,298 km to the central part of Southwest China's Sichuan Province. These stations will be dismantled, merged or expanded to integrate resources and contribute to the new network. The shake-up is in line with the new layout of Shanghai city.

The network integrates five different transportation layers with existing public transport such as railways, subways and buses.

Source: www.smert.gov.cn

Local Bus

Shanghai's buses run everywhere, but constantly face the problem of severe traffic congestion, especially during morning and late evening rush hours. Traveling time is usually long and often rather slow owing to the heavy traffic on most routes.

Bus services operate from around 4am to 10.30pm but certain bus lines have their own schedules. Fares are generally RMB 1 for regular buses and RMB 2 to RMB 3 for air-conditioned ones.

Long-distance Bus

Different levels of comfort are available for long-distance (LD) buses from Shanghai's various LD bus stations:

- **North LD Bus Station** (80 Gongxing Road): handles departures to Jiangsu, Zhejiang, Anhui, Fujiang, Hunan, Shandong and Hubei Provinces;
- **Tianmu East Road LD Bus Station** (100 Tianmu East Road): serves similar destinations (as above);
- **Hengfeng Road Bus Station**: handles departures to Nanjing, Ningbo and Wuxi;
- **Xujiahui Bus Station** (Hongqiao Road, behind Grand Gateway): handles departures to Nanjing and Yangzhou.

Shanghai Tour Bus Lines leave from Shanghai Stadium to various destinations, primarily in the suburban districts. They are cheap and comfortable, providing the best choice for daily trips to the outskirts of town.

Currently, the city is spending RMB 560 million (USD 67 million) to build the largest long-distance bus station of 3.7 hectares in the downtown area. This station will be located near the north square of Shanghai Railway Station. All existing long distance bus stations in the area will be merged into the new one. Construction began at the end of 2002 and will take about three years. Upon completion, the station will be able to transport 20,000 passengers every day on 1,000 scheduled trips.

Taxi services

Taxis are very easy to get hold of in Shanghai and are plentiful, inexpensive and reliable. They are the most comfortable means of transport. However, few drivers speak English and it is advisable to have your destinations written in Chinese to avoid being taken on unnecessarily long trips. Travelers are also advised to watch the meter carefully and to ask for payment receipts before alighting.

Taxis in Shanghai are almost ubiquitously Santana or Passat, manufactured locally by Shanghai Volkswagen Co. Ltd. Fares are calculated at a rate of

RMB 10 for the first three kilometers with RMB 2 per kilometer thereafter. Between 11 pm - 5 am, it rises to RMB 13 for three kilometers and RMB 2.6 per subsequent kilometer. Taxi bookings are available at some big cab operators, such as Dazhong and Qiangsheng, both of which are recommended for high-quality services rendered. Tipping is not mandatory. Some major taxi fleets also offer limousine service with starting rates around RMB 600 per day for an Audi.

Given the large number of taxis in Shanghai, traffic chaos and complicated road signs in Chinese, hiring a car is generally discouraged. Private cars are still not common in Shanghai, although the phenomenon is more visible than almost anywhere else in China. Drivers should also be reminded that there are many bicycles and pedestrians in the streets.

Leading Taxi Companies in Shanghai

Company	Fleet Number	Booking
Dazhong (Turquoise)	7,000	82222, 6258 1688
Qiangsheng (Yellow)	6,000	6258 0000
Bashi (Light Green)	4,700	84000, 6431 2788
Jinjiang (White)	3,600	6258 4584

Civil Aviation

Shanghai has two airports, the Hongqiao International Airport and the new Pudong International Airport (PIA), which was opened more than four years ago. However, most domestic flights now call at the Hongqiao International Airport (HIA), which is only about a half-hour taxi ride (15 km) from the heart of Shanghai.

Currently, the two international airports are managed by Shanghai Airport Ltd, a Shanghai Stock Exchange listed company. In 2001, the two airports handled a total of 194,100 aircrafts and 20.66 million passengers, up 20.9% and 16.8%, respectively.

Hongqiao International Airport

Hongqiao Airport was the principal airport of Shanghai in the past. Due to limited capacity and space, since October 2002, all international (including Hong Kong and Macau) flights to and from Shanghai have called at Pudong International Airport, leaving Hongqiao to serve domestic airlines only.

Shuttle buses depart every 30 minutes starting from 6 am to 9 pm. The fare is RMB 4 to RMB 7, and tickets are sold on board. Transit buses to Pudong Airport are scheduled every 30 minutes from 6 am to 9 pm daily. It is a one-hour journey and costs RMB 30. Travelers are advised to hire taxis from the main taxi stand outside the domestic arrival hall to avoid touts. The average fare is about RMB 65 to reach downtown Shanghai, including toll fees.

Pudong International Airport

The new airport is located in the city's new financial district across the Huangpu River from Shanghai's historic Bund. It is designed to be one of the most advanced airports in the world, providing world-class services to airlines and passengers.

It will ultimately have four 4,000-meter runways and handle 70-80 million passengers and 5 million tons of cargo every year. By the end of December 2003, it was estimated that Pudong Airport handled 15 million passengers for the whole year, a figure due to rise to 20 million in 2004.

Since its opening, it has become Shanghai's new international air hub. Its terminal, which takes the shape of a giant seagull fluttering its strong wings, can accommodate the landing of 36 large aircrafts simultaneously. The throughput of the airport is as high as 126,000 planes, 20 million passengers and 750,000 tons of cargo per year.

Pudong Airport Business Center provides facsimile and computer facilities. Outside the arrival hall, shuttle buses depart every 30 minutes from 6 am to 9 pm to city with a journey estimated to be 1 hour 20 minutes. Transit buses to Hongqiao Airport cost RMB 22 and leave every half an hour from 8 am to 9 pm. The fare of metered taxis is about RMB 170 to get to the city.

An RMB 90 (for international flights) or RMB 50 (for domestic flights) airport tax, or "construction fee", is payable in cash at both airports; children under 12 years of age are exempted from payment. Luggage trolleys are now free for use but luggage bundling service is still chargeable at RMB 10 per unit.

Tips for trips

Bus fare from Pudong International Airport to...

Honqiao Airport	RMB 22
Shanghai Exhibition Center	RMB 19
Zunyi Road	RMB 20
Shanghai Railway Station	RMB 18

Flight Duration

From Pudong International Airport to...

Beijing	1 hr 45 mins
Chicago	15 hrs
Frankfurt	11 hrs
Los Angeles	13 hrs
New York	17 hrs 30 mins
Osaka	2 hrs
Paris	11 hrs
Seattle	12 hrs
Seoul	1 hr 45 mins
Singapore	5 hrs
Hong Kong	2 hrs 15 mins

Port

The Shanghai port serves as the most important gateway to China to the world. Traffic through the port is growing rapidly, particularly in the field of container transport.

Statistics show that container throughput at the Shanghai Port grew a massive 35.8% to 8.631 million twenty-feet equivalent units (TEU) in 2002, accounting for 23.3% of China's total (37 million

TEU). This makes Shanghai the world's fourth largest container port, after Hong Kong, Singapore and Pusan (South Korea).

Shanghai has opened container routes to more than 120 ports around the world. At present, freight vessels sail from Shanghai for Europe or North America everyday.

International Shipping Center

To maintain its status as an international shipping center, Shanghai plans to invest RMB 7 billion (USD 843 million) in port construction in the 2001-2005 periods. Over 80% of the investment will be used to expand existing or build new container ports. According to a port official, the volume of containers to be handled by Shanghai Port was estimated to have exceeded 10 million in 2003.

However, the Huangpu River, with a maximum depth of 8 m, is currently incapable of berthing the 5th and 6th generation container vessels with a draught of about 15 m. The ideal site for a deepwater port is set at the Big Yangshan and Small Yangshan Islands (currently under the administration of Zhoushan, Zhejiang Province) located some 20 nautical miles off Shanghai's Luchao Port.

The islands will be connected to the mainland by grand cross-sea bridges. As the Luchao site is an uninhabited flood plain, large-scale reclamation and major infrastructural works are necessary. The first phase, the resettlement of 80,000 residents is scheduled for 2005. The second and third phases will be completed by 2020.

The development of the grand project kicked off after detailed planning. The Yangshan Deepwater Port is expected to have a deepwater zone 18 km wide and 15 m deep, and be able to accommodate 50 5th- or 6th-generation container liners. It is designed with an annual container handling capacity of 22 million TEUs, which may confer upon Shanghai a leading position in the global transportation network. Upon completion of the first phase, the container handling capacity will immediately rise to 10 million TEUs.

Urban Construction

Urban Development

With globalization and economic development in Asia, Shanghai as the economic center of China is poised to take on the challenge and opportunity to develop into an international metropolis and become one of the world's economic, trading and shipping centers.

Comprehensive Development Plan

- To extend the development area along the sea and rivers into riverside and seaside towns and industrial development zones;
- To further the functional development and image construction of Pudong New Area;
- To build new cities and a central town;
- To build Chongming Island into an important strategic stronghold for Shanghai's sustainable development into the 21st century.

Restructuring the Urban Area

In accordance with the guidelines on integration and coordinated development of the cities and rural areas, where Central City is a major part, a "multi-axis, multi-ring and multi-centre" urban development pattern will be formed as in the following:

Central City Surrounded by Outer Ring Road, the Central City is the political, economic and cultural centre of Shanghai. It is adopting the "multi-centric and open" layout structure. The CBD is the integration of finance, trade, information, shopping, culture, recreation, tourism and business with moderate quantum of residential buildings.

New City The seat of the new medium-sized city based on development of important industries and urban major infrastructure.

Central Town Supported by industries, Central Town is a small-sized city developed from a relatively large and systematically organized rural town with rational layout and superb geographical and economic development conditions.

Ordinary Town An area merged from several existing market towns according to their locations, transportation links, availability of resources and other conditions.

Central Village An area merged from several existing natural villages.

Traffic Management

Over the past 10 years, traffic management has improved in Shanghai and the city is leading the field in China with innovative traffic management practices and advanced technologies.

The scope of traffic management is being broadened to include traffic engineering, planning and design, as well as enforcement and operations, as part of a more coordinated and comprehensive approach.

The first focus for Shanghai was on improving road efficiency for motor vehicles. Significant capacity enhancements have been made through good traffic management, which is complemented by new road infrastructure.

Electronic Toll Collection (ETC)

Plans are in place to expand the Area Traffic Control (ATC) system even further from around 700 junctions to 1,000 by 2005. There is the potential to create ATC links to transport telematics and ITS developments such as Variable Message Signs (VMS), Parking Guidance Systems (PGS), CCTV monitoring and surveillance, •

urban expressway management, area pricing, and Electronic Toll Collection (ETC). Many of these are planned for the 10th Five Year Plan (2001 - 2005). Strategic traffic management measures are poised to become a key set of advanced tools to manage the completed road network.

Urban Redevelopment

Redevelopment of the Huangpu River waterfront

The plan is to set up a mixed-use district to generate activities along the riverfront:

- Relocate the open areas to the riverfront in order to allow people to come into close contact with the natural environment;
- Create accessibility to the riverbank to improve the quality of urban living environment;
- Retain the spirit of Shanghai to form the character of the city;
- Create a unique city landscape to strengthen the image of Shanghai.

Reconstruction of the Suzhou creek waterfront

To further improve the environment, the following plans will soon be carried out:

- To increase the number of public open spaces along the Suzhou creek,

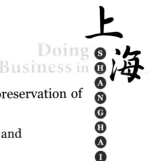
To integrate the conservation of historic blocks with the preservation of historic and cultural buildings;

- To implement flood prevention measures and standards, and construct platforms to reach the water;
- To provide more open spaces;
- To reorganize the local traffic pattern and to provide pedestrian walkways along the river bank.

Urban Conservation

Efforts will be made to preserve the "old style" and features of historic buildings in the Central City. Based on the planned preservation of historic buildings and areas, garden-type apartments, new lanes and alleys, old lanes and alleys and other buildings with unique features within the 80 km² in the old Central City will be preserved.

Readjustment of the Industrial Structure

Industrial Development Strategy

To accelerate industrial development, the city's strategy is to adopt a three-pronged approach using technological innovation as the main stimulus to upgrade the industrial structure of the tertiary, secondary and primary industries. The top priority, however, is to develop the high-level service industry, particularly financial services and high-tech industries, which includes the information industry.

First-level: The tertiary industry is the major concern with due emphasis on the preservation of the urban industry.

Second-level: High-tech, high value-added, non-pollution industries will be the major concerns. Existing industry zones will be gradually upgraded.

Third-level: Development of primary and secondary industries is the major concern.

Information Technology

Shanghai, which hopes to establish itself as a world information center in the near future, has earmarked the information technology industry as one of the key growth areas of local economy.

The IT infrastructure for Shanghai city has created features of high bandwidth, high bit rate, and high performance, which is marked by the completion of the main part of the Info-Port Project.

Over the past few years, the city has turned out integrated circuits, computers, mobile telecommunications facilities and a series of other profitable information technology products.

At the end of 2002, the IT infrastructure is capable of meeting the demands and various requirements of subscribers by providing different options. Therefore, various information services such as Internet browsing, Internet phone, email, e-business, video-on-demand, remote medical treatment, and remote education are available to subscribers. High-speed network services provided by different operators such as Telecom, Unicom, Netcom, and CATV Network are available to enterprises and business subscribers as well as home subscribers.

Telecommunications

The establishment of telecom infrastructure and improvement of communications has helped the development of various telecom businesses and increased the number of subscribers.

In Shanghai city, the number of fixed-line phone subscribers in 2003 was more than 7.33 million. Mobile phone subscribers numbered more than 10.97 million – a figure which is much larger than that of fixed-line phone subscribers. The number of paging subscribers has decreased to 3.01 million, and is still in a downward trend. Frame relay and ATM services have subscribers totaling 5,947. Digital data subscribers increased to 23,000, broadband subscribers up to 0.92 million, CATV

subscribers up to 3.67 million, completed CATV 2-way renovation up to 1.7 million houses, and Internet subscribers up to 4.32 million.

Today, Shanghai produces one-fifth of China's integrated circuits, one-third of telecommunications equipment, and 30% of IC cards, according to available latest statistics.

Urban Environment Protection

Air and water pollution is a major problem in Shanghai. Most of the pollution comes from coal-burning smoke and vehicle emissions. Recent measures to improve air quality include reducing the sulfur content of coal and the use of alternate fuels. The Shanghai area has an abundant surface water supply, but because of the large population and extensive economic development, there are also serious problems with surface water pollution. The major industrial source of water pollution is the chemical industry.

In 2003, the World Bank approved a loan of USD 200 million to launch a project to enhance the environmental quality of the city. The main objective of this project is to tackle pollution problems and improve environmental conditions in Shanghai by progressively developing and implementing integrated, metropolitan-wide measures.

Such measures include the enhanced management of water resources and market-based approaches for solid waste services, testing of alternative approaches for improving urban environment services in less developed areas, and installing, in both the city center and some of the surrounding districts, facilities already known to be high priority in order to achieve metropolitan-wide environmental objectives, e.g., protection of upstream sources for water supply.

Shanghai is also intent on improving sewage treatment. At present, the city can only treat 44% of its 5.04 million tons of wastewater produced daily. To meet the total demand, 27 more sewage treatment factories are to be established with a total estimated investment of RMB 18 billion (USD 2.17 billion).

Urban Ecological Conservation

Currently plans are being implemented to achieve the following aims:

- To build Shanghai into an ecological and sustainable city;
- To form a network of urban open spaces, mainly by constructing large open spaces, open space belts, and forests in the suburbs.

By 2020, 35 locations in the city will be open space. The per capita open space will be increased to 10 m^2.

ADMINISTRATIVE AREAS

Doing Business in 上海

S H A N G H A I

Introduction

Shanghai is made up of 19 administrative areas – 18 of which are "districts", and the remaining one, Chongming, a "county". Most of these districts have developed quickly in recent years. Their development has fueled economic growth in the Yangtze River Delta and helped build a new and modern Shanghai.

Land Area and Population of Shanghai Administrative Areas

Administrative Area	Land Area (km²)	Population (10,000 persons)
Districts		
Huangpu	12.41	57.45
Luwan	8.05	32.89
Xuhui	54.76	106.46
Changning	38.30	70.22
Jing'an	7.62	30.53
Putuo	54.83	105.17
Zhabei	29.26	79.86
Hongkou	23.48	86.07
Yangpu	60.73	124.38
Pudong New District	522.75	204.23
Minhang	371.68	121.73
Baoshan	415.27	122.80
Jiading	458.80	75.31
Jinshan	586.05	58.04
Songjiang	604.71	64.12
Qingpu	675.54	59.59
Nanhui	687.66	78.51
Fengxian	687.39	62.43
County		
Chongming	1,041.21	64.98

Source: Shanghai Statistical Bureau

The opening-up and development of Shanghai is part of the national strategy for economic reforms. It is also a major strategic decision aimed at encouraging social and political progress in China. The development of Special Economic Zones (SEZs) and Pudong New District of Shanghai leads the country in its innovation in administration system and in the upgrading of industrial structure. Shanghai is poised to play an exemplary role for the rest of the country.

Pudong New District

Pudong, literally meaning the east of Huangpu River, has been attracting foreign attention since April 1990 - when the central government in Beijing announced its decision to open up and develop Pudong New District.

The territory has a total land area of 522 km² and a floating population of 2.04 million. In the past, due to the infrastructural lack of bridges and tunnels, the economic development of Pudong lagged far behind districts in the west of Huangpu River where the old downtown of Shanghai is located. As it embarks on a massive drive to improve its infrastructure and hence, investment environment, Pudong is set to become the most prosperous region in Shanghai in the 21st century.

Economic Development

Since the 1990s, Pudong has played a pivotal role in creating new administrative systems, industrial upgrading and opening-up to the outside world.

In 2001, the GDP of Pudong reached USD 13.1 billion and total industrial output stood at USD 10.7 billion, up 16.1% and 20.1% respectively.

In 2003 however, Pudong's GDP registered a new high, hitting USD 18.2 billion, up 17.5% over the previous year. Total industrial output went up 30% to USD 12 billion. It has undoubtedly become a key growth engine for metropolitan Shanghai.

In 2003 also, Pudong's annual output value of micro-electric products totaled USD 85 million. Its software sector grew by 39%, while the biomedical and service sectors each recorded growths of 15%.

The added value of Pudong's financial institutions made up 12.5% of Pudong's GDP, and the logistics sector, 16.5%. The added value of tourism, exhibitions and conventions surged 10% to USD 97 million.

Pudong's import and export value also rose – up 58% over 2002, to the tune of USD 58.1 billion.

Source: www.china.org.cn

Infrastructure Development

With the aim of building a multifunctional and cosmopolitan new urban area in Shanghai, in order to meet the physical, functional, cultural and ecological criteria of a modern metropolis, Pudong has gone through a series of stages of infrastructure development.

"Infrastructure comes first" has been the overriding strategy in the development of Pudong, and a total amount of RMB 180 billion has been injected into the infrastructure sector. A package of major projects involving bridges, tunnels, metros, deep-water port and infoport as well as energy projects has been completed. The investment environment in Pudong has improved considerably.

Source: www.smert.gov.cn

Investment Climate

Pudong aims to become an international economic, financial and trade center. Plans are in place to establish a modern industrial structure, and several state-level development zones have been earmarked and set aside to serve specific purposes. These include Lujiazui Finance and Trade Zone, Zhangjiang High-tech Park, Waigaoqiao Free Trade Zone and Jinqiao Export Processing Zone.

Pudong constitutes a significant proportion of all FDI inflow to Shanghai. At the end of January 2004, Pudong's contracted FDI was USD 260 million, and its total realized FDI (including previous contracted FDI inflow) was USD 473 million. In addition to the huge influx of overseas investment, Pudong also entices a growing number of domestic investors. Many prominent domestic enterprises have relocated, or are relocating, their headquarters or regional headquarters to Pudong.

Source: www.pudong.gov.cn

Urban Districts

Huangpu District

Huangpu District has long been known as a hub of commerce. Nanjing East Road and the newly developed Jinling East Road make the district a shopping haven. In addition, Beijing Road is famous for hardware shops and Fuzhou Road for bookstores and cultural antiques. Also popular with tourists is Yuyuan Garden, with its traditional Chinese architecture, and the opportunity for the visitor to shop, sightsee and indulge in fine gourmet cuisine.

Many renowned specialty stores, which manifest and bring together the quintessence and sophistication of the Shanghainese, originated from Huangpu District a century ago. Among them are "Heng Deli Clock and Watch", "Cao Sugong Ink Stick", "Shao Wansheng Groceries", "Wu Liangcai Glasses" and "Zhang Xiaoquan Knives and Scissors". "Tong Hanchun", "Cai Tongde", "Hu Qingyu Tang" and "Lei Yunshang" are the four major traditional Chinese medicine pharmacies in Shanghai.

The Bund, lined with 52 impressive buildings of varied architectural design and style, reflecting influences from the Gothic, Renaissance and Baroque periods, is not only a popular tourist belt, but also a prime location for many world-class banks and other financial institutions.

The district is also strong in scientific and technical expertise. It has attracted many professionals and this has hastened the development of high-tech industries, particularly, in fields such as electronic instruments, machinery, metrology technology and energy-saving technologies and products.

Source: hpq.sh.gov.cn

Luwan District

Luwan District lies to the south of Huangpu District. With a mere land area of 8.05 km² and population of 328,900, it is also one of the most populous administrative regions in Shanghai.

A bustling classic shopping street for the rich, Huaihai Middle Road showcases the fashion trends of the Shanghainese. Along the road, there are luxury hotels like Jinjiang Hotel and Okura Garden Hotel, as well as giant shopping malls like Parkson, Shanghai Ninth Department Store, Pacific Department Store, Lippo Plaza, Hong Kong Plaza, Cyber Digital

Square, Times Square Shanghai, Goldbell Plaza and Radisson Plaza. There is also a newly developed area for gourmets and tourists called Xintiandi.

To date, more than 400 FIEs have invested in Luwan with total FDI of over USD 1.1 billion. 42 Fortune Global 500 MNCs are located in the district, including IBM, DuPont, Bayer, Cisco, Pfizer and P&G. Exports by FIEs now account for nearly half of the district's total exports.

Following the redevelopment of its urban infrastructure and residential districts, Luwan will be a leading commercial area for Shanghai in the future.

Source: www.luwan.sh.cn

Xuhui District

Xuhui District is located in the southwestern part of urban Shanghai. With an area of 54.76 km², or nearly one-fifth of the downtown area, it is one of a few urban districts that are still able to offer land for industrial purpose.

Xuhui is one of the fastest growing districts of Shanghai. Six parks have been started to develop Xuhui into an innovative technology-intensive area. These include the high-profile state-level Caohejing Economic and Technological Development Zone, Xujiahui Technological Zone, Shanghai Jiaotong University Science Park, Xuhui Park, Huajing Industrial Park and East China University of Science and Technology Industrial Park. The Longhua Diamond Processing Zone is also under construction.

In 2003, 104 new foreign-funded enterprises were registered in Xuhui, and of the total amount of contracted FDI, USD 290 million was utilized, an increase of 7% over the previous year, and the highest since 1997. Of the 104 foreign-funded enterprises, 79 belonged to the service sector, and they chalked up a contracted foreign investment amount of USD 170 million.

The educational facilities at Xuhui District are equally comprehensive. Shanghai Jiaotong University – the alma mater of the Chinese top leader Jiang Zemin, the Medical College of Fudan University, East China

University of Science & Technology and Shanghai Chinese Medicines University are located in the district.

Source: www.xh.sh.cn

Changning District

Changning District is situated in the western part of the city. The area of Changning District measures 38.3 km², with a population of 702,200. With an integrated transportation network, the district is well-connected by expressways and viaducts.

Hongqiao International Airport is located in the west of the district, linked to the city by Yan'an Road Viaduct. The only airport in Shanghai for the past century, before the completion of Pudong International Airport, Hongqiao International Airport continues to play a key role in welcoming foreign guests to the metropolis today. Hongqiao Economic and Technological Development Zone, a state-level development industrial park, is an important foreign business area in Shanghai.

Changning is the leading district in Shanghai in terms of per capita green space. Given the advantageous location and ecological living environment, many foreign expatriates are now living in nearby Gubei New Area or along Hongqiao Road.

Since the 1990s, three economic clusters have been planned at district level to propel the local economy. These are Hongqiao Foreign Trade Center, Zhongshan Park Commercial Center and Hongqiao Airport Industrial Zone. As the district places top priority on the robust development of the IT industry, the "Digital Changning" blueprint has been pinned on the area for the development of a comprehensive test field.

Supporting academic institutions within Changning district include Donghua University, East China Institute of Politics & Law, Shanghai Foreign Trade College and Shanghai Engineering University.

Source: cnq.sh.gov.cn

Jing'an District

Jing'an derived its name from the Jing'an Temple, a Buddhist monastery originally built in 247 AD. The district is the smallest in Shanghai in terms of land area. However, it is the second most crowded district in terms of population density. The district has plans to develop into a "high-class business district and high-quality residential area".

Nanjing West Road is the heart of the district. Grand office buildings like the Shanghai Mart and the Shanghai Exhibition Center, and many elegant hotels such as Hilton, Portman Ritz-Carlton, J. C. Mandarin and Equatorial line this 2.9 km road.

Like other urban districts, Jing'an's economy is largely dominated by the tertiary sector that accounts for 77% of its GDP. Commerce, real estate, as well as financial and professional services are the three vital components of this sector. The secondary sector is represented by a few urban light industries, such as garments, food processing, household appliances, and high-tech products such as telecommunication instruments, fine chemicals and bioengineering technologies.

At the end of January 2004, total contractual FDI stood at USD 280 million. Foreign-funded projects are distributed in various industries of real estate, entertainment, consultancy, property management, software development, IT services, chemicals, garments and medical appliance etc.

Source: www.jingan.gov.cn

Putuo District

Putuo District is the northwest gateway to the city of Shanghai. The Shanghai-Nanjing, Shanghai-Jiading Expressways, and the Shanghai-Beijing Railway run through its territory. Putuo has a land area of 54.83 km², and has long been the traditional industrial base of Shanghai.

The district has several industrial parks, such as Changzheng, Xinyang, Changfeng and Taopu, and many state-owned enterprises. Three science parks are supported by local universities and research institutes.

Putuo is an emerging trade and distribution center of commodities in Shanghai. It is also host to the only silver spot transaction market in China. Local government encourages investment in urban industry, real estate, commerce, logistics and tourism services. Specifically, it hopes to channel investments into the areas of paper packaging, IT, biopharmaceuticals, education, healthcare facilities and the establishment of regional headquarters.

At end-2002, Putuo's total import and export value was USD 293 million, showing an increase of 32.3% over the previous year, and total contracted FDI stood at USD 130 million.

Source: www.ptq.sh.gov

Zhabei District

Zhabei lies to the north of Suzhou Creek. The Shanghai Railway Station for passenger travel and the North Station for cargo transportation are located here. Zhabei is at the south end of the Shanghai-Beijing Railway. Plans are afoot to build a terminal station for long-distance buses.

The district has an established structure of industry. Since February 2002, Zhabei has started the development of so-called metropolitan industrial zones intensively. There are two models now, namely, the North New Industrial Zone and Pengpu Town Industrial Park. The former, leveraging on the expertise of Shanghai University, emphasises high-tech developments in information technology and software; the latter is a conglomerate of industries in electrical and electronic manufacturing, printing, engineering plastics, fireproof materials, mechanical processing and garment manufacturing.

Many MNCs and domestic enterprise groups have established subsidiaries in Zhabei, including Philips, Honeywell and Alcatel.

Source: zbq.sh.gov.cn

Hongkou District

Situated in the north of urban Shanghai, Hongkou District covers an area of 23.48 km². It has a population of 860, 700.

Wholesale and retail, F&B and Real Estate are the mainstay industries of the tertiary sector in Hongkou. "Holiday economy" and chain stores are the two new phenomena in the district's retail market. The manufacturing enterprises in Hongkou are mainly involved in the production of suitcases, garments, lamps, automotive parts and jewelry processing.

Sichuan North Road is one of the most famous shopping areas in Shanghai, and appeals to many middle-class consumers. Many specific business outlets cluster in Dabaishu. These outlets deal with home electronics, steel products, decorative materials, furniture, kitchen and sanitary wares etc. Ace Group, a major suitcase producer, is in the process of building a world-class exhibition and trading center.

One of Shanghai's major education districts, two acclaimed universities are located in Hongkou – the Shanghai University of Finance and Economy and Shanghai Foreign Studies University.

Source: hkq.sh.gov.cn

Yangpu District

With a total land area of 60.73 km² and a population of 1.24 million, Yangpu District is the largest among all nine urban districts. Located in the northeast of urban Shanghai, it is linked via the Yangpu Bridge to Pudong New District, its closest neighbor.

Yangpu is known for many prestigious universities and research institutions. These include Fudan University, Tongji University, and the Second Military Medical University. Altogether, there are 15 universities and over 100 research institutes with 110,000 students in Yangpu. Nearly 200,000 professionals work in the universities and research institutes, including 33 fellows of CAS (Chinese Academy of Science) and CAE (Chinese Academy of Engineering).

上海

Yangpu has four major industrial parks, namely Wujiaochang High-tech Park, Tongji University Science Park, Fudan University Science Park, Fudan Software Development Center and Shanghai Yangpu Incubation Center.

Yangpu is also famous for being one of the birthplaces of China's modern industry. Over 100 large and medium-sized enterprises, such as Shanghai Mechanical Factory, Shanghai Diesel Engine Factory and Yangshupu Power Station were started in Yangpu.

Source: ypq.sh.gov.cn

Suburban Districts

Besides the nine urban districts, nine suburban districts (including Pudong New District) and one county also fall within the purview of the Shanghai Government.

Industries in the suburban districts have been developing at an alarming rate, particularly in IT, biopharmaceutical, chemistry, metallurgy, automobile and environmental protection technologies.

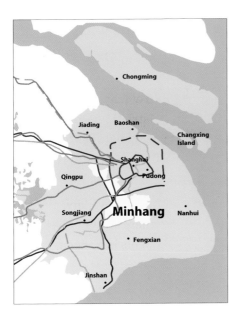

Foreign investment has been the new growth engine for the suburbs. An increasing number of investors, aware of the locational advantages and cost-effectiveness of these districts, have relocated their businesses accordingly.

Minhang District

Minhang District lies at the southwest border of the urban area. The Huangpu River cuts through it from north to south. Minhang has an area of 371.68 km^2 and a population of 1.21

million. It is Shanghai's southern gateway –Shanghai-Hangzhou Expressway, Shanghai-Hangzhou Railway and the Outer Ring Road run across this area. Hongqiao International Airport lies just next to the district.

Minhang is a key industrial base for the municipality. There are a couple of well-developed industrial parks in this region, such as the state-level Minhang Economic and Technological Development Zone, and industrial parks at Xinzhuang, Mindong and Minbei.

MNCs such as Mannesmann, BASF, Itochu, Tomen, Hyundai and Alcatel Alsthom have established subsidiaries in Minhang.

Source: mhq.sh.gov.cn

Baoshan District

Baoshan District is located in the northern part of Shanghai where Huangpu River joins the Yangtze River. The total area of Baoshan is 415.27 km² and the population stands at 1.23 million.

There are three container terminals in the district, which make up as much as 70% of the total handling capacity of Shanghai. Ships from Baoshan call at over 400 ports worldwide.

Baoshan is famous for Baosteel Group, which is one of the largest iron and steel producers in China and a world-class conglomerate in this trade. In addition, the local government has been urging the growth of industries such as storage, transportation services, logistics, tourism, real estate and modern agriculture.

The western area of Baoshan has witnessed the gradual development of a new residential area. Baoshan is determined to develop the district into a garden city and an ideal place to live in. Changxing Island, famous for its clean water and fresh air, has been identified as an ideal manufacturing base for healthcare products and "green food".

There are a few industrial parks for investors to choose from. The 5 km² municipal-level Baoshan City Industrial Park aims to be a manufacturing base for new materials, telecommunications equipment, mechanical instruments and automotive parts. Shanghai University Nanometer Technology Park is a specific high-tech park for the commercialization of nano technology.

Source: bsq.sh.gov.cn

Jiading District

Jiading District, with a total land area of 458.8 km², lies in the northwest region of the city. The population stands at around 753, 000. The State Council upgraded it from a county to a district in October 1992. The district has strong cultural heritage and was historically an established township in Shanghai.

The district is also famous for its automobile industry. The Sino-German joint venture, Shanghai Volkswagen Co. Ltd., is located at Anting town. With annual sales of more than USD 3.62 billion, it ranked as the largest foreign joint venture in China for seven consecutive years. In fact, the automobile industry and the related components manufacturing industry has become the

mainstay of the district's economy. In addition, the district is also strong in the manufacturing of household appliances, textile, metal products, and high-tech products like optical electronics, microelectronics, new materials and software etc.

Led by the automobile industry, the district has also built up its strength in trade, banking and finance, and other services. Now, Jiading is host to the Anting Automobile Market, Shanghai Light Textile Market, Shanghai Decoration Market and Shanghai Dongfang Auto Components Market.

As for agriculture, the district offers a great variety of vegetables, fruits and poultry, such as white garlic, grapes, strawberry, pigeon and black bone chicken. As the local government encourages environmental protection, some well-designed farms attract a great number of international tourists and local people.

Jiading District has a well-developed infrastructure. In 1988, China's first expressway, Shanghai-Jiading Expressway, was completed here. Shanghai-Nanjing Expressway and Shanghai-Beijing Railway run through its southern part.

In the district there are over 10 high-level research institutes like the CAS Shanghai Optics Fine Mechanical Institute and East China Computing Technology Institute. Shanghai University's Jiading Campus and Shanghai Science and Technology Institute are also located here.

Jiading Industrial Zone is one of Shanghai's nine municipal-level industrial parks. There is also the Jiading Civil Technological Park, which comprises Jiading High-tech Park, Fuhua High-tech Park and CAS Shanghai High-tech Industrial Park.

Many district-level parks are also situated in towns like Nanxiang, Tanghang, Jiangqiao, Huangdu, Caowang and Malu. Most impressively, Shanghai International Automobile City is taking shape at Anting town, and the area aims to become the "Detroit of China".

Source: jdq.sh.gov.cn

Jinshan District

Jinshan lies in the southernmost part of Shanghai. With a 586 km² land area and a 23.3 km deepwater coastline, Jinshan enjoys great advantage in geography and location. The Jinshan branch of Shanghai-Hangzhou Railway and a number of highways run through the district. A cross-sea bridge to Zhejiang is also under construction.

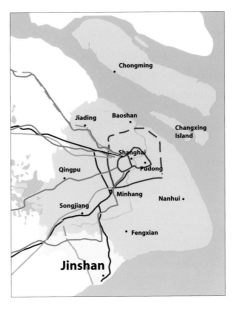

The district places heavy emphasis on industrial development. Nearly 5,000 enterprises, engaged in petrochemicals, mechanical components, textile and garment, electronics, pharmaceuticals and automobile components, form the mainstay of its industry. The petrochemical sector is one of the most prominent sectors. Shanghai Petrochemical, a conglomerate in China's petrochemical industry, is located here.

There are a few industrial parks in Jinshan, each with distinctive characteristics, including Jinshanzhui Industrial Zone, Jinshan No. 2 Industrial Zone, and Shanghai Chemical Industrial Park Jinshan Zone. In addition, Shanghai International Garment Machinery City is located in Fengjing Town of Jinshan District. Zhuhang High-tech Park is meant for pharmaceuticals and there is also a Jinshan International Small & Medium Enterprise Park in Tinglin Town.

Jinshan is also a major agricultural base for Shanghai, supplying rice, edible oil, vegetables, poultry, pork, egg, milk and aquatic products.

Source: jsq.sh.gov.cn

Established in 1995, the 16.16 km² municipal-level Qingpu Industrial Park is

Songjiang District

It is claimed that Songjiang is the original birthplace of indigenous Shanghainese, as the establishment of Songjiang county can be traced back to 751 AD during the Tang Dynasty. In 1998, Songjiang was made a district under Shanghai Municipality's jurisdiction, with a territory covering 604 km² and a population of 641, 200.

As both Shanghai-Hangzhou Expressway and Shanghai-Hangzhou Railway run through its entire region, the district attracts many investors and this has, to some degree, led to land scarcity. A new town with a planned area of 36 km² is under construction to meet the increased demand, and upon completion, would be able to accommodate 250,000 residents.

Universities and colleges in Songjiang include the Shanghai International Studies University and Shanghai Institute of Foreign Trade.

The Songjiang Export Processing Zone (SEPZ), a state-level industrial park, and the 20.56 km² Songjiang Industrial Zone, the first municipal-level industrial park in Shanghai are located in Songjiang. In addition, the Songjiang Modern Agricultural Zone in the southwest part of the district has been designated for development as a green agricultural base for the municipality.

Source: sjq.sh.gov.cn

Qingpu District

Qingpu is located in the area surrounded by Shanghai, and the provinces of Zhejiang and Jiangsu. The famous Dianshan Lake is found in Qingpu.

home to five industries, namely, textile, machinery and electronics, food processing, fine chemicals and modern agriculture. Major investors include Dupont, Suzuka International, BASF, Fuji Electric, Yingji DTF and ISEA LORENZI. Further development of the district is expected to be tightly integrated with that of Shanghai and the Yangtze River Delta Region.

Source: www.shqp.gov.cn

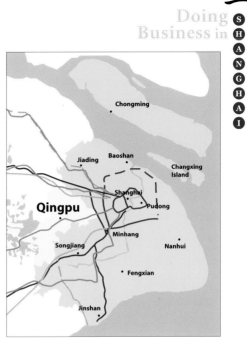

Nanhui District

With an area of 688 km², Nanhui is the largest district in Shanghai and is also one of two newest districts approved in 2001. It is located in the southeast part of Shanghai, and south of Pudong New District. With Pudong International Airport Phase II and

the grand Yangshan Deepwater Port project under construction, the district is poised for great opportunities in its future development. In fact, Nanhui has already been designated as a key district in Shanghai for further development.

Nanhui has one municipal-level and three local-level industrial parks. The municipal-level 26.88 km² Shanghai Pudong Kangqiao Industrial Park, located in Nanhui, was founded in May 1992. Nanhui Industrial Park is another important industrial park in the district. A 6.23 km² Huinan New Town Technological and Educational Zone has also completed the first phase of construction.

Source: nhq.sh.gov.cn

Fengxian District

Approved by the State Council as a district in January 2001, Fengxian is located in the south of Shanghai, and lies on the north side of Hangzhou Bay. Since acquiring its district status, it has become a hot new place for attracting investment.

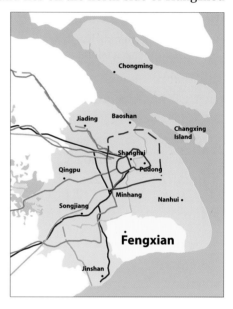

In 2003, its total value added amounted to USD 1.55 billion, and the district received a total financial revenue of USD 370 million. Its foreign trade also progressed steadily, with a total export value of USD 990 million. Total investment in fixed assets was USD 550 million, and its total contracted FDI reached USD 250 million.

The Shanghai Comprehensive Industrial Development Zone (SCIDZ) and Shanghai Chemical Industrial Park Fengxian Zone (SCIPFX) are located in the district. Besides domestic investors from other parts of China, foreign investors from over 50 countries or regions worldwide have already placed their stakes in Fengxian, such as GE, Mannesmann, Pioneer and Fuji etc.

SCIDZ, formerly known as Shanghai Fengpu Industrial Zone, is a 20.8 km² municipal-level industrial park. Strategically located in the center of the district, the industrial park has grown very rapidly in recent years. SCIZFPX, situated in the southwest corner of Fengxian, is a 23.5 km² area fully dedicated to the development of the chemicals industry. Tianyuan PVC,

Gaoqiao Petrochemical and Bayer's USD 400 million chemical projects are currently in progress.

Source: fxq.sh.gov.cn

Chongming County

The last remaining county in Shanghai, Chongming County, has a total land area of 1041 km², and is Shanghai's biggest administrative region. Its population is around 650,000. Sitting in the middle of Yangtze River Estuary, Chongming Island is the third largest island in China, after Taiwan and Hainan.

Chongming's economy has been developing rapidly. In 2003, the county's value-added reached USD 850 million, an increase of 12.1% over 2002. Its financial revenue in 2003 was USD 200 million. Total investment in fixed assets was USD 140 million, an increase of 16.3% of the previous year. Total export value was USD 220 million.

In October 2001, Chongming fulfilled inspection criteria on its development of a State Ecological Exemplary Zone which was first started in 1996. This is a milestone in the county's pursuit of a "green economy"- led by the tertiary sector, followed by the primary and secondary. "Encouraged" (or state endorsed) industries include ecological tourism, conference and exhibition, transit logistics, organic and ecological agriculture, biotechnology and export-oriented processing industries.

Chongming Industrial Zone, established in 1996 with a size of 9.97 km², is one of the nine municipal-level industrial parks in Shanghai. Chongming Green Food Zone is a 3.21 km² giant modern agricultural development zone to be built in the eastern part of the island.

Source: cmx.sh.gov.cn

Island to Develop into a Tourist Haven

Chongming Island, China's third largest island in Shanghai, will focus its future development on tourism, resorts and exhibition centers, with no large-scale industrialization plans.

The long-awaited general development plan for the island, which is regarded as "Shanghai's last piece of pristine land," has been completed and is waiting for final approval from the local and central governments, according to the general office of Shanghai municipal government. ...

The plan, which looks at the island's progress up to 2020, is considered another key strategic step by the Shanghai government in the coming two decades following its successful development of Pudong into a prosperous financial district in the 1990s, according to Li. ...

Under the plan, the island's gross domestic product per capita is also expected to reach around USD 20, 000 by 2020, equaling or slightly surpassing Shanghai's expected average.

To meet the goal, the 1,200 km^2 island will be divided into five areas, with a special function for each.

The eastern part of the island will be reserved as a showcase of the island's friendly ecological environment.

The central area of the island will have its forest area expanded and be converted into Shanghai's largest public recreational area.

The north part will be scheduled for large-scale theme parks and stadia, with certain land reserved for the development of ecological agriculture.

The southern area, where Chongming county government is now based, will be an area for residence and certain pollution-free industries.

And the western part, with the 200-hectare Mingzhu Lake, will be built into an international exhibition and convention area.

Source: (Excerpt) China Daily, 6th January 2004

FOREIGNERS IN SHANGHAI

The Foreign Community

Shanghai has a population of 13.4 million permanent residents, making it one of the largest metropolitan areas in the world. Typically the first choice for foreigners who wish to do business in China, Shanghai has absorbed billions of dollars of overseas investment and witnessed double-digit economic growth over the past two decades.

To date, Japanese citizens account for one third of foreigners in Shanghai, while Americans are a close second with a proportion of 11%. The numbers for Koreans, Singaporeans and German are about 6% each. Recently, a growing number of Malaysians are also choosing to work in Shanghai.

About 95% of foreign citizens employed in Shanghai have received university education. In fact, 8 out of 10 foreigners working in Shanghai hold senior management positions, such as CEOs, general managers and accountants, or technical posts like engineers and IT professionals. Around 81.9% of foreigners are employed by foreign enterprises, and 5% are working in state-owned enterprises or in the growing private sector. A good example is Shanghai Eastern Airlines which has employed 90 stewards from Japan, France, Germany, the United States, Spain and Korea to improve face-to-face interactions with overseas passengers on board.

With a growing number of foreigners working in Shanghai, bars, beauty salons, and restaurants serving Japanese food, Argentina-style roast meat and French food, have mushroomed around town. Along the busy streets in Shanghai, one finds popular food and beverage outlets such as Kentucky Fried Chicken, MacDonald's, Starbucks, Haagen-Dazs and Hard Rock Café. Foreign boutiques and cosmetics are also readily available in Shanghai.

Chinese Holidays

China has her own set of commemorative dates. For example, March 8 is for women, June 1 for children, August 1 for servicemen and September 10 for teachers. The anniversary of the founding of the Communist Party of China, an event which took place right in Shanghai itself, is on July 1. Important holidays include National Day on October 1 and Labor Day on May 1 – both celebrated with a seven-day-long "Golden Week" to promote domestic tourism. Other festivals include the Tour Festival, Peach Blossom Festival, Osmanthus Flower Festival, Orange Festival and Tea Culture Festival.

For the Chinese, the Spring Festival is the most important traditional holiday. The first day of the Festival, or Chuyi in Mandarin, falls on a day in either January or February. This date is derived from the lunar calendar. The whole festive season usually lasts for two weeks. Foreign businessmen are advised to avoid this period as many Chinese organizations and companies are closed or in partial operation. In Shanghai, a general cleanup of the city begins two weeks before October.

Employment Permits

Foreigners who wish to work in Shanghai are required to obtain an Employment Permit before they apply for a z-type visa (for work) to enter China.

The applicant must submit a Chinese resume, photocopies of academic qualification, a letter from the employer and company registration certificate to the Shanghai Municipal Labor and Social Security Administration for processing. It normally takes five days. With the approval letter, the Shanghai employer can, on behalf of the employee, proceed to the Shanghai Foreign Trade and Economic Cooperation Commission for relevant visa application. The permit certificate is valid for six months and renewable upon expiry. Foreign employees must get the Employment Permit in person within 15 days after arrival in Shanghai.

Shanghai Municipal Labor and Social Security Administration

Block A, 865 Zhongshan South Road, Shanghai 200011

Tel: 833666 (enquiry); 86 21 6365 0095 (complaint)

Office hours: 9:15-11:15 hrs (Mon-Fri), 13:30-16:30 hrs (Mon-Thu)

Source: www.sh.lss.gov.cn

Shanghai Foreign Trade and Economic Cooperation Commission

Tel: 86 21 6275 2200, 86 21 5878 8388 (Pudong Office)

According to official statistics, there are about 60,000 people from 120 nations and regions working in the city. The administration issued 27,800 such permits to foreigners in 2003, a 10.2 % year-on-year increase. A total number of 6,733 foreigners obtained their employment permits in Shanghai in the first quarter of 2002, up 30% over the same period in the previous year. The administration also received 33,801 employment applications from Taiwan, Hong Kong and Macau people.

Chinese Visa (Classification)

Type	Applicants	Validity
L (Tourist)	Tourist	30 days
F (Business) Businessmen with invitation	Multiple entry	3-6 months
D (Resident)	Family members of expatriates	-
G (Transit)	Individuals on transit	Overnight stay
X (Student)	Students with invitation from accredited Chinese institutions	-
Z (Work)	Foreigners working in China	6 months renewable

For Z and D Visa application

Foreign Entry and Exit Permit Division, Public Security Bureau

333 Wusong Road, Shanghai Tel: 86-21-63577925

For Z, X and D Visa holders' physical exam

Shanghai Entry and Exit Inspection and Quarantine Bureau

1701 Hami Lu, Shanghai

Green Cards

Shanghai has started to issue so-called "green cards", or permanent residence permit, to overseas residents in order to attract overseas investors and talent. The green card allows the holder to engage in scientific research activities, to start a business, to send his/her children to school under the same conditions as locals, and to enjoy preferential taxation treatment. This has been recognized as a breakthrough in the city's bid to attract domestic and overseas talent.

According to the official report of the Shanghai Personnel Administration, about 90% of the green card holders are returning Chinese students, many holding US green cards concurrently. The rest are foreign nationals and overseas Chinese from Taiwan, Hong Kong and Macau.

Settling in

The whole of Shanghai is in transition. An increasing number of foreigners have chosen Shanghai as the city to settle in and start their businesses.

Getting Around

Although Shanghai is a huge city, the layout of its streets and the prominence of new landmarks make it relatively easy to get around. It is advisable to travel with a map. Shanghai offers commuter buses and the Metro, both inexpensive. But newcomers to Shanghai are advised not to ride on the public buses as it may be a challenging, and potentially unpleasant experience.

Foreigners may be amazed by the fact that bicycles are the most commonly used method for commuting. However, bicycle theft is also common and mountain bikes are usually prime targets. On the other hand, taxis are the most convenient means of travel in Shanghai, and they are economical. Foreigners who are not proficient in Mandarin should bring along addresses written in Chinese, since taxi drivers hardly speak English, let alone other foreign languages.

Driving in Shanghai

Those who wish to drive may obtain a Driver's License by surrendering their existing foreign or international licenses, which will be held until they leave the country. They are also required to undergo a physical examination and to purchase third-party insurance. Shanghai residence is a prerequisite. There are numerous traffic rules and one-way lanes which foreigners may not be comfortable with. Drivers should take note of the many bicycles, motor scooters and jay-walking pedestrians on the roads, which makes driving in Shanghai an experience considerably different from most other cities. The wisest choice, however, may be to hire a local driver to avoid the frustration of dodging bicycles and pedestrians.

Steps to getting a local driver's license:

- Get two application forms, which must be duly completed in Chinese, at Department of Automobiles, 1101 Zhongshan North 1 Road (Tel: 86 21 6516 8168 ext. 5332);
- With completed forms and RMB150, applicants must go for a health checkup at the Foreigners' Section, Huadong Hospital, 221 Yan'an West Road (Tel: 86 21 6248 3180);
- Translate the original driver's license at Shanghai International Studies University, Dalian West Road (Tel: 86 21 6542 2912 , 6531 1900 ext. 2360);
- With all documents and four passport-sized photos, RMB20, and a copy of your company's Business License, applicants must pass a written test (in English) at the Department of Automobiles;
- Those with less than 3 years' driving experience must take a road test;
- Pick up the license one week later.

Accommodation

The property market in Shanghai is open to all – the previous restrictions for purchase and lease to both foreigners and locals have been removed. Unlike in Beijing, foreigners may now live wherever they choose in Shanghai, whether in local housing, serviced apartments or star hotels.

The only legislative requirement is that foreigners need to register at the Foreign Affairs division of Public Security Administration within 72 hours after signing a lease agreement.

The types of houses available in Shanghai vary but could be mainly categorized into Old Houses, Grade-A Apartments, Serviced Apartments, Budget Apartments and Villas. Everyday, an increasing number of foreigners are in search for a new home with a certain budget in mind. To avoid frustration and disappointment, foreigners should keep their expectations in line with their budget. Once a property of choice has been located, the inevitable negotiations will begin, and this is why having an experienced agent working on your behalf becomes crucial.

Although often neglected, foreigners should be particularly aware of the Residential Contract of the property. Finally but most importantly, foreigners should ensure that the agency they choose offers satisfactory follow-up services so that assistance will be available throughout the whole process.

Housing Areas

The Shanghai housing market is divided into the areas of Downtown, Midtown, Gubei New Area and Hongqiao in western Shanghai. Foreigners typically live in apartments, semi-detached houses and villas. Apartments are found inside and outside the city, while semi-detached houses and villas are usually found outside the city center. Expatriate housing is generally fully furnished. All foreign housing has IDD telephone lines and satellite TV (which includes CNN, HBO, CNBC, Star TV and others).

Rental prices vary widely, depending on location, type of accommodation, quality, property management and incorporated facilities and amenities. The prevailing rental rates are estimated at USD 20 per sq meter per month, based on gross floor area. Recent trends show that, due to the strong demand in high-end properties, rents for the mid-to-upper market register an average increase of 6%. The average vacancy rate for all types of expatriate housing properties is currently at a level of 30%, though varying in locations.

Generally speaking, rental contracts are for a minimum one-year period and the price for the second year is usually negotiable. Rental is usually paid in quarterly instalments, and a security deposit equivalent to three months' rent is often required. Commission for the agent, if any, typically equals the amount for a one-month rental.

LUXURY VILLAS

Location	No. of bedrooms	Size (m²)	Rent (USD) per month
Downtown	3	180-200	4800-5000
	4	200	6000
Hongqiao	3	130-230	3000-4000
	4	170-350	3000-5500
	5	250-400	4400-6400
Xuhui	3	140-500	3000-4500
	4	300	4000
Pudong	3	240-340	4800-6000
	4	260-300	4500-6800
	5	240-420	5000-6500

APARTMENTS

Location	No. of bedrooms	Size (m²)	Rent (USD) per month
Downtown	3	150-290	4000-5600
	4	240	4200-5800
Hongqiao	3	140-240	2400-6000
	4	200-350	4000-5000
Xuhui	3	140	1600-2400

Note: Figures are approximated   Source: www.worthenpacific.com

The rents of major housing areas are estimated as follows:

Hongqiao and Gubei New Area, a large newly built residential area to the west of downtown, used to be a prime choice for expatriates living in Shanghai. The popularity of these locations was largely due to its proximity to the Hongqiao International Airport and relative convenience in commuting to the city – both within a 15-20 minutes' ride by taxi. Facilities catering to foreigners include international schools, restaurants and supermarkets like Carrefour, making settling in a relatively easy process. Housing, in the form of apartments, serviced apartments and villas are plentiful and often of the highest quality in town – most have their own gardens and playing grounds for kids. Although the area's popularity has been partly compromised by newly emerged residential properties across the municipality, the area remains attractive to newcomers, particularly those with families. It is a suitable place where one may enjoy the peace and tranquility.

Pudong has recently emerged as a hot spot for foreigners who want to be in closer touch with Shanghai's latest developments. With the establishment of Pudong International Airport along with the development of Lujiazui Finance and Trade Zone, this area is set to become the new settlement for foreigners in Shanghai. In fact, housing in Pudong boasts green surroundings and fresher air, both precious in the industrialized metropolis. The constant improvement in infrastructure, enhanced accessibility and the establishment of many MNCs in Pudong have promoted the demand for housing in this area. Most of the houses here are new and well designed. Large open spaces, luxurious garden habitat, less traffic, subway and bridges add additional merits to its living environment, but naturally, also raise the cost of living.

Rental in Pudong is now comparable to that in Hongqiao and Gubei. A 3-bedroom apartment can easily cost the lessee a sum more than USD 4,000 per month. For a two to three-storey villa, the price can be as high as USD 9,000.

Puxi area, literally meaning west of the Huangpu River, is Shanghai's old town. It is currently still undergoing an urban redevelopment. Most of Shanghai's shopping centers, commercial streets, service providers and municipal-level government bodies are located here. Living downtown ensures convenience to work, public transportation, bars, restaurants, and business partners. However, there is also noise, air pollution and traffic congestion to put up with.

Districts like Xuhui, Luwan, Huangpu and Jing'an have been foreigners' favorites as these areas are often equated with prosperity, elegance and the nobility of Shanghai. A large number of architecturally-aesthetic old houses and villas are set back from major roads and lie quietly in peaceful lanes and alleys, adding much character to the city landscape of Shanghai. Many foreigners find that old houses in the Puxi area are the perfect choice in trying to find "a home away from home".

Despite the lack of green space and the all-too-often traffic jams, demand for these properties far exceeds supply. Most of the available properties appear on the market only for a few days, before they are quickly snapped up. Of course, brand-new condominiums are also numerous in town, providing another alternative for expatriates and their family members.

Monthly rental in Puxi may be as low as USD 1,200 for a one-bedroom apartment for singles, with a space measured between 80-120 m². Normally, unit rent hardly exceeds USD 20 per m² per month unless tenants ask for very high-end facilities or amenities. With a monthly budget of USD 3,000, expatriates are able to lead a decent and comfortable life in the heartland of Shanghai.

Source: www.worthenpacific.com

HOTELS

While Shanghai continues to grow into one of the world's most expensive cities in terms of expatriate living expenses, hotels in Shanghai still maintain fairly reasonable prices and services for overseas visitors who need a short stay in the city.

The hotel business was among the first sectors in China which opened for foreign investment. International leading hoteliers and foreign funds have been flooding Shanghai since the early 1980s.

SIMPLY GRAND

Spectacularly positioned on the upper floors of the landmark Jin Mao Tower.
The city's most luxurious accommodation with views to take your breath away.
12 acclaimed restaurants and bars to send your taste-buds soaring.
Why settle for down-to-earth travel when we can bring you closer to the stars.

FEEL THE HYATT TOUCH®

GRAND
HYATT
SHANGHAI

Jin Mao Tower, 88 Century Boulevard Pudong, Shanghai Phone: 86.21.5049.123 www.shanghai.grand.hyatt.cor

In China, only tourist hotels are able to accept foreign guests. Under the China National Tourism Administration (CNTA), most of them are star-rated hotels.

By the end of 2003, Shanghai had 338 such hotels with an average occupancy rate of 67.5%. With China's entry into WTO, Shanghai's high-end hotels are showing great potential, but are facing fierce competition too. To date, there are 20 five-star and 26 four-star hotels in Shanghai, among which are many of the international renowned chains of hotels, such as the Marriott, Four Seasons, Sofitel, Novotel, Hilton, St. Regis, Holiday Inn and Shangri-La. Most of them manage to maintain an occupancy rate of above 70%.

Jin Jiang, the largest hotel management company in China and Shanghai's local brand, now manages 53 hotels nationwide; in Shanghai, four five-star hotels, five four-star hotels and 10 three-star hotels are under its brand name, including Jin Jiang Hotel, Jin Jiang Tower, Huating Hotel, Peace Hotel and Park Hotel, most situated at the city's premier locations.

With the ever-growing power of web community, discounted rates, often involving substantial savings, are readily available for budget-conscious travelers.

Education

For foreign children accompanying their parents to Shanghai, it is recommended that they first consult an international school.

In recent years, an increasing number of international schools have emerged to meet the ever growing expatriate population in Shanghai. These include Shanghai American School, Shanghai Singapore International School, Yew Chung Shanghai International School, Concordia International School Shanghai, Shanghai Changning International School, French, German and Japanese Schools.

Shanghai American School

Established in 1912, the Shanghai American School (SAS) is the first international school in mainland China. As the largest international school in Shanghai, SAS offers pre-kindergarten courses through grade 12 classes to more than 1,700 students from about 50 nationalities, most being Americans, Koreans and Taiwanese. It offers American curriculum on two campuses in Puxi (elementary through high school) and Pudong (pre-kindergarten through grade 8).

Fully accredited by the Western Association of Schools and Colleges (WASC), SAS is an independent non-profit school owned by the SAS Parent Association. The annual school fees for 2002-2003 range from USD 11,500 for pre-kindergarten to USD 20,000 for grade 9 though 12.

Source: www.saschina.org

Shanghai Singapore International School

Founded in 1996, the Shanghai Singapore International School (SSIS) offers a balanced curriculum in line with the educational policies of Singapore. Located in Zhudi town of Minhang district, SSIS is near to Shanghai American School's Puxi campus.

Besides a bilingual education system, SSIS enables its pupils to access authentic Singapore-produced textbooks and learning materials. Offering pre-school (aged 3 to 6), primary school (aged 7 to 12) and secondary school (aged 13 to 16) education, SSIS maintains competitive rates in tuition. Full day program for pre-school is between USD 7,000 and USD 8,000, and ranges from USD 8000 to USD 12,000 for primary and secondary school per year.

Source: www.ssischool.com

Yew Chung Shanghai International School

First established in Hongqiao by the Hong Kong-based Yew Chung Education Foundation in 1993, Yew Chung Shanghai International School now boasts two other campuses in Gubei and Pudong. It also has sister schools in Hong Kong, Beijing, Yantai and Chongqing.

Yew Chung offers an international curriculum based on the National Curriculum of England, with a bilingual approach. It provides programs for 1 to 2 years old up to secondary school students. The Infant and Toddler Learning Program is priced at USD 4,000-USD 11,000 per year, depending on number of days per week; Kindergarten (K3 and K4), Primary (Year 1 to 6), and Secondary (Year 7 to 13) schools are at USD 17,000, USD 17,500 and USD 18,000 per year, respectively, excluding miscellaneous charges.

Source: www.ycef.com

Healthcare

Foreigners in Shanghai should be vaccinated against hepatitis A and B, typhoid, tetanus and polio. They should also avoid drinking tap water, and use boiled or distilled water instead. Mineral water is widely available, as are a wide range of water purifiers and distillers. Vegetables should be thoroughly washed in water that contains a drop of iodine.

Shanghai is home to a number of well-equipped hospitals that have special foreigner departments. Some hospitals have also formed joint ventures with organisations from Hong Kong, Australia and Japan, and this has improved the level of services and skills they offer. At the same time, they are also seeking to enhance their capability in providing emergency treatment that meets international standards.

Famous hospitals in Shanghai include Huadong Hospital, Zhongshan Hospital, Shanghai No. 6 People's Hospital, Huashan Hospital, Shanghai No. 1 People's Hospital and Xinhua Hospital. In Shanghai, foreigners are familiar with World Link Medical and Dental Centers, whose international team of medicals and dental professionals provide primary healthcare, pediatrics, obstetrics-gynecology, and a full range of dental services. Premier members even have 24-hour access to physicians.

Places of Worship

Shanghai is home to a number of places of worship for all beliefs. There are mosques on Xinle Road, while Xujiahui Cathedral and Shanghai

Community Church at Hengshan Road serve the Catholic and Protestant communities respectively. Buddhists may choose to go to the Jade Budda Temple at Anyuan Road, Longhua Temple at Longhua Road, and Jing'an Temple at Nanjing West Road, which are also attractions for sightseers. A 780-year-old Confucius Temple is located in Jiading District of Shanghai, where people may show their respect to the greatest philosopher and educationist of ancient China.

Shopping

Shops and department stores in Shanghai are among the most well stocked in China. They boast a wide variety of stylish local and foreign goods. The three major shopping streets are Nanjing Road, Huaihai Middle Road and Sichuan North Road.

Often cited as China's No.1 Commercial Street, Nanjing East Road was formerly a small street in the British Settlement in Shanghai. It was not until the 1930s that four big Chinese department stores pushed it into the forefront of the business center of the Far East. The 5.5 km road now comprises the Nanjing Walking Street and a shorter extension linking it to the Bund. Along the street are Shanghai No.1 Department Store, New World, Isetan, Shanghai Landmark Tower, the Century Park and many other elegant commercial centers and hotels.

Huaihai Middle Road is all about shopping, with newly erected spacious department stores shining under the sun along a road colorfully lined with flowerboxes. Called Xiafei Road in the past French Settlement, Huaihai Road has always been equated with sophisticated

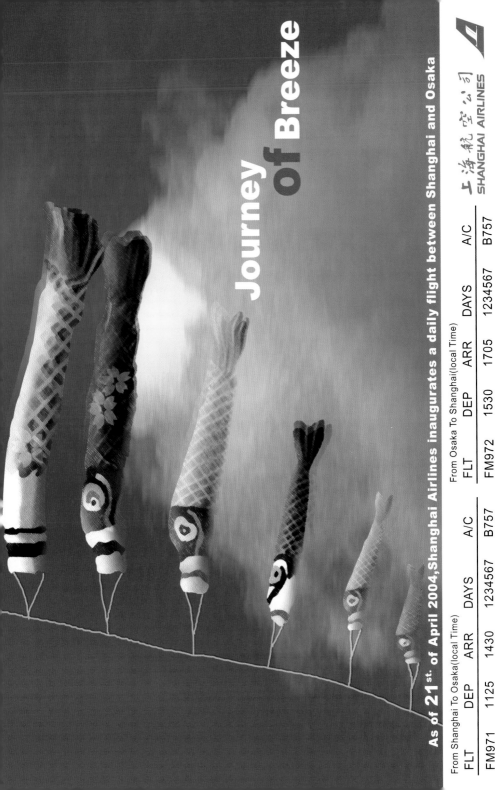

Journey of Breeze

As of 21ˢᵗ of April 2004,Shanghai Airlines inaugurates a daily flight between Shanghai and Osaka

上海航空公司
SHANGHAI AIRLINES

From Shanghai To Osaka(local Time)

FLT	DEP	ARR	DAYS	A/C
FM971	1125	1430	1234567	B757

From Osaka To Shanghai(local Time)

FLT	DEP	ARR	DAYS	A/C
FM972	1530	1705	1234567	B757

Shanghai Airlines Center Ticket Office：Great Hall of No.212 Jiangning Road Shanghai   Reservation Hotline：800-6208888(Shanghai) 021-62550550

shopping and stylish hospitalities. Shopping malls like Times Square, Hong Kong Plaza and Shanghai Square line the east side of the road.

Xintiandi, or "New Heaven and Earth" in Chinese, is a newly constructed area near Huaihang Middle Road. It now hosts a wide range of boutiques selling fashionable goods, creative home furniture, as well as arts and crafts, and many trendy restaurants with exotic and fusion cuisines. Supermarkets and department stores can be found here too, such as Metro, Carrefour and Isetan.

To experience the incredible pleasures in "bargaining" (or "haggling" with the hawker), shoppers may also patronise Xiangyang Market near Huaihai Road, Dongtai Road Market and Fuyou Road Market, where branded products of different qualities and antiques can be found.

Foreigners may easily locate foodstuffs and household goods at chain supermarkets and convenient stores all over the city, including Carrefour, Tops, Metro, Hualian, Lianhua, Watson's and Wellcome. The supermarkets offer foodstuffs ranging from fresh meat and seafood, vegetables, wines and liquors, bread, to pet food. Some supermarkets, such as City Supermarket, also provide free home delivery services.

Leisure

Nightclubs, pubs, discos, and karaoke lounges catering to all styles and tastes abound throughout the city. As one of China's cultural centers, Shanghai offers a wealth of entertainment options, from theatre and Chinese opera, ballet and symphony, to museums. Gourmets will appreciate the city as it is also home to a variety of restaurants, be it German, Italian, Spicy Sichuan or Crude Cantonese.

Health-conscious foreigners will find an abundance of health clubs, mainly in the city's large hotels. Most are well equipped with the latest gym apparatus, and supervised by trained professionals. Facilities include swimming pools, squash and tennis courts, and aerobics rooms. Memberships are available, but prices could be expensive and services vary.

Some leading clubs for foreigners include Shanghai International Club, Portman Health Club, Holiday Inn Health Club and Hilton Health Club.

Shanghai offers the visitor a great city life. Taking a cruise drifting down the Huangpu River at night or having a family picnic at Dianshan Lake in the suburbs are just two of the many pastime options.

Attractions in Shanghai

The Oriental Pearl TV Tower and the Jinmao Tower

With a height of 468 meters, the Oriental Pearl TV Tower is the tallest TV Tower in Asia and the 3rd highest in the world, after the 553-meter CNN Tower in Toronto, and the 535-meter Moscow TV Tower. Eleven spheres with various sizes are inlaid "from the blue sky down to the green lawn", resembling a string of pearls. The sphere at a height of 263 meters is an observation hall from where a breathtaking panorama of the metropolis is clearly presented.

Within walking distance of the Oriental Pearl Tower is the 88-storey Jinmao Tower. At a dizzying height of 420.5 metres, it was completed in August 1998 and cost USD 560 million to build. Grand Hyatt Shanghai occupies the 53rd to 87th floors, which makes it the tallest five-star hotel in the world.

The Bund

The Bund originates from an Anglo-Indian term for the embankment of a muddy waterfront. Called "wai tan" in Chinese, it refers to a stretch of the west bank of the Huangpu River. It was Shanghai's Wall Street, a place of feverish trading and an unabashed playground for Western business sophisticates.

Still a grand strip of hotels, banks and shopping streets, the Bund remains an intrinsic part of Shanghai's character. Everyday, Chinese and foreign tourists pad along the Bund's grand edifices reminiscent of neoclassical 1930s downtown New York or renaissance in any European citiy. The 52 buildings are a great collection of different architectural styles such as Gothic, Baroque, Roman, Renaissance, British, French and East Indian. Among them are the old  homes to Hong Kong and Shanghai Bank, the Banque de l'Indochine, and AIA. Today, the Bund is a spectacular symbolic illustration of the financial and economic development of Shanghai.

Yu Garden

Yu Garden, or "yu yuan" in Chinese, offers a wide variety of delicious snacks, souvenirs, and arts and crafts in a traditional Chinese setting. Its original  owners, the Pan family in China's Ming Dynasty during the 15th century, spent 18 years developing the area. It was used as headquarters during the Shanghai Little Dagger Society Uprising of 1853.

Today, it has been restored and attracts throngs of Chinese and international tourists amazed by its perfect combination of halls, pavilions, terraces, rockeries, ponds and bridges – typical components of a traditional Chinese garden.

The People's Square

Located at the heartland of Shanghai, between the bustling Nanjing Road and the raised Yan'an Viaduct, the garden-style square undertakes multiple functions to promote the city's culture, transportation and commerce. Extensive renovation was carried out from the end of 1993 to 1 October 1994, the National Day. A racecourse in the years preceding 1949, the People's Square is now the home to Shanghai Municipal Government, the Grand Theater, Shanghai Museum and the Urban Planning Exhibition Hall. It is a must-visit place where one can feel the modernisation and diversity of the city of Shanghai. Century Park is on the north, with an underground Metro Line 2 station.

The Shanghai Museum

The Shanghai Museum is situated in the heart of People's Square. It is 24 meters high with five floors, covering a total area of 38,000 m². The design springs from the overall environment of China, displaying symbols and artifacts of Chinese culture and tradition. The building uses an artistic conception of a round dome (sky) and square building (earth).

The museum was constructed with the best in modern architectural technology, and provisions are made for any special demands on the structure, such as earthquakes, fire, theft prevention, and flood, dust and light damage or contamination.

A museum of ancient Chinese art, it was founded in 1952. With a collection of over 120,000 pieces of cultural relics in twelve categories, including bronze, ceramics, calligraphy, paintings, jades, numismatics, furniture, seals, sculptures, minority art and foreign art, Shanghai Museum is especially famous for its collection of bronzes, ceramics, paintings and calligraphy.

As you view Shanghai Museum from a distance in People's Square, you will find that the building itself is a work of art, featuring multiple orientations, multi-visual angles and many distinctive characteristics. The elegant construction perfectly combines traditional cultural themes with modern technological innovation. Shanghai Museum portrays a cross-century image, and is one of the true scenic spots in metropolitan Shanghai.

The Shanghai Zoo

The Shanghai Zoo is more than a simple animal display area. It is an extensive cultural park. The Zoo was opened May 25, 1954, on the fifth-year anniversary of Shanghai's liberation.

After forty years of constant construction and improvements, the Shanghai Zoo now has a total area of more than seventy hectares. It has become a large integrative and interactive zoo with over five hundred animal exhibition areas exhibiting over 3,000 animals. The Zoo is especially proud of its Rare Animal Group exhibition areas, which contain displays of animal species that can be seen nowhere else on earth.

Three Longhua Marvels

The Old Temple, Flying Pagoda and Peach Garden are known among the locals as, loosely translated, the "Three Longhua Marvels." At the end of each year, pilgrims flood the site to attend the seasonal ceremonies and ring the bell to bring in the New Year. The temple, whose designs are based on Buddhist culture and local folk customs, bring together the temple, pagoda and garden into a beautiful whole. This area has become one of the greatest attractions and is actively promoted by the Chinese State Tour Administration.

Source: www.sh.com

ECONOMIC INDICATORS 2003

General

	Amount/ Quantity	Percentage Change (%)
GDP	USD 75.5 billion	+11.8
Government Revenue	USD 34.18 billion	+28.5
Government Expenditure	USD 13.3 billion	+25.6
Value Added		
• Primary Industry	USD 1.12 billion	+2.3
• Secondary Industry	USD 37.82 billion	+16.1
• Tertiary Industry	USD 36.57 billion	+8

Domestic Investments

	Amount/ Quantity	Percentage Change (%)
Fixed Assets	USD 29.63 billion	+12.1
• Infrastructure	USD 11.2 billion	37.8% of total Fixed Assets Investment
• Real Estate	USD 10.9 billion	36.8% of total Fixed Assets Investment
Industrial	USD 9.67 billion	+16.2

Foreign Investments

	Amount/ Quantity	Percentage Change (%)
Total FDI Contracts	4321	+43.5
Total FDI Contract Value	USD 11.06 billion	+23.5
Total Value Added, Tourism Enterprise	USD 4.08 billion	+3.3

Trade

	Amount/ Quantity	Percentage Change (%)
Total Foreign Trade	USD 122.4 billion	+54.7
Total Imports	USD 63.9 billion	+57.4
Total Exports	USD 48.48 billion	+51.2
• Exports to USA	USD 12.76 billion	+63
• Exports to Russia	USD 18 million	+71.8
• Exports to EU	USD 10.6 billion	+84.5
• Exports to Asia	USD 21.78 billion	+34.7
• Exports to ASEAN	USD 3.86 billion	+36.3

Social Development

	Amount/ Quantity	Percentage Change (%)
Total Population (residents only)	13.41 million	-3.29
Total No. of Employed Persons	5.8 million	+57,000
Foreign Employees		
• from outside China	1,400	-
• from other parts of China	26,400	-
Unemployment Rate	4.9%	-
Average Annual Per Capita Income	USD 2,680	+13.8
Household Annual Disposable Income	USD 1,798	+12.2
Consumer Price Index (CPI)	+0.1%	-
Number of Credit Cards Issued	40.8 million	-
Total Expenditure, Credit Cards	USD 18.8 billion	+46

Property Market

	Amount / Quantity	Percentage Change (%)
Real Estate Sales Prices		+20.1
• Commercial Property Sales Price	-	+20.5
• Residential Property Resale Price	-	+21.6
• Residential Property Rental	-	+2.1

Economic Production

	Amount/ Quantity	Percentage Change (%)
Agricultural Production Value	USD 23.95 billion	+2.3
Industrial Production Value	USD 286.58 billion	+17.6
High-Tech Production Value	USD 298 billion	+43.5
Value Added Construction	USD 3.2 billion	+1.3

Information Infrastructure

	Amount / Quantity	Percentage Change (%)
Mobile Phone Users	10.9 million	+1.85 million
Internet Users	4.3 million	+120,000
Users with Broadband Connection	924,900	+57,700

Financial Development

	Amount / Quantity	Percentage Change (%)
Banking and Finance Revenue	USD 7.6 billion	+7.6
Total Assets of Foreign Financial Enterprises	USD 3.3 billion	-
Total No. of Foreign Financial Enterprises	89	-
• Banking and Financial branches	62	-
• Insurance Companies	41	+5
Total Value, RMB Assets	USD 6.35 billion	-
Total Value, Insurance Premiums	USD 3.5 billion	+22
Total Value, Securities Transaction	USD 1,000 billion	+70.6
• Shares Transaction Value	USD 251 billion	+22.8
• Bonds Transaction Value	USD 744 billion	+70.6
• Funds Transaction Value	USD 4.37 billion	-35

Transportation

	Amount/ Quantity	Percentage Change (%)
Total Value Added, Transportation, Warehousing and Postal	USD 3.76 billion	+4.5
Total Cargo Volume	6.1 billion tons	+7.7
• Port Cargo	316 million tons	+19.9
• Air Cargo	1.6 million tons	21.9

Source: Shanghai Bureau of Statistics

THAMES TOWN

Thames Town. A unique English town in China
Sightseeing, entertainment, commercial and residential

Come experience the true-blue English town life now!

The 1 km² English-inspired Thames Town, with 350,000m² of building area, is designed by a British company WS Atkins. This picturesque town is a core project of the "One City & Nine Towns" initiatives actively put forward by the Shanghai Municipal Government.There will be commercial and residential areas, as well as facilities including a church, hospital, school, kindergarten, hotel etc. UK companies are welcome to partake in business opportunites in Thames Town.

General Developer:
Shanghai Songjiang New
City Construction &
Development Co.,Ltd.

Developer:
Shanghai Henghe Real
Estate Co.,Ltd.

**Reception Center
(Temporary):**
11F No.339,Le Du Road,
Songjiang District, Shanghai

+86 21 6781 2088

FORMS OF FOREIGN INVESTMENT

Introduction

China is relatively restrictive when it comes to setting up businesses although this is changing. The government is keen to attract foreign investment but most are in the form of joint ventures (JV) between foreign and Chinese companies.

Joint ventures are particularly encouraged in industries such as the media. Telecommunications equipment makers are usually all joint ventures. Some sectors, such as that of telecommunications service providers cannot even permit foreigners as minority shareholders.

However, more and more companies are being given special approvals. Even smaller foreign companies have succeeded in setting up wholly-owned foreign enterprises. It is increasingly common for a foreign investor to begin with a JV partner to facilitate setting up a business and dealing with government officials. Eventually, these foreign investors simply buy out the JV partner and start on their own.

The best rule of thumb is to investigate thoroughly any business opportunity before talking to any prospective partner. Chinese partners are often invaluable for navigating the murky depths of business in China and facilitating the setting up of a business.

Opportunities and Restrictions

Generally the best way to find out how to set up business in Shanghai is to contact your local consular office and inquire about the opportunities and restrictions which affect people of your nationality.

Usually there is a government agency that can provide basic information on the steps a foreigner needs to take, contacts he needs to establish and various documentary requirements.

Shanghai and its surrounding areas all have special economic zones (SEZs) which offer, for instance, different tax incentives. The best way to get this information is to contact your consulate in Shanghai or the Chinese consulate in your home country. The new financial and industrial/manufacturing center of Pudong is also one of the best places to approach to apply for tax write-offs and other incentives. You can try contacting the Economic and Trade Bureau of the Shanghai Pudong New Area:

Economic and Trade Bureau of the Shanghai Pudong New Area

Room 7Q, First Trade Tower 985 Dongfang Rd., Pudong New Area, Shanghai
Tel: 86 21 6876 7019; 6876 1766   Fax:86 21 6876 1766

Major Forms of Foreign Investment

There are three main types of foreign direct investment in China, namely, the equity joint venture (EJV), the cooperative joint venture (CJV) and wholly-owned foreign enterprise (WOFE). Collectively, they are referred to as "foreign invested enterprises (FIEs)".

By definition, joint ventures (including EJV and CJV) are jointly invested and established between one or more Chinese business entities or individuals and one or more foreign business entities or individuals in accordance with the Equity Joint Venture Law and Regulations or the Cooperative Joint Venture Law and Regulations. The fundamental feature of a joint venture in China is that the foreign party or parties hold 25% or more in the ownership of the joint venture. In contrast, a WOFE refers to a separate legal entity with limited liability status set up in China based on the Wholly Owned Foreign Enterprise Law and Regulations. In such an entity, the foreign investors hold 100% ownership.

Apart from the above three, other forms of foreign investment are also available, such as:

- Foreign Invested Holding Companies
- Foreign Invested Joint Stock Companies
- Build-Operate-Transfer (BOT)
- International Leasing
- Compensation Trade
- Processing and Assembling

Equity Joint Venture vs. Cooperative Joint Venture

JVs are legal persons under Chinese law and may own assets, sue and be sued. EJVs operate in the form of a limited liability company, which means that the personal wealth and property of the shareholding partners are shielded from corporate loss.

In comparison, CJVs can choose to acquire or not to acquire a legal person status. In other words, a CJV with non-legal person status is allowed to be set up, which is legally equivalent to a partnership establishment. It does not enjoy limited liability protection. In practice, the majority of CJVs are set up as limited liability companies.

The most significant difference between EJV and CJV is the allocation of profits and liabilities. In an EJV, profits and liabilities are allocated according to the ratio of the capital contributions made by the partners. It simply means that if one party contributes 30% of the capital investment, they will be rewarded 30% of the total profits and required to take up 30% of the liabilities.

CJV allows for greater flexibility in the agreement between the joint venture parties. In a CJV, profit sharing is generally prescribed by the joint venture agreement between the parties. In practice, the foreign party generally receives a higher percentage of profit in the early years of the CJV while their Chinese partner will become the owner of the fixed assets of the CJV at no cost after termination of the joint venture.

Wholly-Owned Foreign Enterprises

To promote more foreign investment, greater flexibility was introduced more than three years ago for foreigners to set up wholly-owned enterprises. WOFEs are now an alternative to joint ventures in some specific sectors. The restrictions imposed on WOFEs in areas such as foreign exchange balance, export obligation, priority of domestic sourcing, and the reporting requirements for production and operation plans have been removed. Due to a more liberalized and transparent regulation system, WOFEs have overtaken JVs in recent years to become the most popular form of foreign investment.

Export obligation

Under the revised law, WOFEs no longer have to export all or the majority of their products. According to the original law, enterprises with foreign capital "shall" be established in such a manner to help promote the development of China's national economy and they "shall" adopt advanced technology and equipments, and market all or most of their products outside China.

But the amended laws state that foreign enterprises are "encouraged" to market their products outside China and use advanced technology. This change gives a greater degree of autonomy to WOFEs to sell their products in China's domestic markets.

Sourcing

According to past regulations, WOFEs should purchase their production equipment and raw materials in domestic markets. The revised law now stipulates that when purchasing raw materials within the permitted scope of its operation, an FIE "may purchase the goods in China and may also buy them in the international markets." With these new amendments, WOFEs in China can enjoy greater freedom in purchasing.

Foreign exchange

The original regulation on WOFE required a WOFE to achieve the balance of foreign exchange income and expenditure. In the current amendments, the provisions on "foreign exchange balance" requirement for WOFEs have been removed.

Production and Operation Plans

WOFEs were also previously required to submit their production and operation plans to the authorities for filing. This requirement has, to a certain extent, impeded the daily operations and management of WOFEs. The revised laws on Foreign Capital Enterprises and Sino-foreign Equity Joint Ventures have deleted this item. WOFEs now have greater autonomy in operation.

Industrial restrictions

On the other hand, the industrial restrictions on WOFE have also been gradually lifted. According to the 2002 Industrial Catalogue promulgated by the Ministry of Foreign Trade & Economic Cooperation (MOFTEC), WOFEs can be set up in all the "Encouraged" and "Restricted" sectors except those specified as "exclusive for joint ventures".

Currently, the areas in the "Encouraged" category exclusively reserved for joint ventures are considered strategic or of great importance to the nation's social and economic development and security:

- Construction and operation of municipal light railways;
- Construction and operation of civic airports;
- Construction and operation of nuclear power plants;
- Exploration and mining of copper, lead, zinc and aluminum;
- Repairing, designing and manufacturing of special type or high quality ships;
- Manufacturing of nuclear power units (more than 600 megawatts);
- Construction and operation of comprehensive water irrigation systems;

- Construction and operation of trunk railway line networks;
- Airlines;
- Postgraduate-level education institutions;
- Manufacturing of air transportation control network equipment;
- Designing and manufacturing of civilian airplanes and airplane engines;
- Designing and manufacturing of satellites for civilian use; and,
- Designing and manufacturing of rocket launchers for civil purposes.

The areas in the "Restricted" category that are exclusively for joint ventures are:

- Development and production of grain, cotton and oil seeds;
- Processing of wood from precious trees;
- Exploration and mining of special and rare types of coal;
- Printing of publications;
- Smelting and separation of rare earth;
- Manufacturing of automobile cranes with capacity under 50 tons;
- General services (used in areas such as photography, mineral exploration and industries);
- Development of large tracts of land;
- Medical facilities;
- Senior high schools; and,
- Construction and operation of cinemas.

New Forms of Investment

In addition to setting up EJV, CJV or WOFE, other forms of investment are now available to foreign investors. Foreign investors can set up holding companies and foreign-invested joint stock limited companies in China. These two new forms of investment are expected to become more and more popular as China relaxes its laws and regulations in accordance with China's WTO entry agreement.

Foreign-Invested Holding Companies

Foreign-invested holding companies (FIHCs) refer to those EJVs or wholly-owned subsidiaries engaging in direct investment activities set up in China by foreign investors. They are set up as separate legal entities with limited liability status and independent from enterprises in which they invest (i.e. their subsidiaries).

In terms of business activities, FIHCs are restricted to only direct investment activities. Since 2001, FIHCs can also act as a promoter or shareholder of a joint stock company in China.

Unlike foreign manufacturing and trading enterprises, which are restricted to carrying out business only in the location specified in its business registration, FIHCs are able to invest in projects all over China.

However, there is a capitalization requirement for FIHCs. An FIHC is required to have registered capital of at least USD 30 million. The total loan amount that a foreign-invested holding company can borrow should not be more than four times its actual paid-up registered capital unless approved by MOFTEC. This is clearly different from the case of the more general forms of Foreign Investment Enterprises, where the limit of debt financing is determined by the total investment of the relevant foreign invested enterprises.

Foreign-Invested Joint Stock Companies

A foreign-invested joint stock company refers to an enterprise or a legal person that meets the following conditions:

- Its capital consists of shares of equal denomination;
- The liabilities of its shareholders are limited to the respective subscription of shares by such shareholders;
- Its liabilities are limited to the value of all its assets; and,
- The shares are held by Chinese as well as foreign shareholders and the foreign investors together hold more than 25% of total shares.

A foreign-invested joint stock company is considered as a type of foreign investment enterprise. With regards to foreign investment in China, all laws and regulations are applicable. In other words, it would be legally impossible to set up a foreign-invested joint stock company in the industrial sectors that prohibit foreign investment.

The minimum capitalization requirement for registering a foreign invested joint stock company is at least RMB 30 million (USD 3.62 million), of which foreign investors must subscribe and contribute more than 25%.

BOT

BOT (Build-Operate-Transfer) refers to the cooperative pattern in which the government signs a contract with a project company which will, according to the contract, collect funds and construct infrastructure projects. Over an agreed period of time, the project company will own, operate and maintain the project while reclaiming investment and making reasonable profits by charging fees. When the contract period is over, the ownership of the project will be transferred to the government. BOT is mainly adopted in developing infrastructure projects such as toll roads, power plants, railways, wastewater processing facilities and subways etc.

Forms of Indirect Foreign Investment

International Leasing

Primarily, there are three kinds of leasing trade called financial lease, operating lease and comprehensive lease. Under financial lease, long-term credit is extended by a leasing company to its client, that is, the leasing company will first pay for the purchase of the equipment selected by the client and then lease it to the client.

For the duration of the use of the equipment, both parties shall not arbitrarily terminate the contract; the lender shall retain ownership of the equipment while the client shall possess the right to use it. The client is responsible for the maintenance of the equipment and the leasing company shall collect rents from the client. Upon expiry of the lease, the client may require an extension of the lease or purchase the leased equipment at a negotiated price.

With this method, the leasing company provides equipment needed by the client and is responsible for the maintenance and repair of such equipment while the client pays rents according to the lease contract and returns the equipment upon termination of the lease.

Operating lease is limited to the period the equipment is used. It is usually applicable to short-term projects. The lease expires when the project is completed.

The comprehensive lease is a method whereby lease is combined with equity or contractual joint ventures, or lease is combined with inward processing and compensation trade. However, the method of combining lease with equity or contractual joint ventures shall be the portion outside the registered capital of the joint venture.

Compensation Trade

On the basis of credit, the foreign party provides the Chinese party with capital or equipment, technology and raw material, and undertakes to buy a certain quantity of products from the Chinese party. The Chinese partner compensates by installments to the foreign party directly or indirectly by using the products manufactured and the equipment and technology provided by the foreign party, or other products agreed upon with the foreign party. Inward Processing and Compensation Trade has been very popular since the beginning of the reforms.

Processing and Assembling

The foreign investors provide raw material, auxiliary material, parts, components or drawings, while the Chinese partner processes them or assembles them into finished products which are then returned to the foreign party for marketing. The Chinese party charges a fee for the processing. Alternatively, the foreign party provides production equipment with or without a price and funds for building the plant premises where the Chinese party collects a processing fee. The cost of production equipment purchased by the foreign partner shall be transferred to the Chinese party in installments using the processing fee.

Land Use Rights in Shanghai

Various types of foreign investment have been adopted in Shanghai, but the main forms of FDI remain Sino-foreign EJV, Sino-foreign CJV, and WOFE. Inevitably, setting up business involves land use. In China, the ownership of all urban land belongs to the State. Land transactions only involve land use rights and do not affect ownership of land. Underground natural resources, minerals, and objects buried or hidden in the land are not part of the transfer of land use rights.

Currently, investors may acquire land use rights through a grant or assignment from the government. The maximum terms for granting of land use rights are as follows:

- Residential purpose – 70 years
- Land for industrial purpose – 50 years
- Land for the purposes of education, scientific research, culture, public health and sports – 50 years
- Land for commercial, tourism and recreational purposes – 40 years
- Land for comprehensive purpose or other use – 50 years

Unless otherwise stated in the grant contract, or disallowed for planning reasons, the term may be extended on application by the grantee. Unless otherwise stated in the grant contract, land use rights may be assigned or mortgaged by the grantee. Land use rights may also be inherited. If grantees are FIEs, they are given the privilege of not paying ground rent, as stipulated in "Measures of Shanghai Municipality for Administration of Land Use by Joint Ventures Using Chinese and Foreign Investment".

SETTING UP BUSINESS

Introduction

Foreign entrepreneurs may now at their discretion determine organizational structure according to the operation of their enterprises. Shanghai, which is at the forefront of China's push for deeper reforms, is offering a more liberal environment to promote international investments.

Many measures are being taken to cope with the new challenges. These measures offer foreign entrepreneurs considerable advantages when they set up businesses in the metropolitan city.

Adopting the Right Approach

Foreigners intending to invest in Shanghai however, should approach the appropriate government departments to understand the legal procedures to save effort and time. First of all, you may consult People's Republic of China's embassies or consulates stationed in your home country or region for the right procedures.

Or you can directly contact the Shanghai Chapter of China's Council for the Promotion of International Trade, Shanghai Foreign Investment Service Center, or the overseas offices of Shanghai Foreign Investment Board regarding specific issues related to doing business in Shanghai. You may request for an invitation letter by stating the purpose of visit, proposed dates of stay, and the intended investment projects. Upon receiving a letter of invitation, you may proceed to the nearest embassy or consulate to apply for an entry visa to China.

Setting up JV or WOFE in Shanghai

Before doing business in China, foreign investors need to produce required documents in order to go through the process smoothly. The procedures and required documents for direct investment vary in the forms of business entity, such as Joint Ventures (JVs) and Wholly-owned Foreign Enterprises

(WOFEs). In general, there are some basic procedures that FIEs have to follow (see also *"FORMS OF FOREIGN INVESTMENT"*).

Letter of Intent (LOI) or Memorandum of Understanding (MOU)

This stage is for investors who wish to establish a joint venture in Shanghai. They need to reach a preliminary understanding with their Chinese partners in the form of LOI or MOU. These documents provide a basic description of the project, planned equity distribution among the partners and the amount of proposed capitalization. The latter will determine to which level the project approval application should be directed. Although LOI or MOU is not legally binding on both parties, it should nevertheless expressly specify provisions concerning exclusivity and confidentiality.

The preliminary agreement is attached to a project proposal to be submitted by the Chinese partner(s) to one of the authorities – MOFTEC, Shanghai Development and Planning Commission (SDPC), Shanghai Foreign Economic Relations and Trade Commission (SMERT), or the Shanghai Foreign Investment Board – for approval, depending on the scope and scale of the project.

Project Proposal

For JVs, the next stage is the submission of a project proposal. Chinese partner(s) should be solely responsible for preparation and submission of the proposal.

For WOFEs, to draft a proposal is the first step to setting up the business. It should be prepared by the foreign investors and submitted directly to the authorities in Shanghai. The foreign investor may appoint a local agent to liaise with the government. The foreign investor should thus sign an authorization letter stipulating the agent's scope of services, responsibility and fees.

Generally, the authority will give an official reply within 20 days upon receipt of the proposal and other relevant documents. The approval or disapproval letter will be issued to the foreign investor, if it is a WOFE, or to the Chinese partner, in the case of a JV. The foreign party in a JV should thus request a copy of this document from the Chinese partner to confirm that the approval is consistent with the agreed terms of the project.

Having received a favorable reply, the Chinese party of a JV or the foreign investor in a WOFE may apply to Shanghai Industrial and Commercial Administration for registration of company name.

Feasibility Study Report

Once the preliminary approval on the project proposal is obtained, a feasibility study is to be prepared. This involves all investing parties. A feasibility study is in fact a more detailed and expanded version of the previous project proposal. However, it must include:

- A general description of the project and the parties involved in the venture;
- Production plans and basic market research;
- Location of the project and reasons for the selection;
- Description and explanation of purposes of equipment and technology to be utilized;
- Organizational structure of the enterprise;
- Environmental protection, employment, construction plans and timetable;
- Capital sources; and,
- Attachments such as certificate of incorporation and business license, financial reports of the investing company, background information of legal representative, etc.

One important issue in drafting the feasibility study is the "scope of business" for the enterprise. The scope of business should be carefully defined, as it is likely to be repeated in the JV contract, articles of association and on the enterprise's business license. The scope of business on a Chinese business license delineates what activities the company is authorized to conduct; the language is usually narrowly construed.

Therefore, investors must make sure that the scope of business covers all categories of business activities planned for the enterprise. However, Chinese authorities will reject overly broad or vague language and narrowly interpret those broad or ambiguous words. So the scope must be described in precise terms. This might prevent the enterprise from engaging in business activities that the investor might have thought they were authorized to engage in.

Another key issue to be addressed in the feasibility study is capital contributions. Chinese authorities have a series of guidelines that must be followed with respect to the minimum amount of capitalization for each type of FIE. The specific amount should be confirmed with local agencies and it normally involves no less than USD 200,000. There is also a timetable. It is based on the size of investment and is meant for the foreign partners to fulfill commitments for capital contributions. In addition, investors should be aware of the maximum ratio of debt to equity allowed for a JV. There are also regulations requiring audits to confirm the valuation of state-owned assets to be counted as the Chinese partners' contributions to capitalization. Finally, foreign investors' contributions in kind require appraisals from Chinese import and export authorities.

The feasibility study is to be approved by MOFTEC, SDPC, SMERT, or the State Council, depending on the amount of investment. Usually, investments more than USD 30 million require state-level approval. However, due to the recent decentralization, those projects that fall in the "encouraged" category of the industrial catalogue may be approved by the Shanghai government itself

Contracts, Articles of Association

For JVs, the next step is the completion of contract, articles of association and the application for formal approval. While the feasibility study is under review, JV partners can work out the actual contract and articles of association. The contract incorporates all understandings and terms from the preliminary agreement, project proposal and feasibility study, though there may be some modifications. Chinese law views the joint venture contract as the fundamental document for the establishment of joint ventures. The contract must meet the conditions in China's joint venture law (for equity JVs) or cooperative enterprise law (for cooperative JVs). The feasibility study and preliminary project approval documents are included as appendices when the contract is submitted for formal approval.

As WOFEs involve no contract, the documents include a written application for the establishment of the WOFE, a feasibility study report, the articles of association, a list of board directors, an authorization letter of legal representatives, the foreign investor's certificate of incorporation and evidence of credit standing, the written approval of the project proposal and other necessary documents.

For both JVs and WOFEs, the articles of association must be drawn up and submitted as part of the formal application. Under Chinese law, the articles of association are viewed as the code of company governance – similar to the company by-laws or memorandum of association in other legal jurisdictions. Chinese law (JV regulations) contains detailed provisions regarding issues that must be addressed in the joint venture contract and articles of association.

It should include basic information about the enterprise: the enterprise's name and address, scope of business, total capital and organization chart. The JV regulations require that the JV contract and articles of association be written in Chinese. However, a foreign language version of the documents is frequently prepared and the parties may agree that both language versions have equal validity.

Generally, the authority that examines such applications will give a reply within 30 days on receipt of the feasibility study report, contract and the articles of association. After this approval, the Chinese party of a JV or the foreign investor of a WOFE may apply for the approval certificate. Shanghai Foreign Investment Board will issue the approval certificate within three days upon receipt of the application.

Business License

The WOFE or JV will need to register with Shanghai Industrial and Commercial Administration (SICA) and apply for a business license within 30 days upon receipt of the approval certificate. SICA will issue the business license within 10 working days to projects that have passed the examination. The enterprise is deemed as established on the date when the business license is issued.

Having acquired the business license, the enterprise must register with the State Tax Bureau, the Local Tax Bureau and the Customs House within a month, and must seek approval from the People's Bank of China in order to open a foreign exchange account or an RMB account with banks in Shanghai. FIEs are also required to register with the Shanghai Public Security Bureau to obtain residence permit for foreign personnel and approved family members; and to approach Shanghai Foreign Service Co. Ltd. for the recruitment of local staff.

Preparation of Documents

Apart from the key documents like project proposal, feasibility study report, contract (if any) and articles of association, a number of forms and documents have to be prepared. In the case of a WOFE registration, documents to be submitted include:

- Company registration application form;
- Application for company name;

- Appointment letter of directors;
- Name list of directors;
- Registration form of the legal representative (chairman of Board);
- Environment Impact Report;
- Letter of authorization in case the investor wishes to appoint a representative to handle the registration matters relating to the company in Shanghai;
- Lease agreement with local landlord (foreign investor should enter into a tenancy agreement before processing the registration);
- Certificate of incorporation of the investing company;
- Board resolution that approved the investment in Shanghai;
- Original copies of bank reference; and,
- Brief resume and photocopies of passports of directors, general manager and assistant general manager.

Setting up Representative Office in Shanghai

An overseas enterprise that wishes to establish a Representative Office (RO) in China may entrust a local agency to handle the matter and submit application on its behalf. Approving authorities may vary in respect to industries:

Approving Authorities for Representative Office Set-up*	
Trading, manufacturing, forwarding agency	SMERT*
Finance, insurance	People's Bank of China
Shipping and agency	Ministry of Communications
Airfreight	Civil Aviation Administration of China
Others	Relevant ministries in accordance with their nature of operations

*In Shanghai, most RO applications are filed with SMERT.
Source: SMERT

Preparation of Documents

The applicant should complete the form, "Application for registration of foreign enterprises' permanent office in China" issued by Shanghai Industrial and Commercial Administration (SICA), and prepare the following documents:

- The original Application letter, stating scope of business, trading history with China and reasons for RO establishment, etc;

- Brief introduction of the company. This document should include the company's registered capital, turnover, business scope, staffing, and business setups in other parts of China;

- Certificate of incorporation (photocopy is acceptable);

- A bank reference letter regarding the capital, transactions and credibility of the company;

- The Letter of Authorization of the chief representative. In the case that the chairman of the board is the chief representative, the other two directors should sign. In the case that general manager is the chief representative, signatures of the chairman and two other directors are necessary; board resolution is not compulsory but definitely appreciated;

- A brief resume, passport-sized photographs, photocopies of identity card and every page of passport of the Chief Representative;

- The Letter of Attorney by appointed chief representative to authorize relevant consulting firms to handle the application on behalf of the foreign company; and,

- Original rental agreement with local landlord. The original title deed and permit of RO of the property must be produced for verification upon submission of the application.

The foreign company should note that offices for ROs are pre-designated by SMERT and mostly located in the CBD area in Shanghai. As Chinese regulations regard "registered office" the same as "operating office", one office premise is allowed to be registered by one company or RO only. Furthermore, Chinese translation shall be provided throughout the documentation if the original documents are in foreign languages. However, Chinese versions produced by those appointed translation houses, often under SMERT, are acceptable.

Examination and Approval

The foreign company or its appointed consulting agent should complete and submit all the relevant documents to SMERT. SMERT will examine the RO applications of overseas enterprises, and, if satisfactory, issue an approval certificate within 30 days upon receipt of the application.

EMPLOYMENT PERMIT, EXPERT CERTIFICATE & RESIDENCE CERTIFICATE

A foreign-invested enterprise, which is intending to employ foreigners, is required to apply for employment permits for foreigners at the Shanghai Labor and Social Security Administration with the following documents:

- business license,
- approval certificate for setting up enterprise,
- application letter, and
- the employees' personal information.

After receiving the employment permit, the enterprise may apply for professional visa notification at SMERT, which is authorized by the Ministry of Foreign Affairs. Alternatively, the foreign employee can apply for a professional visa to enter China at a local Chinese embassy or consulate with the faxed copy of professional visa notification.

After entering China, and within 15 days, the foreign employee can apply for an employment certificate at Shanghai Labor and Social Security Administration with the following documents: professional visa, employment permit, employment contract, health certificate and photos of the foreign employee. With the employment certificate, the foreign employee can apply for residence certificate at the Exit and Entry Division of Shanghai Public Security Administration.

The appointed Shanghai agent of a foreign company can apply for professional visa notification on behalf of the chief representative and representatives. After receiving the professional visa notification, the chief representative and representatives may apply for professional visas at a local Chinese embassy or consulate. Upon entering China, they can apply for employment permit certificates at SICA.

Registration with Other Authorities

After receiving the approval, the foreign representative office will need to further register with various government bodies before its official opening:

- Registration with the SICA to obtain a registration certificate as well as a representative card;
- Registration with the Public Security Administration and preparation of company stamp;
- Registration with the Quality & Technical Supervision Administration to obtain a special identification number;
- Registration with the Authority for Foreign Exchange and opening a foreign currency account with the Authority;
- With approval from the Authority for Foreign Exchange, opening foreign and local currency accounts with banks in Shanghai;
- Registration with Local Tax Administration;
- Registration with State Tax Administration;
- Registration with the Customs House;
- Registration with Shanghai Foreign Service Co. Ltd. and completing proper formalities for hiring local employees;
- Application to the Labor and Social Security Administration for employment permits for foreign employees; and,
- Application to the Public Security Administration for residential permit and visas for foreign employees.

The entire registration process will probably take two months. The RO approval certificate is valid for three years. The registration of the RO is only valid for the duration of one year and has to be renewed annually.

TRADE OPERATIONS

Introduction

In line with China's booming trade, Shanghai put in a sterling performance in foreign trade in 2003, with high-tech products making major inroads into the overseas markets.

For more than a decade, Shanghai has experienced unprecedented growth in its foreign trade. The European Union, Japan and the United States are, and remain, the city's key foreign trade partners.

As at the end of 2003, total foreign trade hit USD 112.4 billion. Exports jumped 51.22% to reach USD 48.4 billion. Total imports amounted to USD 63.8 billion, a hefty increase of 57.4% over the previous year. Foreign-invested enterprises accounted for 60.75% of the total exports and 59.17% of the total imports respectively.

The momentum of growth continued unabated in 2004. In the first two months of 2004, foreign trade reported a year-on-year 51.4% rise. This

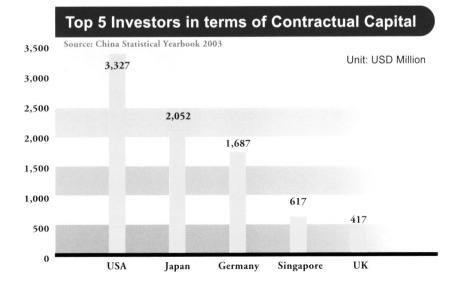

Top 5 Investors in terms of Contractual Capital

Source: China Statistical Yearbook 2003

Unit: USD Million

total included USD 17.3 billion in imports and USD 20.9 billion in exports, up 51.1% and 51.7% respectively.

Again, overseas-funded enterprises accounted for 67% of the imports, with the volume imported by private enterprises soaring 110% to reach some USD 1.1 billion, and that by State-run enterprises rising 28.5% to USD 4.6 billion.

Promoting Foreign Direct Investment

In its efforts to promote foreign direct investment, the city strongly favors investment in its manufacturing sectors, especially in the emerging industry of equipment manufacturing. Other major manufacturing sectors keen on attracting capital are micro-electronics, chemicals, fine steel and shipbuilding.

As most major manufacturing enterprises are State-owned, the city government will further give the all-clear to foreign companies wanting to take over or merge with State-owned firms.

Further Opening up of Service Sector

Meanwhile, as the most cosmopolitan city on the Chinese mainland, Shanghai will continue to lead the country in opening up the service sectors to international investors.

Commerce, medical services, tourism and education are the main sectors which will open wider to foreign funding, according to the local trade authority.

By late January 2004, the number of foreign firms in China was 468,200 with a total contracted investment up to USD 953.3 billion and actual investment of USD 505.55 billion.

Creating a Congenial Investment Environment

In order to create a congenial investment environment for overseas firms, the Chinese Central Government has gradually set up a relatively complete

legal system. In the past 20 years, the Chinese government has promulgated and issued a series of laws and statutes concerning the establishment, operation, termination and liquidation of foreign-invested enterprises.

Currently, the Chinese government is re-examining its existing laws and statutes in accordance with the framework of the WTO. It has abolished certain obsolete laws and regulations, and will gradually revise the laws and regulations that are incompatible with the rules of the WTO.

For instance, in 2000, China revised The Law of the People's Republic of China on Chinese-Foreign Contractual Joint Ventures and The Law of the People's Republic of China on Wholly Foreign-Owned Enterprises, and discarded certain restrictions regarding the balance of foreign exchange account and localization of supplies. In 2001 The Law of the People's Republic of China on Chinese-Foreign Equity Joint Ventures was also revised.

In March 2003, the State Administration of Industry and Commerce, State Taxation Administration and State Administration of Foreign Exchange further announced the temporary rules for foreign investors to buy enterprises in China.

The new rules, which came into effect in April 2003, are aimed at encouraging import of advanced technology, and managerial and administrative skills from abroad, in order to help perfect the economic environment in China. The rules stipulate that foreign investors should not wholly own the enterprise concerned. On the other hand, their total shares should not be less than 25% of the enterprise's equity.

Key Fields in which Investment is Encouraged

Shanghai will further improve the investment environment so as to absorb domestic and foreign investment, and encourage foreign business people to make further investment.

While implementing state policies and regulations on encouraging foreign investment is encouraged, Shanghai has singled out the following projects where investment is encouraged:

1. Communications, energy and important raw and processed materials industries and agricultural technological development projects urgently needed by the state;

2. Projects that meet the needs of the international market, help open up new foreign markets, promote the technological transformation of the existing enterprises in Shanghai, raise the grades of products and increase foreign earnings through product exports;

3. New equipment and new materials projects that import advanced technologies, improve the functions of products, and save energy as well as raw and processed materials, that help raise enterprises' technological and economic benefits, fill in the gaps in domestic production, and meet the needs of the market;

4. New-tech and new-design projects that utilize natural resources and regenerative resources in a reasonable and comprehensive way;

5. New- and high-tech industrial projects that suit the demands of the international and domestic markets;

6. Establishment of import and export trade enterprises, international entrepot trade enterprises and processing, packing, storing and transportation enterprises which serve international trade in the Waigaoqiao Free Trade Zone in Pudong; and,

7. Investments in the development of large tracts of land, especially in the transformation of the shanty towns in the old city area of Shanghai, and projects that can accelerate the development of other projects.

Import and Export

Foreign Trade Sector Opens Further

From March 2003, following the Ministry of Foreign Trade and Economic Cooperation announcement on the Provisional Measures on the Establishment of Sino-Foreign Joint Venture Foreign Trade Corporations,

Shanghai Import & Export Monthly Sheet by trade 2003, USD 10,000

Date	Accumulative Export						Accumulative Import					
	General trade value	change%	Processing Trade value	change%	Others value	change%	General Trade value	change%	Processing Trade value	change%	Others value	change%
Jan. 2003	139915	41.96	165706	57.19	3979	-12.75	210270	81.76	117345	66.43	109953	70.62
Feb. 2003	255230	38.97	326827	42.56	9942	-2.1	369109	67.51	217158	52.74	209862	69.65
March 2003	394372	39.02	521339	38.96	17983	.05	584517	62.85	349973	57.85	348239	78.76
Apr. 2003	566617	43.35	775297	48.04	33729	19.58	812530	55.64	488570	52.12	483571	71.64
May 2003	734974	46.34	1008770	55.91	41058	25.81	1046767	61.73	629823	52.07	618712	75.91
June 2003	896579	47.63	1235506	53.81	51450	27.7	1261156	62.64	765741	51.11	758469	77.07
July 2003	1082394	48.69	1496183	58.89	63202	31.15	1498303	60.4	926296	50.45	927061	72.35
Aug. 2003	1266221	47.09	1723318	57.29	77829	32.35	1746201	58.85	1086236	50.39	1083945	68.84
Sep. 2003	1455287	46.17	1999392	59.06	92760	34.76	2030937	56.81	1260845	47.75	1256080	67.28
Oct. 2003	1631268	45.94	2252515	58.06	104332	36.59	2264260	56.91	1431981	49.09	1411335	68.51
Nov. 2003	1814538	45.8	2551166	61.75	121223	44.9	2535526	56.52	1617861	49.56	1576832	67.68
Dec. 2003	1940559	41.54	2761895	58.56	143366	56.42	2813645	55.88	1815819	50.93	1760203	67.41

Source: http:www.investment.gov.cn/english/tjsj/ie_fmy.asp

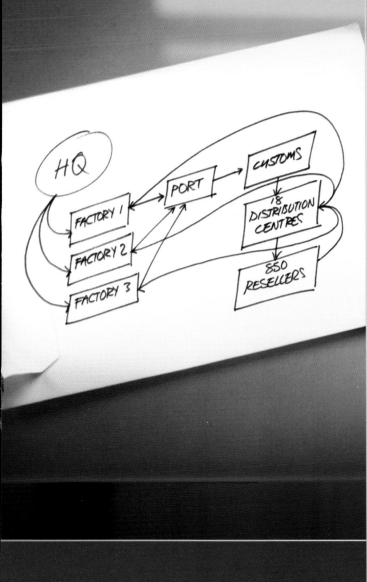

foreign investors now enjoy easier access to China's import-export sector. The most important step taken is the lowering of the "threshold" for foreign firms, as they will no longer be required to have a turnover of at least USD 5 billion in the year prior to submitting their application. This policy change is particularly favorable to foreign small- and medium-sized enterprises.

The new measures are expected to attract more foreign capital into China's import-export sector. For those establishing JVs in the central and western regions, the minimum requirement is much lower. The requirement that the foreign party must have had a representative office in China for at least three years has also been dropped.

Geographical and quantitative restrictions have also been lifted. However, JV import-export companies intending to operate in Shanghai's Pudong New District are still subject to some restrictions. The new measures are formulated by the Chinese government in a move to fulfill its WTO commitment to the granting of import-export rights to all FIEs in China three years after accession.

More liberal legislations in the pipeline

Changes have been made to most provisions of the law governing trading activities. There will soon be basic amendments in three major areas:

1. New provisions on the scope of foreign trade operators, foreign trade rights for trade in goods and technology, state trading, and voluntary import-export license. Under the amended law, foreign trade operators include natural persons, legal persons and other organizations. Foreign trade operators can engage in the import and export of goods and technology after registration.

2. New provisions on designated operation, restricted and prohibited imports/exports, intellectual property rights protection, foreign trade order, foreign trade investigations and foreign trade subsidies in line with WTO rules for the protection of China's industries and market; and,

3. New provisions on the establishment of an alert mechanism, a public information service system and other systems to meet the actual needs of foreign trade.

In view of the absence of punitive measures other than the revocation of foreign trade rights under the existing foreign trade law, the draft strengthens sanctions against illegal operations through the adoption of more severe forms of punishment, ranging from criminal and administrative penalties to business ban.

Lower Export Tax Rebate

The State Council is currently in the process of phasing out China's export tax rebate policy. The rate of export tax rebate will be gradually lowered in 2004. It is expected to be lowered from the present 15% to 11%, and a further cut of 3% to reach 8% eventually. Initially, however the export rebate of five products – wool, lead, coke, rare earth and tungsten has been totally abolished, and the entire policy will be scrapped by 2010.

The export rebate policy was aimed at boosting the competitiveness of export goods in world markets by avoiding double taxation on these goods in case import tariffs are imposed by the importing countries. But the policy has run into problems in that payment for large sums of export rebate due to export enterprises has been long delayed. According to statistics from the Ministry of Commerce (MOFCOM) and State Administration of Customs, overdue export rebates amounted to RMB 250 billion (USD 30.19 billion) at the end of 2002 and rose to RMB 350 billion (USD 42.27 billion) at the end of 2003.

Reform in export tax rebate policy is led by vice premier Wu Yi and the State Development and Reform Commission, with support from a number of related ministries. Although various ministries and research institutes have tabled different proposals before, they have now agreed that the export rebate policy should be phased out. Such a move would offset efforts made since 1998 in raising export rebate on a basic rate of 9.3% in a bid to boost the Chinese economy after the Asian financial crisis.

The impact of abolishing the rebate is expected to be minimal. For one reason, foreign companies will continue to source from China. Chinese export goods will remain competitive even without export rebates, as the country's key advantages lie in its highly affordable land/office rentals and skilled labor costs.

Setting up Foreign Trade Companies

Enterprises that wish to engage in the import and export business either for "foreign trade" purpose or for "self-operation" are required to apply for Import and Export Rights at the authorized foreign trade and economic cooperation commission (department or bureau) of all provinces, autonomous regions, and municipalities. In the case of Shanghai, Shanghai Municipal Foreign Economic Relations and Trade Commission (SMERT) is the approving authority.

Foreign trading companies may import and export all kinds of products and technology, except those specified as prohibited by MOFTEC. The applicants must meet the following requirements:

- The enterprise must have legal person status with at least one-year history and valid business license;
- Registered capital no less than RMB 5 million(USD 604,100), or RMB 3 million for those operating in central and western China;
- The enterprise has tax registration and passes the tax audit exercised by relevant taxation authorities; and,
- A qualified legal representative.

Application materials include:

- Formal application letter produced by the enterprise;
- Certified copy of corporate business license;
- Photocopy of certificate of tax registration;
- Photocopy of the legal representative's identity card; and
- Other relevant documents.

General View of Shanghai Import and Export, in USD 10,000, Dec 2003

Item	Value	Change%	Item	Value	Change%
Total Export	**4,845,820**	**51.22**	**Total Import**	**6,389,667**	**57.4**
by Trade			**by Trade**		
General Trade	19,040,559	41.54	General Trade	2,813,645	55.88
Processing Trade	2,761,895	58.56	Processing Trade	1,815,819	50.39
Others	143,366	56.42	Others	1,760,203	67.41
by Enterprise			**by Enterprise**		
State-owned	1,518,715	26.67	State-owned	2,005,582	44.3
Foreign-invested	3,079,444	60.75	Foreign-invested	4,115,782	59.17
Others	247,661	175.45	Others	268,302	220.04

Source: Shanghai Foreign Economic Relation & Trade Commission, Shanghai Foreign
Investment Commission

As the final decision is made at state level, SMERT will transfer the application to MOFTEC for approval. Upon receiving the documents, MOFTEC will check and reply within 10 working days. After receiving approval letter from MOFTEC, SMERT will issue the certificate of import and export enterprise qualification within five working days.

Import and Export for Self-Operation

Enterprises that wish to import machinery, components and materials for their own production purposes or export goods of their own are required to meet the following criteria in order to apply for an import and export permit:

- The enterprise has a valid business license;
- Registered capital of no less than RMB 3 million (RMB 2 million for those in central and western China, and RMB 1 million for research institutes, high-tech enterprises and enterprises that engage in machinery and electronic products);
- Tax registration; and,
- A qualified legal representative.

Application materials include:

- Formal application letter produced by the enterprise;
- Certified copy of corporate business license;
- Photocopy of certificate of tax registration;
- Photocopy of certificate of identification number issued by the Quality & Technical Supervision Administration;
- Photocopy of the legal representative's identity card;
- For high-tech enterprises or enterprises that engaged in machinery and electronic products, relevant certificates are required; and,
- Other relevant documents.

Upon receipt of the complete set of documents, SMERT will give its official reply within 10 working days and issue certificates for approved enterprises.

Usually, applicants will be asked to produce official approval letters from the local customs house and local foreign exchange administration, and a reference letter from banks indicating the enterprises' performance in the past three years.

Application forms can be downloaded from the following website: www.lbn.trade.sh.cn/banfa/biaoge.htm

Other Matters

According to SMERT's regulation in March 2002, enterprises registered in Pudong New District that apply for import and export rights can enjoy certain privileges with regard to application procedures and qualifications:

- For enterprises wishing to engage in foreign trade business, the requirement for the minimum one-year business history is waived;
- The registered capital can be as low as RMB 1 million for applicants for foreign trade business;
- For enterprises that wish to import and export for own operations, the registered capital minimum requirement could be RMB 500,000.

After receiving SMERT's approval and certificate, the enterprises need to proceed to other authorities, such as the Shanghai Industrial and Commercial Administration, tax bureaus, customs, quality supervision, foreign exchange administration etc to complete the formal procedures. They are also required to send a certain number of staff to familiarise themselves with the latest regulations on foreign trade and economic cooperation.

Every year from 1st January to 30th April, those enterprises are subject to SMERT's annual routine examination. Failure in participating or passing the examination will result in disqualification. The enterprise in question may not continue its import and export business and will be barred from re-applying for the certificate within that year. All enterprises are required to submit reports indicating that they were not ever fined in the past year by the local customs house, foreign exchange administration, taxation administration and other related authorities. For enterprises that had changes in enterprise's name, legal representative or registered capital, they have to apply for renewal of certificates.

In order to enhance the efficiency and to simplify the procedures, the 2002 annual examination adopted the E-registration method. Eligible enterprises could choose to go through the application by filling forms on a website (www.lbn.trade.sh.cn). For those not eligible for direct internet application, they could authorize the Shanghai Foreign Trade Enterprises Association for registration on their behalf.

Shanghai Foreign Economic Relations and Trade Commission
New Hongqiao Plaza, 55 Loushanguan Road, Shanghai, P. R. China 200335
Tel: 86 21 6275 2200   Fax: 86 21 6270 4708   Email: smert@online.sh.cn
Office hours: 9:30-11:30, 13:30-16:30 (Mon, Wed); 9:30-11:30 (Fri)
Source: www.smert.gov.cn

HUMAN RESOURCES AND RECRUITMENT

As Shanghai's economic growth continues to accelerate, the number of foreign companies entering China has increased dramatically. Intense business competition in recent years has caused significant shortage of qualified, highly skilled professionals. It is imperative that companies setting up businesses be fully aware of current trends and conditions in the Chinese job market in order to be effective in their recruiting strategies.

Recruitment

The trend towards localization of employees has increased salaries of locals and continues to level the playing field between foreign and local recruits. Recent surveys indicate that Shanghai will experience an average of 10% pay increase annually for management employees.

With greater foreign competition, unemployment figures are expected to rise as inefficient and unprofitable state-owned enterprises (SOEs) are forced out of business. Unemployment rate has reached 7% in recent years, much higher than the official rate estimated at just under 4%. The current movement of workers from agricultural and manufacturing-based economy to the service sector had resulted in an abundant supply of unskilled workers. Training and retaining employees has become a crucial task for the management.

Recently, more and more companies are beginning to localize their employees rather than hire foreign candidates. Higher education and better training facilities in China have raised the quality of skilled labor. Thus, many companies are choosing to staff locally rather than recruit expatriates from abroad. Human resources management is becoming more and more important in major cities like Shanghai. Competition for skilled professionals will be more vigorous than at any other time in the past.

Human Resource Market

When recruiting candidates in China, it is necessary to be aware of the different candidate options that are available to fill a position. The four types of candidates that are most often considered are: local Chinese employees, overseas Chinese, Chinese returnees, and expatriates. Each group has different strengths and weaknesses. Companies should carefully consider the position they are filling and compare the pros and cons of hiring candidates from each of these groups.

Executive Remuneration Levels 2002

Gross Monthly Base Salary (in RMB)	Shanghai	Beijing
Chief Executive Officer	24.255	15.376
Business Unit Manager	12.903	6.897
Production Manager	8.621	4.471
Project Engineer (Production)	4.741	3.448
Foreman (Production)	2.991	1.678
Manager (Engineering)	8.621	6.517
Proccess Engineer	4.741	5.503
Technical Employee	4.140	3.330
Project Engineer (Quality)	5.267	4.741
Sales Manager	7.759	6.034
Sales Support Assistant	3.448	3.736
Marketing Manager	6.914	7.851
Accounting & Finance Manager	8.621	4.741
Accountant	3.060	3.772
Human Resources Manager	4.677	5.603

Source: DeWitte & Morel

Local Employees

In recent years, local Chinese have become more familiar with western business practices. Training programs as well as more opportunities for higher education have afforded many practical skills. The percentage of the population with university education has risen significantly. By allowing more people access to private educational systems, the government is

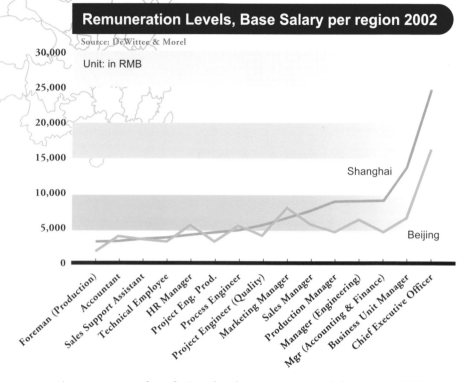

Remuneration Levels, Base Salary per region 2002

Source: DeWittee & Morel

Unit: in RMB

Shanghai

Beijing

Foreman (Production), Accountant, Sales Support Assistant, Technical Employee, HR Manager, Project Eng. Prod., Process Engineer, Project Engineer (Quality), Marketing Manager, Sales Manager, Production Manager, Manager (Engineering), Mgr (Accounting & Finance), Business Unit Manager, Chief Executive Officer

creating a stronger foundation for the country's workforce. Local Chinese candidates are increasingly being looked upon to fill not only entry-level positions but also middle and upper management.

Lower salary levels, as compared to expatriates or returnees, make local Chinese very attractive to businesses interested in cutting costs. Many companies have chosen to intensively train promising local Chinese candidates to take the place of the higher-salaried, hence more "expensive" expatriates.

Foreign Recruits

On the other hand, the Chinese government has also instituted changes in the immigration laws in order to lure overseas professionals into China. According to the China Daily, these changes include granting long-term or permanent residency status to professionals from abroad. These changes in the immigration laws are designed to facilitate the hiring of foreign recruits and to ease the shortage of qualified professionals in high-tech industries.

The newly established immigration law changes will apply to overseas Chinese, Chinese returnees, as well as expatriates. New regulations have also been introduced to make it easier for foreign headhunting firms to gradually enter the Chinese job market. Beginning on 1st October, 2002, foreign headhunting firms will be allowed to form joint ventures with local recruiters in China. This will further facilitate the hiring of foreign recruits.

Chinese Returnees

Returnees are people who were born in China, and who currently reside abroad for employment or educational purposes, but who wish to return to China for good employment opportunities. In the past, Chinese students or professionals leaving for countries abroad tended to remain overseas. Fewer than half of the students that have left China for higher education have returned. However this statistic has risen by 13% per year in recent years, indicating a greater desire to pursue opportunities back home.

A recent survey conducted in five prestigious Chinese universities such as Tsinghua and Peking found that over 140,000 students have returned to China after completing their education in the West, bringing with them new ideas and technology. Returnees reportedly have started nearly 4,000 new businesses in the country worth over RMB 10 billion (USD 1.2 billion).

The reason for the great demand for returnees in China is clear. Chinese returnees are familiar with both western culture and some may also have a knowledge of or experience with western business practices if they had worked overseas. Similar to overseas Chinese, however, the skills of returnees must also be scrutinized in order to arrange an appropriate compensation package.

In the past two years, the Chinese government has implemented many changes in order to attract the return of its citizens from abroad. For

Personal Income Tax Rate -
Applicable to Income from Wages and Salaries

Annual Taxable Income	%
Less than RMB 500	5%
RMB 500.01 ~ 2,000	10%
RMB 2,000.01 ~ 5,000	15%
RMB 5,000.01 ~ 20,000	20%
RMB 20,000.01 ~ 40,000	25%
RMB 40,000.01 ~ 60,000	30%
RMB 60,000.01 ~ 80,000	35%
RMB 80,000.01 ~ 100,000	40%
More than 100,000.01	45%

Source: China Income Tax Agency

Personal Income Tax Rate -
Applicable to Income of privately owned business and from contracted management or leasehold management for enterprises or institutions

Annual Taxable Income	%
Less than RMB 5,000	5%
RMB 5,000.01 ~ 10,000	10%
RMB 10,000.01 ~ 30,000	20%
RMB 30,000.01 ~ 50,000	30%
More than 50,000 .01	35%

Source: China Income Tax Agency

example, they have established 60 industrial or high-tech parks throughout the country for the purpose of attracting professionals to return and set up a targeted 2,000 enterprises. The Caohejing New Technology Development Zone in Shanghai, comprising over 600 enterprises and research institutions is one such park.

Increasing Localization

With the current trend to increase localization of employees, the hiring of expatriates in China has been slowing down dramatically. Current compensation packages offered to new expatriates are neither as high nor as comprehensive as they were a few years ago. The rise in living standards in many of China's cities provides ample reason to do away with many older, very generous, compensation schemes.

Overall, recruitment of expatriates from the West has fallen substantially in China. However, the recruitment of expatriates from Hong Kong and Taiwan has increased and will continue to grow with China's entry into the WTO. It is predicted that as more and more Hong Kong people and Taiwanese enter the job market in China, these professionals will soon become undifferentiable from local Chinese professionals, thus, minimizing the need to identify where they are originally from in order to determine their skills or compensation.

Personal Income Taxes

Foreign companies should be aware that they must apply for tax registration within 30 days of receiving a business license to operate in China. The process is fairly straightforward and usually takes about one day to complete. Under Chinese law, companies are considered "income taxpayers" with similar responsibilities as employees in the so-called "double declaration system."

Employees are required to file annual employee income tax returns while employers must file monthly withholding reports. Foreign companies would then pay employee taxes from their withholding accounts. According to China's Individual Income Tax Law, individuals that qualify as a resident and have income from the following sources (below) are liable for taxation. Foreigners who are resident in China for more than 90 days are liable for income tax.

Duration of Stay	Liability for Income Tax
Foreigners resident in China between 90 and 183 days	Liable only from income earned from "Chinese source"(i.e. income derived from work performed in China)
Foreigners resident in China for more than 183 days	Liable for taxes on work performed outside China, unless the work is clearly differentiated by a separate work contract.

COMMERCIAL PROPERTY

Introduction

Shanghai recorded a double-digit economic growth in 2003, with GDP reaching USD 75.3 billion, a hefty jump of 11.8% over the previous year. The booming economy and China's recent entry into WTO, have led to an influx of foreign companies needing office space. Although the full effect has yet to be felt, its impact on the commercial property market is already apparent.

The increase in the number of foreign companies, in part due to the Chinese government's recent decision to grant wider access to the financial and service sectors, is expected to fuel the demand for office space. Half of the Fortune 500 companies have already set up offices in Shanghai, attracted by the city's improving infrastructure, cosmopolitan environment and quality of life.

According to the Shanghai Real Estate Index Office, the Shanghai Housing Index rose 4.5% to 1,045 points in July 2003. For the whole year, the index had surged 18%, compared to 15% the previous year. Investment in real estate as at end of 2003 also increased by as much as 20.3%.

Source: Shanghai Municipal Statistics Bureau

Grade A Office Rents

District	Monthly Rental USD/sq m	% Change end of 2003	Short Term Trend
Grade A Overall	29.51	6.0%	↑
Hongqiao	25.86	4.6%	↑
Central Puxi	31.21	8.1%	↑
Lujiazui CBD	31.45	5.2%	↑

Source: Shanghai Municipal Statistics Bureau

Office Rental

For most businesses, leasing office space is a major commitment. The cost of office leasing significantly affects the bottom line, but also has many other important consequences. Operational efficiency and corporate image

Signing a Lease

Rental Rates and Costs

HOW ARE RENTS QUOTED AND PAID?

Rents are quoted in U.S.dollars per month, and usually RMB payment is made on the first day of each month, and one month in advance.

IS SECURITY DEPOSIT REQUIRED?

A security deposit of 1-3 months' rent, rates and service charges are usually required and are refunded at the end of the term without interest.

WHAT IS TYPICALLY INCLUDED IN THE RENT?

The rent includes the usage of the furniture, house/apartment and common space. Most developments provide its own club membership, which is included in the rent. Other costs may include electricity and other utilities.

WHAT DOES THE SERVICE CHARGE COVER?

Service charge typically covers maintenance, use of communal facilities, security and cleaning of the common areas.

Lease Term

WHAT IS THE TYPICAL LEASE TERM?

Usually one year fixed lease. Some service apartments offer fully-furnished suites for short periods (1-6 months); most two year leases will include a tenant's break-clause allowing the tenant to give 2 or 3 months' written notice at any time after 9-10 months of the lease. This means that tenants have a minimum stay of 12 months without incurring a penalty should they decide to leave.

DO TENANTS HAVE AUTOMATIC RENEWAL RIGHTS?

No, renewal options or extensions have to be negotiated separately with landlords.

WHAT IS THE PROCESS TO RENEW A TENANCY?

The landlord issues a written notice to the tenant between 2 and 3 months prior to the expiry of the tenancy to indicate his/her intention regarding renewing the tenant's lease. Negotiations of the new terms can take place right up to the expiry of the old tenancy.

are considerations which should not be overlooked.

For this and many other reasons, demand for quality office space is expected to remain strong in the foreseeable future. The top four industries demanding up-market office space are the manufacturing, technology,

Major Office Supply in 2004

Project	Location	Office Space (est sq m)
The Center	989 Chang Le Road	85,350
Jun Yao International Plaza	789 Zhaojiabang Road	50,000
Resource Plaza	268 Zhongshan Road South	40,800
Zhang Jiang Mansion	Zhang Jiang Hi-tech Park	44,000
Fortune Plaza	Dong Chang Road	35,000

DO TENANTS HAVE AUTOMATIC SUBLET OR ASSIGNMENT RIGHTS?

No. The right to assign the lease to a third party is rarely granted.

IS IT POSSIBLE TO TERMINATE LEASE? WHAT IS THE PROCESS AND IS THERE A PENALTY?

Normally, there are break lease rights within the contract. Early terminations for one year lease usually have to be negotiated with the landlord who may ask for payment of a penalty or the introduction of a replacement tenant.

AT THE CONCLUSION OF A LEASE TERM, WHAT IS THE PROCESS FOR HANDING BACK THE PROPERTY?

At the end of the lease, the tenant is responsible for reinstating the premises to the same condition as it was at the commencement of the term, subject to normal wear and tear. Landlords will prepare an inventory of the condition of their premises and the list of fixtures and fittings at the commencement of the term.

Tenant Improvements & Decoration Works

DOES THE TENANT HAVE THE RIGHT TO MAKE IMPROVEMENTS?

A request must be submitted to the landlord and approved before the work begins.

DO LANDLORDS PROVIDE BASIC FURNISHING?

Prior to the handover of the premises to the tenant, landlords will undertake to do the following works:

- Sand and polyurethane wooded floors - most houses/apartments have wooden parquet or strip wood flooring.
- Repaint all walls and ceilings.
- Check that all electrical wiring, gas appliances and all sanitary and water apparatus are in good, safe and working condition. Most landlords will supply air-conditioning units and ensure that they have been well maintained. Most landlords will expect the maintenance of such appliance to be borne by the tenant. Non-

professional services and financial services industries. Currently more than 80% of the world's top 50 banks have established their presence in Shanghai. With an increasing number of banks permitted to do retail and corporate banking business with local residents and enterprises, demand for top-grade office space is also likely to edge up further.

However, for the year 2004, market analysts do not expect rentals to surge dramatically. Office vacancy rates are still on the high side and some new developments are already in the pipeline. Increased supply is expected to put pressure on the rental market.

According to the Shanghai Municipal Statistics Bureau, average rental for major commercial buildings as at the end of July 2003 had gone up 5.2% to reach around USD 320 per m².

working appliances are replaced at the cost of the landlord.

ARE UTILITIES CONNECTED AND INCLUDED?

Landlords shall read the meters as a new record when tenants check in. Utilities are usually connected but tenants will have to change the name of the occupant. Except in some service apartments, the landlords are responsible for the payment of the utilities. All utilities are charged monthly.

WHAT IS THE PROCESS FOR APPLYING FOR TELEPHONE LINES?

Most buildings have extra telephone lines. Tenants may get one more line upon signing the relevant application form with the landlords.

Other

ARE EXPATRIATES CLUSTERED IN CERTAIN AREAS?

Most expatriates prefer to live in the downtown area which is the prime location with a quiet environment. For those with

families, particularly if they attend the American School, SIS or some other foreign schools, then the Pudong New District and Hongqiao Area are popular, where most of the villa properties are located.

HOW IMPORTANT IS THE REPUTATION OF THE OWNER, FOR EXAMPLE, DO YOU ONLY RECOMMEND CERTAIN OWNERS OR DEVELOPERS?

With the major landlords providing excellent management of their portfolios it is beneficial to lease a unit in one of the single owned buildings. Tenants should avoid renting a separately/individually-owned property unless it is managed by a good management company.

WHICH TYPES OF PROPERTY DO EXPATRIATES TYPICALLY OCCUPY? FOR EXAMPLE, HIGH RISE BUILDINGS OR LOW RISE BUILDINGS?

Major residential buildings in Shanghai are fairly new and in the downtown area, most properties are high-rise. There are a number of houses and low-rise properties in Pudong New District and Hongqiao Area, which are close to Pudong International Airport and Hongqiao Domestic Airport.

Residential Rental

The residential market in Shanghai has slowly recovered to normal levels since early 2003. Multi-national companies (MNCs) have started to increase their expenditure on leasing of apartments and houses for their expatriate staff.

The average rental of low-end housing has been raised to RMB 5,000 per m^2 from RMB 4,000 per m^2, while that for apartments cost between RMB 5,000 per m^2 and RMB 7,000 per m^2 in 2003. The rental for Grade A residences had increased by 6% in the same year.

Despite the Chinese government's efforts to reign in the housing market and a feeling among many investors that apartments and villas in Shanghai are overpriced, housing prices jumped by the fastest rate in eight years in July 2003 to set a record high.

Protection of Private Property

China is in the process of approving some Constitutional amendments to give greater protection to private properties. Economists and legal experts believe the amendment will help better protect the property of private businessmen, and that the recognition means they will be given a level playing field in the competition with state-owned and foreign enterprises.

The constitutional amendment, will, for the first time, enshrine the protection of private property. This has brought the country's newly-rich private entrepreneurs, who have accumulated wealth in the past two decades of reform and opening-up, into the spotlight. The amendments are likely to bring China's legal framework in line with its market-oriented commercial strategy.

Economists believe the constitutional protection of legally accumulated wealth will spur investment and consumption, and further promote development of the country's economy. They say the guideline in the constitution will in time lead to the law being adapted to business practices such as trading in real estate, stocks and bonds.

One benefit for entrepreneurs might be an easier time getting loans from state banks, which now lend mostly to state-run enterprises. With their private property protected, businesses could use it as collateral to obtain loans.

English Sentiments Life at Thames Town

Airscape

Thames Town is located in Songjiang, which lies southwest of Shanghai and is founded more than a thousand years earlier than Shanghai. It is well-connected to the city centre, as well as other neighbouring provinces and cities such as Zhejiang, with the Huhang Expressway, Huhang Railway and Tongsan Expressway. And the planned Shanghai Light Rail Route R4 directly links Songjiang new city to Xujiahui. Establishments such as several universities, technological parks and tourism resorts are located here. Under the planning of the Shanghai Municipal Government, Thames Town, an English-inspired town with an area of 1 km^2 which fully integrates residential life, vacations, leisure, shopping and nature, has become the pioneer model of the development of the new Songjiang.

Picturesque Thames Town is made up of a business nucleus which radiates out to outlying residential areas of English villas and houses. A natural lake with an area of approximately 30,000 m^2, which originates from the famous Dianshan Lake and runs through Huangpu River, winds throughout the whole satellite town, making good use of the town's geographical advantages. Beginning from the yacht dock, it meanders through the civic square, to the central business district, then down the natural slopes, and eventually ending at the wedding church.

This core waterfront route is designated as pedestrian paths. Along this route, there are various lifestyle-related facilities, public buildings, a four-star hotel, and a cultural centre housing a swimming pool with constant temperature control, tennis courts and other leisure facilities. In addition, there is a supermarket, clinic, kindergarten etc. along the waterfront.

Upon entering the business district, it is divided into several zones according to its functions. The dazzling array of food and beverage outlets along the banks, such as coffee joints, pubs, cafes etc. is simply a feast for all; and you may find private Manchester United collections or the Beatles classics on sale at the medieval marketplace located at the northern end...... Live the way as the English do, a promise of a truly unique experience.

The outlying residential areas consist of waterfront low-rise apartments (just beside the business district), townhouses (between the church and school) and 57 English architectural detached villas. These different housing types outline the image of a small bustling English town. You are welcome anytime, to experience the ultimate English lifestyle.

Many developers who signed short-term leases with their tenants are renewing them in the next few years. These owners are expected to seek higher rents as market demand becomes stronger.

Property Investment

For long-term property investment, market analysts are generally optimistic about the prospects. They believe that no other place in East Asia has a better investment environment than Shanghai, whose economic growth is expected to accelerate in the coming years.

They observe that property prices are not likely to fall unless a large amount of low-end housing is available, but a shortage of land has prompted developers to target high-end consumers. Some analysts, on the other hand, believe a bubble is building up, particularly if prices continued to rise unchecked.

It should also be noted that the People's Bank of China has given directives to domestic banks in mid-2003 to tighten controls on mortgages for luxury housing and on financial lending to developers.

Property investment, after all is a long-term commitment. Companies should be prudent in making such decisions. They must realize that the current demand has the risk of being distorted out of proportion.

FINANCIAL SERVICES

Introduction

Shanghai was the first city in China to form the largest financial credit rating system for companies and consumers. Since then, many improvements have been made in order to cater to the changing needs of the expanding business community.

In Shanghai today, a viable finance industry is fast emerging. Housing loans currently account for 80% of consumer loans. Auto loans are also rising, though automobile financing has yet to keep pace with the growth in passenger car sales.

While foreign banks are actively preparing to play a bigger role in the city's finance business, domestic banks are also rushing to expand their market share. In addition to the competition to offer mortgages and business loans, the big four state banks – the Agricultural Bank of China, the Bank of China, China Construction Bank, and the Industrial and Commercial Bank of China – and second-tier banks, particularly China Merchants Bank, are offering credit card and wealth-management services.

While China had agreed to allow foreign investment in auto financing companies upon WTO entry, the People's Bank of China has yet to finalize rules on automotive financing and related regulations on interest rates and collateral. Such rules are expected soon.

Influx of Foreign Funds

In 2002, the People's Bank of China approved the capital-adding applications of 28 foreign-funded banks in Shanghai. The added capital totaled more than USD 506 million. To the Shanghai service sector, the capital-adding of foreign-funded banks has become an important financing channel.

Most major Chinese banks have set up branches in Shanghai. In addition, a large number of local and foreign banks now have transaction networks all around Shanghai, offering a diverse range of banking services. This has provided great convenience for people and businesses in Shanghai.

Banking Service

Generally, banks operate from Mondays to Fridays, 9 am to 5 pm. The operating hours of foreign banks are slightly different: Japanese banks end the day at 4:30 pm, and American banks at 6 pm. Half-days are the rule on Saturdays. Chinese banks in the tourist areas are often open on Sundays so that travelers can convert their foreign currencies.

Most foreigners living in Shanghai do not have accounts with Chinese banks. Money is typically deposited overseas and cash is accessed at Automated Teller Machines (ATMs) around Shanghai.

The main banks offering this service are Bank of China (daily limit of RMB 2, 500), Industrial and Commercial Bank of China (daily limit of RMB 3, 000) and Citibank. ATMs using the Cirrus (toll free 800-424-7787) and Plus networks are easily found throughout the city. You will receive the official bank exchange rate on all transactions and may be charged a withdrawal fee by your home bank. In addition, credit cards are becoming popular and are accepted at most of the department stores, airline companies and hotels.

To open a multi-currency account in a local bank, for example, Bank of China, you should take your passport and Residential Card. You may open a passbook account in either US dollars or Chinese currency. Accounts are interest-bearing. To withdraw cash, you need to visit the bank with your passbook.

Shanghai Pudong Development Bank (SPDB)

Shanghai Pudong Development Bank is China's ninth largest commercial bank and was the first commercial bank to list on the Shanghai Stock Exchange. Established in 1993, the bank has a nationwide network of 290 branches across 30 cities. Its 7000 strong staff provide financial services to both corporate and consumer clients.

The bank is listed No. 308 among the top 1,000 banks in the world by core capital according to the British magazine, "The Banker", and is ranked No. 15 among the top 300 Asian commercial banks by the "Asian Banker" magazine in terms of ROE, capital adequacy ratio, NPL ratio and increase in profits and assets. The bank has also been nominated by "Asian Weekly" for four consecutive years as one of the top 100 listed companies in China, with a total market value of RMB 5.69 billion.

SPDB provides retail and commercial banking services, such as accepting deposits from the public, providing short-term and long-term loans, handling domestic and overseas settlements, discounting bills and notes, issuing financial bonds, acting as an agent for issuing, cashing and underwriting of government bonds, trading government bonds, conducting inter-bank financing, trading in, and acting as an agent for foreign exchange trading, providing letter of credit (LC) services and guarantees, acting as agent for accounts receivable and payable, acting as agent for insurance, and providing safe deposit box services.

Currently, SPDB is expanding its loan services. People who wish to travel but are temporarily short of money can apply for loans of up to RMB 50,000. The maximum loan term is one year.

Source: www.spdb.com.cn

Financing Issues

China implements a highly regulated system of foreign exchange control and strictly monitors foreign debt levels. FIEs are free to take foreign currency loans from foreign banks under certain conditions. However, when borrowing from overseas parties (including offshore branches of foreign banks and other parties such as foreign shareholders) or from foreign banks in China (such as mainland branches of foreign banks or joint venture banks), FIEs are required to undertake foreign debt registration at State Authority for Foreign Exchange (SAFE). Failure to do so may cause penalties to the borrower and the inability to remit money or to repay the debt.

FIEs can also seek Chinese currency financing, especially when foreign exchange controls are tightened and exchange rate risks are high. Chinese currency financing is available from Chinese banks and, subject to some geographical and other restrictions, from licensed foreign banks in China.

When lending to FIEs, banks usually require credit support. The most common forms include guarantees from foreign shareholders, bank guarantees with standby letters of credit (particularly in RMB borrowings), and mortgages over real estate and equipment. Security given by FIEs in favor of foreign banks (including mainland branches of foreign and joint venture banks) must be registered at SAFE.

Foreign-funded enterprises in China are permitted to apply for loans from Chinese domestic banks using the foreign partner's overseas assets as mortgage. Inter-company loans (i.e. loans between Chinese domestic companies) are not permitted except through a financial intermediary. Foreign-funded enterprises are permitted to apply for A- or B-share issues. Insurance services may be provided to foreign invested firms in some areas.

Foreign Banks in Shanghai

Many foreign banks have established either branches or representative offices in Shanghai. These banks are now playing increasingly important roles in Shanghai's financial sector.

By the end of 2002, there were over 70 foreign financial institutions in Shanghai, of which 53 were foreign banks. Most of them are among the top banks in the world. Of these foreign-invested banks, 45 are the branches or representative offices of foreign banks and the rest are foreign-invested but locally-registered banks. The total assets of these foreign banks reached USD 23.6 billion, which accounted for more than half the foreign financial institutions' assets in China.

At the end of May 2002, the total number of foreign banks operating in Pudong alone had risen to 37, 18 of which were authorized to conduct Chinese RMB business. Foreign currency deposits and loans with the banks totaled USD 1.63 billion and USD 9.71 billion respectively. Four of the banks are from North America, while 18 are from Europe and 15 from Asia. Their assets totaled USD 12.9 billion.

So far, the major business of foreign banks remains at financing large joint-venture projects and serving foreign customers who need access to foreign banking services. But China's accession to the WTO will soon see foreign banks increasingly gain government approval to offer retail banking services to the Chinese people.

TAXATION

Tax applicable to foreign invested enterprises

China's rapidly-changing corporate and individual tax regulations make ongoing tax planning an essential part of doing business in China.

Tax incentives serve as one of the most important factors to be considered by foreign investors while making decisions to invest in China. Currently, the major taxes applicable to foreign invested enterprises (FIEs) include enterprise income tax, value-added tax, consumption tax, business tax, personal income tax, resource tax, land appreciation tax, stamp duties, tax on urban real estate, tax for vehicle usage and license, customs duty and vessel tonnage tax. Various tax concessions or breaks are available to FIEs under certain circumstances.

Major Taxes Applicable to FIEs

Currently, the major taxes applicable to foreign invested enterprises (FIEs) include:

- enterprise income tax,
- value-added tax,
- resource tax,
- stamp duties,
- tax for vehicle usage and license,
- tax on urban real estate,
- personal income tax,
- business tax,
- land appreciation tax,
- consumption tax,
- customs duty,
- vessel tonnage tax.

Over the past 20 years, China has made significant progress and has gained more experience in its tax legislation, in particular, those related to foreign invested enterprises. While China continues to use preferential tax treatment as an important means to attract FDI, it has shifted its emphasis from the amount or quantity of foreign investment onto the quality of foreign investment, believing that this will help promote the country's overall and sustainable economic development. It is widely perceived that, with China's WTO accession, tax incentives will be focused on encouraging investment in specific industries (e.g. high-tech industries) and specific locations (e.g. Western China).

Enterprise Income Tax (EIT)

So far, China maintains two sets of EIT laws, one for domestic enterprises and the other for FIEs. For domestic enterprises, the EIT is 33%, while for FIEs, the EIT is 30% plus 3% local sur-tax when no preferential tax treatments are applicable. There are, however, quite a number of tax incentives available to FIEs tailored to the specific industries and locations.

For those foreign enterprises that do not have an establishment in China but derive profits, interests, rents, royalties or other income from sources in China, or those who have an establishment or a few establishments in China but their income is not effectively connected with those establishments, a withholding tax of 20% on such income is payable.

If an FIE is terminated before the prescribed 10-year period, the amount of income tax exempted or reduced shall be repaid to the tax authorities.

In addition, if an FIE is engaged in the building of municipal infrastructure with a business period of over 15 years, the EIT can be exempted for the first five years after making profits, and the EIT can be reduced by 50% for the next five years. For an FIE involved in building infrastructure in Pudong New District, the EIT rate is 15%.

Those who reinvest their profits to set up or extend export enterprises or technologically advanced enterprises with a business period no less than five years will get a full refund of EIT paid on the reinvested amount.

Individual Income Tax (IIT)

Individual income tax shall be levied on the following:
- Income from wages and salaries;
- Income from production or business operation derived by individual industrial and commercial households;

- Income from contracted or leased operation of enterprises or institutions;
- Income from remuneration for personal services;
- Income from author remuneration;
- Income from royalties;
- Income from interest, dividends and bonuses;
- Income from lease of property;
- Income from transfer of property; and,
- Contingent income and other income specified as taxable.

Income from wages and salaries is taxed at nine progressive rates, ranging from 5% to 45%. For foreign taxpayers, the monthly deduction is RMB 4, 000 (RMB 800 for domestic employees). Income from compensation for personal services, royalties, interest, dividends, bonus, lease of property, transfer of property, contingent income and other kinds of income shall be taxed at a proportional rate of 20%.

Individual Income Tax Rates (applicable to Monthly Salaries)

Grade	Monthly Income Taxable (RMB)	Tax Rates (%)
1	The part less than 500	5
2	The part from 500 to 2,000	10
3	The part from 2,000 plus to 5,000	15
4	The part from 5,000 plus to 20,000	20
5	The part from 20,000 plus to 40,000	25
6	The part from 40,000 plus to 60,000	30
7	The part from 60,000 plus to 80,000	35
8	The part from 80,000 plus to 100,000	40
9	The part exceeding 100,000	45

Note: The Monthly Income Taxable refers to the remaining sum of an individual's monthly income after RMB 800 or an extra deductible sum is deducted as stipulated by Article 6 of the Law on Individual Income Tax. With regard to foreigners, it refers to the remaining sum of his monthly income after RMB 4, 000 is deducted.

Value Added Tax (VAT)

There are three kinds of rates for VAT:

- For taxpayers selling or importing goods, or providing services of processing, replacement and repairs, the tax rate is 17%.
- For taxpayers selling or importing grains, edible vegetable oil, coal gas, natural gas, coal or charcoal products for household use, books, newspapers, magazines, chemical fertilizers, agricultural chemicals and agricultural machineries etc., the tax rate is 13%.
- For taxpayers exporting goods, except otherwise stipulated by the State Council, VAT is exempted.

For enterprises and individuals engaged in production or providing taxable labor service with annual sales volume less than RMB 1 million, those engaged in wholesale and retailing with annual sales volume less than RMB 1.8 million, and those designated by the tax authority as small VAT payers, the tax rate is 6% on a taxable price basis.

Business Tax

Business tax shall be levied on organizations and individuals involved in supplying taxable labors, transfer of intangible assets and sale of real estate. The rate of business tax is 3% for communications and transportation, civil construction, post and telecommunications, culture and sports industries; 5% for banking and insurance services, transfer of intangible assets, and real estate sales industries. The business tax rate for entertainment industries is 5% - 20%. Generally, the tax is applicable to companies in the service industries.

Resources Tax

Foreign enterprises that mine and explore mineral and natural resources within the territory of China are subject to resources tax.

Land Appreciation Tax

Land appreciation tax is levied on the income from the transfer of state-owned land use rights, buildings and their attached facilities. The appreciation amount shall be the balance of proceeds received by the taxpayer on the transfer of real estate after deducting the following items:

- The sum paid for the acquisition of land use rights;
- Cost and expenses for land development;
- Cost and expense for the construction of new building and facilities, or the assessed value for used properties and buildings;
- The taxes related to real estate transfer; and,
- Other items as stipulated by the Ministry of Finance.

Stamp Duty

Activities involving purchases and sales, processing, contracting, leasing, transportation, storage, loan lending, property insurance, technology contract and property transfer vouchers, business account books and licenses are subject to stamp duty. The minimum rate is charged at 0.005% and the maximum is 0.1%.

Stamp Duty in Detail

Item	Taxable Amount	Tax Rate (%)
Purchasing and sales contract	Purchasing and Sales amount	0.03
Processing and Contracting	Income from Processing	0.05
Construction project, exploration and survey and design contract	Fee collected	0.05
Building and installation project, contract preparation	Sum from the lease	0.03
Property leasing contract	Sum from the lease	0.1
Goods transportation contract	Transportation fee	0.05
Storage and preservation contract	Fee collected	0.1
Money lending contract	Sum lent	0.005
Property insurance contract	Income from insurance fee	0.1
Technology contract	Sum specified	0.03
Property rights transfer contract	Sum specified	0.05
Business account book	Each account book	RMB 5

Consumption Tax

Consumption Tax is levied on the sale of goods and covers 11 taxable items and 25 tax rates (for details refer to the rules for the Implementation of Interim Regulations of the People's Republic of China on consumption tax), with 3% as the minimum and 45% as the maximum. The tax on the goods used in the production process shall be levied on the basis of the price of the goods, whereas the tax levied on yellow rice wine, gasoline and diesel shall be on the value per unit quantity basis. Consumption tax shall be exempted for the taxable consumer goods exported by the taxpayers, except those taxable consumer goods subject to export restrictions imposed by the Government.

Vehicle Usage and License Tax

The rate for vessels and vehicles is assessed on the basis of weight capacity and vehicle type or number of seats if they are passenger vehicles. The tax payable for passenger vehicles with no more than 10 seats is RMB 55 per six months; for those with 11-30 seats, the tax payable is RMB 65 per six months; for those with 31 seats or more, the tax payable is RMB 75 per six months. The tax payable for heavy vehicles is RMB 24 per net ton per six months; for small motorcycles, it is RMB 10 per six months; for general motorcycles, it is RMB 18 per six months; and for motor tricycles, tax payable is RMB 24 per six months.

Customs Duty

After China's entry into the WTO, the aggregate import duty was lowered to about 12%. According to a notice given by the General Customs Administration at the end of 2001, 7,316 items are still taxable. However, tariffs are categorized into four groups, namely, most favored nation rate, conventional tariff rate, special rate and normal rate.

Imported goods are taxed on its normal C.I.F. (cost, insurance and freight) prices. Customs has the authority to determine the taxable price if the goods'

C.I.F. is not quotable. The tariff rates are set in a detailed checklist. For some special imported goods, tariff is exempted. For specific imports, the rates may be found at the Shanghai Customs' website, www.shcus.gov.cn.

Export commodities produced by the FIE itself, except those prohibited from export by the State and those subject to other State regulations, shall be exempted from export tariff.

Goods imported out of necessity, such as raw materials, fuel, parts and components, accessories or packaging materials for FIEs to produce export products, are regarded as bonded goods and are supervised by customs.

Taxation Administration

The Law on Taxation Administration is the basic law on taxation and is also a procedural law. All enterprises, domestic and foreign, are treated equally under this law.

Taxation Authorities

Shanghai Municipal Finance Administration (SMFA) is the department of the municipal government in charge of fiscal revenue and expenditure, financial and tax policies and state-owned capital funds of the municipality. It also combines the functions of Shanghai Municipal Administration of State Taxation and Shanghai Municipal Administration of Local Taxation.

SMFA provides operational guidance to district and county bureaus of finance and exercises administrative powers over all taxation establishments within the municipality.

Tax Registration

Joint ventures (JVs), wholly-owned foreign enterprises (WOFEs), representative offices and other similar organizations in China are required to register with tax authorities within a specified time given in the relevant regulations. In general, this has to be completed within 30 days after the business license is issued. Registrations are to be filed with both the State Taxation Administration and Local Taxation Administration. The two administrations have their own tax jurisdictions. To qualify as an ordinary VAT payer and be able to issue VAT invoices, a taxpayer has to undertake VAT registration as well.

Upon completion of the tax registration, the tax authorities will issue the applicant a tax registration certificate that must be renewed every year. During the registration process, you should discuss with the tax officers and confirm the basis for tax calculation and filing. The consequence of late registration involves a maximum penalty of RMB 10, 000 or even the repeal of your business license. Any changes in business license or operating office require re-registration with the tax authorities.

Taxation Control

The tax year is the calendar year, i.e., from 1 January to 31 December. If a foreign enterprise experiences difficulties in computing its taxable income on the calendar-year basis, it may apply to the tax authorities to adopt its own financial year as the tax year. For an enterprise that commences business within a calendar year or has operated for less than 12 months in a calendar year, the actual operating period will be treated as the tax year.

An FIE is required to file its annual tax returns, audited financial statements and the auditor's report to the tax administrations within four months after the end of the year. The application for deferring the filing of the above documents should also be submitted within this period of time. The penalty for failure to file the above documents within the prescribed time limit is calculated on 0.2% per day on the tax amount overdue.

Any taxpayer or withholding agent who fails to perform tax registration procedures, fails to set up an accounting system and fails to keep its business records within a prescribed time limit is required to redress these within a prescribed period. Any failure to comply with this will be subject to a fine of up to RMB 2,000; if the violation is serious, a fine up to RMB 10, 000 will be imposed. A fine of over RMB 2, 000 but under RMB 10, 000 will be imposed if the taxpayer or withholding agent fails to meet the due date the second time.

The fine for tax evasion which involves such unlawful activities as forgery, falsifying or concealing relevant information, fraud, or failure again to pay tax within the prescribed time period is up to but not more than 500% of the tax due. In most of the above cases, serious offenders will be prosecuted by law.

Tax Audit

The tax authorities have the power to carry out tax audits to examine taxpayer records and relevant documents. Refusal of tax examination will be subject to a maximum penalty of RMB 50, 000. In general, tax authorities shall provide an enterprise a written notice about the impending tax audit. You should adopt a cooperative attitude, but do not forget to check with the tax officers on the exact scope of audit and ensure that they show you their staff identity cards.

Tax Reporting and Payment

Different taxes have different reporting periods and payment due dates. In general, Foreign Enterprise Income Tax (EIT) is paid on a quarterly basis, VAT and Business Tax are usually on a monthly basis, and Individual Income Tax (IIT) is on a monthly basis too. Tax authorities will not send you tax returns. Instead, you should collect blank tax returns from tax offices, complete them and file accordingly.

Acceptable ways of submission differ from place to place and depends on the nature of the tax. For some locations, reporting via mail is acceptable, while at some other locations, submission must be made in person. Shanghai has recently launched electronic filing.

Late payment of tax will involve a fine of 0.05% a day on the tax owing. Withholding agents who fail to observe these obligations will be subject to a maximum penalty of 500% of the tax involved. Under the tax regulations, you may apply to the tax authorities for deferred tax filing and payment.

Preferential Tax Policies in Pudong New District

- The income tax of foreign-invested manufacturing enterprises shall be levied at a reduced rate of 15%.

- Foreign-invested enterprises scheduled to operate for a period over 10 years shall be exempted from income tax in the first two years starting from the profit-making year and be granted a 50% reduction in the next three years.

- High-tech projects invested by foreign investors in Pudong New District may enjoy 10% income tax rate for another three years after the period of tax exemption and reduction. Export enterprises with foreign investment shall pay their income tax at a reduced rate of 10% when their annual export sales value amounts to more than 70% of the annual sales value.

- The income tax of foreign-invested enterprises in the field of ports, energy and transportation shall be levied at a reduced rate of 15%. If the operation period of the above-mentioned enterprises is over 15 years, the income tax shall be exempted for the first five years starting from the first profit-making year and entitled to a 50% reduction for the next five years.

- The buildings or houses built or purchased by foreign investors for their own use shall be exempt from property tax for five years, starting from the transaction date.

- Foreign financial institutions, such as foreign banks and JV banks, with its paid up capital over USD 10 million in Pudong New District or its operating fund as a branch allocated by its headquarters over USD 10 million, may enjoy a reduced income tax rate at 15% upon approval by the relevant authorities. Starting from the first profit-making year, the abovementioned institutions may enjoy income tax exemption for one year and 50% income tax reduction for another two years.

INDUSTRIAL PARKS AND EXPORT-ORIENTED PROCESSING ZONES

Introduction

The development of industrial parks in China gained great momentum in the last few years. Overwhelming demand by foreign investors is one important factor.

Export-oriented processing zones have become a bridge connecting the domestic and overseas markets. Since the first such zones appeared in 2000, export-oriented processing zones have seen an expansion both in size and number, in part due to preferential taxation policies in their favor.

China currently has 38 such zones, mostly in coastal provinces and municipalities. Shanghai alone has 11. By June 2003, 447 enterprises invested USD 4.75 billion in such zones, achieving a total foreign trade volume of USD 11.73 billion, over USD 5.9 billion of which was from import and USD 5.83 billion from export. Exports and imports in these zones in the first half of 2003 increased 450% over the same period the previous year.

CAOHEJING HIGH-TECH PARK

Economic and technological development zones (Etdzs) and high-tech parks (Htps) enjoy different preferential policies, as granted by the state government. Caohejing High-Tech Park (CHTP) however, is the only state-level development zone that enjoys preferential policies granted to both Etdzs and Htps.

Established in 1986, the 189 ha CHTP was among the first batch of state-level development zones in China. CHTP is located in Xuhui District, southwest of Shanghai, and has proven to be an attractive area for investors. It is only 11 km from the main town area in Shanghai, four km from Xujiahui – the center of the district, and seven km from Hongqiao International Airport. Among all development zones in Shanghai, it is one of the nearest to the city.

More than 800 enterprises so far have already resided in CHTP, among which more than 300 are foreign-invested. More than 20% of the enterprises are recognized as high-tech enterprises by the municipal government.

Major domestic enterprises include Datang Mobilecom, Zhongxin Telecommunication, China Unicom, China Netcom, Fuxin Group and Huaxin Bio-technology, while Taiwanese enterprises include Acer, Inventech, Microtek, Sinowealth Electronics, Kimpo Electronics etc.

Over 40 world-renowned enterprises have invested and set up subsidiaries in the park, such as GE, Lucent, 3M, Intel, Emerson, AMP, Raychem, Dupont, Agilent, Tandem, Lattice and Foxboro from the USA, Air Liquid and Schneider from France, Philips from the Netherlands, Clariant and Mettler-Toledo from Switzerland, Bell from Belgian, Spirax Sarco from Britain, NTT, Toshiba, Mitsui, Epson and Ricoh from Japan, and Nortel from Canada.

The zone is dedicated to the development of advanced technologies in the fields of microelectronics, IT products, software, aerospace technology, telecommunication, laser, bioengineering and new materials.

CAOHEJING HIGH-TECH PARK DEVELOPMENT CORPORATION
Tel: 86 21 64859900, 64850000
E-mail: contact@caohejing.com
Website: www.caohejing.com

SHANGHAI CHEMICAL INDUSTRIAL PARK

Shanghai Chemical Industrial Park (SCIP) is an RMB 150 billion municipal project undertaken jointly by Sinopac Shanghai, Huayi Group, Gaoqiao Petrochemical, Shanghai Industrial Investment Group and Shanghai Jiushi in early 2001. It is one of the four key industrial bases designated by the municipal government for the development of petrochemical industries. With registered capital of RMB 2.16 billion (USD 260 million), SCIP Development Corporation is the sole developer of this mega project, offering a one-stop service to all qualified foreign investors.

With a total development area of 23.4 km^2 and a first phase area of 10 km^2, SCIP is mainly located in Jinshan District in the southernmost part of Shanghai, with another part hosted by Fengxian. Perched on the north bank of Hangzhou Bay, it is 60 km away from downtown Shanghai and 50 km from both airports in Shanghai.

Major MNCs such as Bayer, BASF and British Petroleum have joined SCIP. The total investment for the Bayer project will be USD 3.1 billion, and a joint venture between Sinopac, Sinopac Shanghai Petrochemical and British Petroleum will cost USD 2.7 billion. It is expected that by the end of 2005, 12 major projects will start operation.

SHANGHAI CHEMICAL INDUSTRIAL PARK DEVELOPMENT CO. LTD.
10, Lane 18, Gaoan Road, Shanghai, P. R. China 200030
Tel: 86 21 64713298   Fax: 86 21 64713301
Email: webmaster@scip-cn.com
Website: www.scip-cn.com

MINHANG ECONOMIC AND TECHNOLOGICAL DEVELOPMENT ZONE

Minhang Economic and Technological Development Zone (MHETDZ) was among the first 14 state-level ETDZs approved by the State Council in 1986. Its total development area is 3.5 km².

Located at the southwest part of Shanghai, near the upstream of the Huangpu River, it is 30 km away from downtown Shanghai, 27 km away from Hongqiao International Airport, and 15 km away from Longwu Port.

MHETDZ has so far attracted 154 projects, of which 48 were invested by MNCs, including 28 Fortune 500 companies, such as Bristol-Myers Squibb, Coca Cola, Fuji-Xerox and Ingersoll Rand. Contractual investment amounted to USD 2.2 billion.

Major industries in the zone include mechanical and electronic equipment manufacturing, bioengineering, pharmaceuticals, and food and beverage. A branch of Shanghai Normal University has also been set up within the zone.

MINHANG UNITED DEVELOPMENT CORPORATION

1251 Jiangchuan Road, Minhang, Shanghai, P.R. China 200245
Tel: 86 21 64300888   Fax: 86 21 64300789
Email: smudc@online.sh.cn
Website: www.smudc.com

HONGQIAO ECONOMIC AND TECHNOLOGICAL DEVELOPMENT ZONE

Established in 1983, Hongqiao Economic and Technological Development Zone (HQETDZ) is a new commercial and business zone in Shanghai that comprises office and exhibition facilities, residential areas, restaurants and shopping malls.

Land has also been reserved as consular areas for foreign consulates. Japan, the US, Australia, Korea, Singapore and Pakistan have already signed land use or exchange contracts, and general consulates of India, Denmark, Korea, the Netherlands, Switzerland, Argentina, Romania, Israel and Cuba in Shanghai have set up their offices in the zone.

HQETDZ is located in Changning District, west of Shanghai's urban district. It is bounded by four roads – Zhongshan West Road, Gubei Road, Xianxia Road and Hongqiao Road. It extends over an area of 65.2 ha, including 31.09 ha for construction, 19.54 ha of green land and 14.39 ha for roads. The development zone is only 5.5 km away from Hongqiao International Airport.

Total contractual investment is more than USD 3.2 billion, with utilized foreign investments totaling USD 2.26 billion. Major investors come from Hong Kong, Taiwan, Japan, Singapore and the US. MNCs which have set up offices in the zone include 3M, GE, Nokia, Ericsson and LG.

HONGQIAO ECONOMIC AND TECHNOLOGICAL DEVELOPMENT ZONE

34-35th Floor, New Town Center, 83 Loushanguan Road, Shanghai, P.R. China 200336

Tel: 86 21 62756888   Fax: 86 21 62194505

Website: www.shudc.com

ZHANGJIANG HIGH-TECH PARK

Zhangjiang High-Tech Park (ZJHTP) is located in the central part of Pudong New District. It was approved by the State Council in July 1992 and is one of the four industrial bases of Shanghai. For its prominence and importance in the country's high-tech developments, it is one of two widely known industrial parks in China, for which the phrase has been coined, "Zhongguancun in the north, Zhangjiang in the south". "To focus on Zhangjiang" has emerged to be a national strategy to expedite the development of high-tech areas in China.

ZJHTP covers an area of 25 km² and is surrounded by a vast golf course, villas, parks, international exhibition centers and a foreign language school. It is linked conveniently to the downtown area of Shanghai and the Pudong International Airport by highways. In addition, Metro Line No. 2 ends in the ZJHTP. The emphasis of ZJHTP has been placed on information technologies, bioengineering, pharmaceuticals as well as real estate. By the end of June 2002, ZJHTP had successfully attracted 457 projects with total contractual investment of USD 6.6 billion.

It now hosts the State Biotech and Pharmaceutical Base (Shanghai), National Information Technology Industrial Base, National Science and Technology Innovation Base, Pudong Software Development Park, Pudong Java Application Research Center, Motorola, Afataike, LG, SmithKlineBeecham, Roche, Rhodia and United Signals.

Integrated circuit (IC) industry plays a pivotal role in the development of information technology. Several world-class IC manufacturers have made investments in the park, such as SMIC (USD 1.48 billion), Hongli Semiconductor Shanghai and Tailong Semiconductor (USD 400 million).

The park is divided into six functional sections, namely, technological innovation, research and education, high-tech pilot and test, residential, commerce and service, and industrial sections.

THE ADMINISTRATIVE COMMITTEE OF ZHANGJIANG HIGH-TECH PARK
200 Longdong Avenue, Pudong New District, Shanghai, P. R. China 201204
Tel: 86 21 50801818   Fax: 86 21 50800686
Email: zjpark@zjpark.com
Website: www.zjpark.com

JINQIAO EXPORT PROCESSING ZONE

Introduction

Approved by the State Council in 1990, Jinqiao Export Processing Zone (JQEPZ) was among the first batch of Export Processing Zones (EPZs) in China. Separated by Jinqiao Road, the 6 km² Jinqiao High-Tech Park and a 1 km² commercial district are situated on the eastern side, – as approved by the Ministry of Science and Technology in April 1998; while the western part is designated to be a residential area which will be known as the Biyun International Community.

Located in the middle of Pudong New District with a planned area of 20 km², JQEPZ links Lujiazui Finance and Trade Zone in the west and Waigaoqiao Free Trade Zone in the north, and it is close to Zhangjiang High-Tech Park that sits to its south. The EPZ is 25 km away from Hongqiao International Airport, 15 km away from Pudong International Airport, and 9 km from Waigaoqiao Port.

Investment Climate

The industrial output value of the JQEPZ soared 30% to set a new record of RMB 103.8 billion (USD 12.5 billion) in 2003.

The figure is one-third of Pudong's industrial output value and one-tenth of the total industrial output value of Shanghai. More than 98 percent of the output value was generated by foreign-funded enterprises. In the course of its 13-year development, Jinqiao has attracted 568 Chinese and overseas enterprises with a total investment of USD 11.1 billion.

In 2003 alone, 42 domestic and foreign firms have settled in the processing zone, bringing in USD 420 million. They include a number of big names such as the Swiss ABB company, which poured USD 17.5 million into building a factory for transformer production.

Lured by substantial gains in profits at Jinqiao, 14 foreign-funded firms increased their investments in the processing zone last year, with a total sum of USD 160 million.

To date, one in every two MNCs that have come to Pudong have taken residence in JQEPZ. Among them are global players like General Motors, Siemens, NEC, Nestle, Hewlett-Packard and Bell. JQEPZ encourages development in electronics, information technology, vehicles and The automobile components, electrical household appliances, bioengineering and pharmaceuticals.

JQEPZ was conferred the "ISO 14000 State-level Model Zone" in August 2000, the third industrial park in China and the first in Shanghai to have achieved the status.

JINQIAO EXPORT PROCESSING ZONE ADMINISTRATIVE COMMITTEE
28 New Jinqiao Road, Pudong, Shanghai, P.R. China 201206
Tel: 86 21 58991818   Fax: 86 21 58991812
Website: www.goldenbridge.sh.cn

WAIGAOQIAO FREE TRADE ZONE

Waigaoqiao Free Trade Zone (WFTZ) claims to be China's first and biggest free trade zone. It was approved by the State Council in June 1990 to be set up on an area of 10 km². So far, 7.52 km² has been utilized, occupied by businesses involved in international trade, bonded warehousing, commodity display and export processing.

Located in Pudong, WFTZ is situated at the mouth of the Yangtze River. From there, it is a 40-minute drive to reach Hongqiao International Airport, 20 minutes to Pudong International Airport, 35 minutes to Shanghai Railway Station and 30 minutes to the city center.

By the end of 2001, 5,022 projects had been set up in the zone with total investment reaching USD 6.56 billion. Investors come from 58 countries and regions worldwide.

Major MNCs such as GE, Toshiba, IBM, Philips and Intel have invested heavily in the zone. Among others, Waigaoqiao Automobile Exchange Market and a biochemical and medical instruments market are two key projects.

Administrative Committee of Waigaoqiao Free Trade Zone
2 Huajing Road, Waigaoqiao Free Trade Zone, Pudong New District, Shanghai,
P.R. China 200131
Tel: 86 21 50461100   Fax: 86 21 50461441
Website: www.waigaoqiao.gov.cn

SONGJIANG EXPORT PROCESSING ZONE

Songjiang Export Processing Zone (SJEPZ) was established by the State Council on 27 April 2000. With a development area of 1.98 km², it was founded within the Songjiang Industrial Zone, one of the municipal-level industrial parks of Shanghai.

Key industries encouraged by SJEPZ include IT, biopharmaceuticals, new building materials, fine chemicals and light machinery.

Investors in the zone enjoy special tax incentives. Services and institutions like customs, goods inspection, commercial transactions, taxation, banking, and foreign trade are readily available. Investors can complete all export formalities within the EPZ.

SJEPZ is 20 km away from Hongqiao International Airport, 42 km away from Pudong International Airport, and 47 km from Wusong Port. It is close to the Shanghai-Hangzhou Expressway.

THE ADMINISTRATIVE COMMITTEE OF SONGJIANG EXPORT PROCESSING ZONE
81 Rongle East Road, Songjiang District, Shanghai, P.R. China 201613
Tel: 86 21 57741102, 57741859   Fax: 86 21 57743188
E-mail: sjiz@public.sta.net.cn
Website: www.sjepz.com

QINGPU INDUSTRIAL ZONE

With total development area of 16.16 km², Qingpu Industrial Zone (QPIZ) was approved by the municipal government in 1995. Located in Qingpu District in the west of Shanghai, QPIZ is 17 km from Hongqiao International Airport and 45 km from the Shanghai Port.

The zone is divided into five industrial clusters of IT, biopharmaceuticals, high-tech materials, precision machinery, green food and packaging. QPIZ is one of two incubation bases for high-tech achievements in Shanghai; the other one is Zhangjiang in Pudong.

Major companies that have established operations in QPIZ include DuPont and Suzuka International from the US, Hoechst A.G., BASF and CeDo from Germany, Yongji DTF and TLS International from Singapore, UFI Group and Isea Lorenzi from Italy, Fuji Electric, Sunny, Showa and Jentech from Japan, Happy Goal and HCP International from the Virgin Islands, and Herganies from Sweden.

THE DEVELOPMENT CORPORATION OF QINGPU INDUSTRIAL ZONE
5500 Waiqingsong Highway, Qingpu District, Shanghai, P. R. China 201700
Tel: 86 21 59724619   Fax: 86 21 59722856
Email: sqpiz@sqpiz.com
Website: www.greenin.com.cn

SHANGHAI SOFTWARE DEVELOPMENT PARK

Opened officially in 1999, Shanghai Software Development Park (SHSDP) consists of three parts, Pudong Software Park (located in Zhangjiang High-Tech Park), Fudan Software Development Center, and SJTU (Shanghai Jiaotong University) Caohejing Software Park. With strong backing from the municipal government, funds for development have reached RMB 3.7 billion (USD 447 million).

Over 748 enterprises have registered in these parks and 49 of them have started operations, with foreign capital of USD 224 million. Some prestigious companies in the park include Shanghai Wonders Information, Shanghai Fudan Guanghua Information Industries, Shanghai VSC, SJTU Withub Information Industries, Shanghai Pudong Software Park Development Co., Shanghai Baud Data Communications, Shanghai Fudan Net-Info, Kingstar Group, Shanghai Integra Info Tech, Microsoft and HP.

The establishment of SHSDP is aimed at boosting Shanghai's capacity in software development. It is estimated that by 2005, the turnover of the industry in Shanghai will be at least RMB 50 billion (USD 6.04 billion) and export will reach USD 400 million. The population of software professionals in Shanghai is expected to increase from 32,000 to 100,000.

SHANGHAI PUDONG SOFTWARE DEVELOPMENT PARK CO. LTD.

Zhangjiang High-tech Park, Pudong New District, Shanghai, P. R. China 201203
Tel: 86 21 38954510
Email: spsp@public.sta.net.cn
Website: www.spsp.com.cn

SHANGHAI JIAOTONG UNIVERSITY SCIENCE PARK

Shanghai Jiaotong University Science Park (SJTUSP) was set up in 1999 and was subsequently awarded the status of National University Science Park in May 2001.

SJTUSP mainly consists of four subsidiary zones: Withub, Zhangjiang Zone in Pudong, Mingu and Xinhua. Withub is located at the main campus of Shanghai Jiaotong University (SJTU), and engages in the development of information technology, new materials, new energy and biotechnologies.

Enterprises in SJTUSP are able to tap on the resources and opportunities offered by SJTU which is composed of four campuses, 17 colleges and one graduate school. It hosts 16 State Key Programs, nine State Key Laboratories, and two State Engineering Research Centers.

Among the 1,900 strong university academic staff, there are eight CAS (Chinese Academy of Science) fellows, nine CAE (Chinese Academy of Engineering) fellows, 460 professors and around 700 associate professors. The number of students is 22,000, with 4,900 and 1,900 postgraduates pursuing their master and doctoral degrees respectively.

SJTU enjoys a good reputation in the fields of engineering, IT, management and biological studies, and has established alliances with more than 30 major MNCs and other enterprises to commercialize academic achievements. Among the projects that have brought attractive returns are high-definition digital TV, MCFC fuel battery, micro motors, piston production line for Volkswagen, 6,000-meter deepwater daggling observation system etc.

There are 24 university-affiliated enterprises operating in the park, such as Nanyang Group, Only Group, Shanghai Withub Information Industries and Shanghai GoFly Group. In particular, SJTU Only Group has grown from a small company to become a top player in China's healthcare market with sales turnover running into the hundreds of millions.

SHANGHAI JIAOTONG UNIVERSITY SCIENTIFIC DEVELOPMENT AND COOPERATION OFFICE
Haoran Scientific Building, Shanghai Jiaotong University
1954 Huashan Road, Xuhui District, Shanghai, P. R. China 200030
Tel: 86 21 62932047, 62932048 Fax: 86 21 62932451
Website: www.kejichu.sjtu.edu.cn
E-mail: kaifa@mail.sjtu.edu.cn

FUDAN UNIVERSITY SCIENCE PARK

Similar to SJTUSP, Fudan University Science Park (FDUSP) was inaugurated in April 2000 to leverage on Fudan University's R&D capabilities. It consists of Fudan Software Development Center, Shanghai Yangpu Venture Incubation Center, Fudan-SK Entrepreneurial Center, Guoquan Zone, Fenglin Zone and a few other professional incubation bases.

Founded in 1905, Fudan University has developed into one of the top universities in China. After merging with the former Shanghai Medical University, the university now has 17 colleges and 43 departments, and hosts 45 State Key Programs, 5 State Key Laboratories, 57 research institutes and 80 multidisciplinary research centers.

The academic fields cover humanities, science, social sciences, economics, journalism, international relations, business administration, law, life science, pharmaceutics, IT and software development. Among its 2,400 staff, there are 19 CAS and CAE fellows, 1,300 professors and associate professors.

Currently, Fudan University owns 99 affiliate enterprises with total sales revenue reaching RMB 1.16 billion (RMB 140 million). The industries cover IT, biopharmaceuticals, new materials, environmental protection, chemical engineering, communications, medical instruments and investment funding.

Fudan University Science Park Development Corporation has a registered capital of RMB 100 million (USD 12.08 million). Major shareholders include Fudan University, Shanghai Wujiaochang Square High-tech United Corporation, Shanghai Shangke Investment Corporation, Shanghai Science & Technology Entrepreneur Center, Shanghai Lujiazui Finance & Trade Zone Holdings and Shanghai Yangpu Development Corporation.

FUDAN UNIVERSITY SCIENCE PARK INVESTMENT SERVICE CENTER
139 Handan Road, Shanghai, P. R. China 200437
Tel: 86 21 65311017   Fax: 86 21 65448060
Email: xcqian@fudan.edu.cn
Website: 202.120.224.90/xiaochan/web/kejiyuan.htm

ECONOMIC OVERVIEW

Introduction

Sidelined by the central government in Beijing in its earlier efforts to develop the southern part of China, Shanghai, or the Pearl of the Orient, has in the 1990s made an impressive comeback.

Since then, Shanghai has consistently outperformed the country's overall economic growth rate, averaging between 13% and 14% annually. In 2003, its GDP growth rate reached 11.8%. Its impressive growth goes some way to explain the generally bullish mood among the foreign business community in the metropolitan. With the forthcoming EXPO 2010, expectations are further heightened resulting, hence, in a greater inflow of overseas investment.

Most visitors to Shanghai cannot help but be impressed by the amount of construction work going on in the city, be it in the form of massive infrastructure projects such as railways and elevated ring roads or high-rise office and apartment complexes.

Latest statistics released by the municipal authorities show that foreign-invested enterprises (FIEs) now number more than 18, 000. The FIEs have made great contributions to Shanghai's economy and their business volume now makes up about one-third of the city's total economy.

Economic Transformation

Shanghai's strategic location is a key to its success as a business magnet. The city lies at the confluence of the East China Sea and the Yangtze River, which stretches inland all the way to the Tibetan plateau, making it a natural center for commerce. It has become the leading engine propelling China's economic growth for the challenging years ahead.

Cutting back on much red tape, the Shanghai municipal government has streamlined its approval procedures to the extent that a foreign-invested business applying to set up shop in the city can now expect to go through the process in about two months, as compared to up to one year in other parts of the country.

Foreign companies have benefited greatly from more transparency in the decision-making process, a wider choice of industries in which they are allowed to participate, more freedom in choosing local business partners, a better educated workforce and government officials more in touch with the needs of foreign investors.

Shanghai's infrastructure has been planned and built with careful coordination. Its large and highly skilled work force, broadly-based scientific establishment, tradition of producer cooperation, and excellent transportation and communications facilities have all contributed to the city's stature as the leading industrial center in China.

This industrial center produces a great variety of capital and consumer goods, including specialized dies, lathes, electronic assembly equipment, watches, cameras, radios, fountain pens, glassware, leather goods, stationery products, and hardware.

The city's well-established chemical and petrochemical industries serve as a basis for the production of plastics, synthetic fibers, and other products. Textile manufacturing is also significant.

But the most important indicator of its economic transformation is perhaps the high-tech industry. The rapid expansion of various industrial parks attracted 4321 contracts for foreign direct investment in high-tech products in 2003 – a hefty increase of 43.5% over the previous year. Total actual investment

Latest Economic Indicators

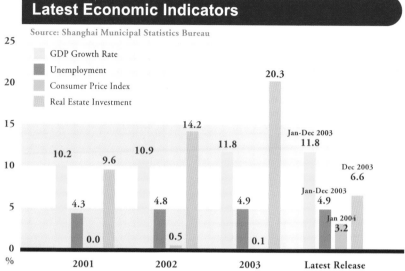

Source: Shanghai Municipal Statistics Bureau

GDP Growth Rate
Unemployment
Consumer Price Index
Real Estate Investment

Note: *1-year lending rate announced by People's Bank of China
USD 1= Euro 1.02, USD = RMB 8.28

value reached USD 11 billion, an increase of 30%.

The current relentless push towards high-tech development will stimulate the economy immensely. It will also generate a multiplier effect that would benefit other sectors, particularly the communications, information and IT industries. It will also have a direct impact on the city's current plan to build a totally new information technology infrastructure known as InfoPort. When this is ready, the whole city will be wired with broadband networks.

Primary Industries

Shanghai's agricultural industry has sustained moderate growths in the past few years. In 2003, the value added of the agricultural sector reached USD 23.9 billion, a 2.3% increase over 2002. Of this total, plantations contributed USD 1.17 billion, down 1.5%, animal husbandry USD 97 million, down 6%, and fishery USD 58 million, up 15.8%.

In addition, total production value of the primary industry in 2003 reached USD 14 billion, an increase of 2.3% over 2002. Export of new varieties of vegetable, high-quality flowers and special fruits increased remarkably.

Shanghai's rural economy has completed its transition from grain, oil and cotton production to a comprehensive suburban economy that is more diversified, integrated and industrialized. By the end of 2003, the basic development of the city's first four modern agriculture parks had been completed, and a group of projects for production and processing of vegetables, flowers and edible mushrooms was launched. The city has set up more than 300 key or overseas-funded enterprises to undertake the production, processing and marketing of agricultural products.

Secondary Industries

The production output of the secondary industry was USD 37.8 billion in 2003, an increase of 16%. Total industrial production for the whole year reached USD 136 billion, a hefty increase of 31.4%. Total profit of all the industrial enterprises was USD 9.73 billion, an impressive increase of 46%.

Shanghai now has more than 42, 000 industrial enterprises, which together, hire about four million employees. In recent years, Shanghai's industrial system underwent an overall restructuring with the aim of strengthening the core industries, nurturing the high-tech industries and reforming traditional ones. Shanghai is also at the heart of China's light industrial sector, home to leading brands in food, cosmetics and textile industries.

In the 1990s, Shanghai's industrial development focused on automobile, communications and information equipment, petrochemical and fine chemical, household electric appliances, steel and iron industries etc. At present, it is making a concerted effort to expedite the development of three major high-tech industries: integrated circuit and computer science, modern biology and pharmaceuticals and new materials.

The six pillar industries of Shanghai, namely, automobile, electronic and telecommunications equipment, iron and steel, petrochemical and fine chemical production, set equipment manufacturing, and biopharmaceuticals, have further consolidated their dominance through innovation and improvement in technology and product.

Tertiary Industries

In the last few years, a series of measures was adopted by both the central and municipal governments in order to stimulate the city's tertiary industry. As a result, the proportion contributed by the tertiary sector to the GDP remained largely stable.

Currently, it constitutes 48.4% of the city's total GDP. Specifically, several industries have gradually become pillar industries over the past 10 years, such as finance and insurance, commerce, transportation, post and telecommunications, real estate and information technology. In 2003, the finance and insurance sector grew by 7.6% to reach USD 76 billion and was one of the fastest-growing sectors in the metropolitan.

Today, Shanghai has become the capital of China's burgeoning service industry. Banking, retail, finance, trade, insurance, and real estate development contribute well over half the city's GDP.

The information industry has also achieved remarkable advancement. In 2003, it grew by another 17% to reach USD 75.15 billion. The prime part of the InfoPort project, featuring broadband, high speed and multi-functions, has already been completed.

In addition, a number of key projects, such as integrated information pipelines, the broadband IP urban network, data network, cable television-Internet transformation, and the broadband information exchange center, have all been completed.

Development of Pudong New District

Less than two decades ago, the Chinese government declared its

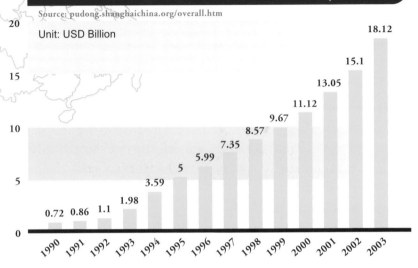

GDP of Pudong New District 1990 - 2003

Source: pudong.shanghaichina.org/overall.htm

Unit: USD Billion

intention to transform Pudong from farmland into a financial, trade and industrial centre.

Today, Pudong has become one of Shanghai's fastest-growing business centers, boasting many world-class buildings, roads and bridges. Several high-tech industrial parks have sprung up in the area.

The GDP of Pudong reached USD 18 billion in 2003, up 17.5% over the previous year. The growth of Pudong's GDP in 2003 was the biggest in the past seven years. The figure was 6 percentage points higher than the growth rate of Shanghai's GDP. Nearly half of the GDP was contributed by the non-state sector.

The annual output value of micro-electric products totaled USD 843 million in 2003. Software and bio-medical sectors registered a growth of 39% and 21% respectively. The service sector recorded a 15% growth. The finance, logistics and tourism sectors have become the pillars of the tertiary industry in Pudong.

In 2003, the import and export value of Pudong came to USD 58.1 billion, rising 58% over the previous year. Foreign direct investment contract value was USD 3.47 billion, an increase of 7.8%.

Today, Pudong has acquired a modern image, with eye-catching highrise buildings of amazing architectural variety, a transformation that is indeed remarkable.

Emphasis on Key Industries

In the next five years, Shanghai will focus much of its energies on attracting foreign capital into six major industries and to open the service market to overseas funds on a larger scale. These six new major industries include IT, financial services, commerce, automobile, set equipment manufacturing and real estate. Unlike the city's previous set of six key industries, the new ones are related to the high-tech industry and service trades.

In the near future, the city will make full play of its advantages in the tertiary sector, so that it may boost the opening up of services like commerce, foreign trade, transportation, accountancy and law firms. Besides directing the introduction of foreign capital, Shanghai has also adopted

new policies to promote private enterprises – especially those in the high-tech area –, to utilize foreign capital and to encourage foreign enterprises' mergers and acquisitions.

Future Development Trends

The six new pillar industries, i.e. the IT, financial services, commerce, automobile, set equipment manu-facturing and real estate industries, have been identified by the municipal government as the most important engines to power the city's economic growth. In particular, the high-tech industry largely represented by IT is considered as the primary thrust for economic growth.

According to the city's economic blueprint, the contribution of the non-state-owned economy to the GDP will be increased to about 40% by 2005. Making room for market-oriented capitalization, state investment will gradually withdraw from traditional industries such as food, drink, plastics, metal products, and switch to the high-tech and pillar industries, such as fine steel, petrochemicals, automobile, electronics and information technology.

By 2005, telecommunications and computer software development are expected to make up 13% of the city's GDP. Meanwhile, the city will give further support to four new industries – biopharmaceuticals, environment protection, new materials and logistics – in the hopes that they become new pillars of economic growth in the future.

REAL ESTATE

Introduction

Shanghai has witnessed exponential growth in both residential and commercial development since the 1990s, and this has continued at a steady rate. Prosperity in the new century further cemented Shanghai's top position in terms of development and demand.

In 2003, Shanghai's investment in real estate surpassed RMB 90.1 billion (USD 10.89 billion). Statistics released by the Municipal Statistical Bureau show that 4.1% of the city's economic growth in the period was from the real estate industry.

Meanwhile, both demand and supply of real estate in the city hit a record high. In the period, the total area of newly completed real estate projects reached 24.92 million m^2, an increase of 25.6%, while total land area of real estate sold reached 23.76 million m^2, up 20.5%.

Due to the surging demand, the land area of real estate left unused continued to decrease. By the end of June 2003, the land area of residential projects left vacant for more than one year was 1.06 million m^2, down 20.9% from the beginning of the year.

During this period, the property industry completed value-added turnover of some USD 5.58 billion, up 13.7% over the corresponding period last year, accounting for 7.4% of the total GDP of the city.

Of the total investment of USD 90.1 billion, individual investors contributed USD 1.07 billion, up 62.9% year-on-year, while shareholding companies contributed USD 1.9 billion, up 3.4%, and overseas investment reached USD 940 million, up 37.5%.

As in many developed countries, the market for resale properties, or so-called stock properties, has flourished in Shanghai. In 2002, 17.9 million m^2 of resale properties were traded, 26% higher than the previous year.

Besides local demand, Shanghai real estate has also attracted both foreign buyers and locals from other parts of China. A good example is the launch of Chrysanthemum Park, developed by Singapore's CapitaLand, where 65% of house owners were from Wenzhou in Zhejiang province.

Market Overview

Value Added

In recent years, Shanghai real estate has enjoyed continuous and healthy growth. Its value-added contribution to the city's GDP has been gaining in significance. Real estate, defined as one of the "pillar industries", together with construction, construction materials, interior renovation and furniture, has become a new and strong booster to the Shanghai's economy.

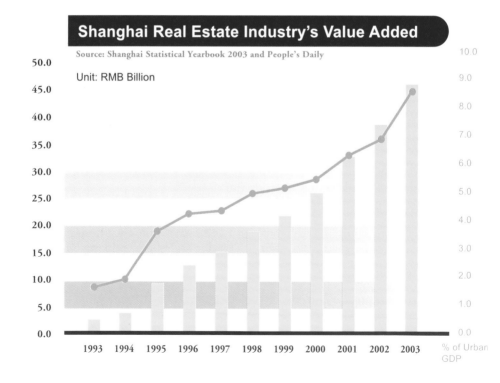

Shanghai Real Estate Industry's Value Added

Source: Shanghai Statistical Yearbook 2003 and People's Daily

Unit: RMB Billion

Top Provinces for Real Estate Development
(by sales) As a Percentage of National Total, 2001

Source: China Major Real Estate Development Enterprises 2002, China Statistics Press

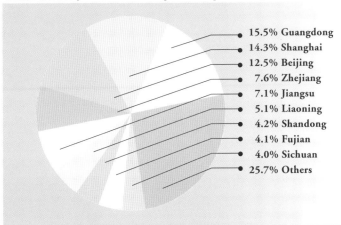

- 15.5% Guangdong
- 14.3% Shanghai
- 12.5% Beijing
- 7.6% Zhejiang
- 7.1% Jiangsu
- 5.1% Liaoning
- 4.2% Shandong
- 4.1% Fujian
- 4.0% Sichuan
- 25.7% Others

In 2003, the real estate industry in Shanghai accounted for 13.7% of the GDP, or USD 5.59 billion, with a few downtown districts even reaching 12-17%. The share of real estate industry in the local economy is forecasted to be well over 15% by 2005, hence closing the gap between Shanghai and major cities elsewhere in the world.

Market Size

In 2003, the Shanghai real estate market was the second largest in China in terms of actual sales at USD 14.69 billion or 49.2% of the total, second only to Guangdong Province. In terms of total pre-sold gross floor area, it was the third largest – 82.67 million m^2, or 20.6% over the previous year. A total floor area of 23.76 million m^2 of properties was sold in 2003, of which 91.5% was bought by individuals, mostly for housing purposes.

Profitability

Total real estate investment in Shanghai in 2003 reached USD 10.89 billion with operating income amounting to USD 11.73 billion. The operating income of the whole industry was increasing at an average compounded rate of 29% between 1999-2003, while profitability as a ratio of profit to total investment or operating income improved too.

Market Structure

Residential Market

In contrast to the situation two years ago, Shanghai's homes are now the most costly in China. In 2001, the average price of a house in Shanghai was RMB 3,658 (USD441.96) per m², while that of a house in Beijing was RMB 4,716 (USD 569.79), or 28.9% higher.

In 2003 however, Shanghai became the country's most expensive housing market when its average price per square meter surged upwards

Shanghai's Homes are Most Costly

Shanghai has surpassed Beijing to become the country's most expensive housing market when its average price per square meter surged more than 24 percent in 2003, according to a report on the real estate sector by the National Bureau of Statistics.

A hefty housing price rise will eventually lead to oversupply and panic selling, analysts cautioned.

Cognizant of the trend, the city government has vowed to rein in development of the industry. Cai Yutian, the director of the Shanghai Housing and Land Administrative Bureau, the local property industry watchdog, said earlier this year that the city government would step in and cool the red-hot market.

He said housing prices in 2004 should not increase more than 12 percent from a year earlier.

The city government rolled out new rules earlier this year to prevent investors from selling houses under construction. Developers are not allowed to sell apartments until the building is topped out. The government has also tightened regulation on mortgage loans.

According to the rules, homebuyers could only buy one apartment using loans; they of 24%, according to a report on the real estate sector by the National Bureau of Statistics.

The average price for Shanghai's residential dwellings topped USD 618.36 per square meter in 2003, up 24.2% from 2002. The national figures for average housing price was RMB 2,379 (USD 287.43) per m^2 in 2003, an increase of 3.8% from the preceding year.

Shanghai was also the fastest-growing housing market in 2003. Investors from other parts of China and foreign countries had driven up pressure on the city's housing market as they bet on further price rises when Shanghai hosts the World Expo 2010.

Office Market

According to Colliers International in a research report put out in February 2004, 2003 had seen steady rental growth with average rental for Grade A office space in the city having risen by 4.4% to USD 21.2 per m^2 per month. Grade A offices in prime locations such as Huaihai Zhong Road, Nanjing

are barred from borrowing money from the banks to buy a second flat.

The Shanghai Housing Index, the benchmark of new housing prices, grew by a scant 0.45 percent in January 2004, compared to 33 percent in 2003.

The city government could also control price hikes through land allocation, industry analysts say.

Source: www.chinaview.cn, 15th March 2004

Xi Road and Lujiazui, Pudong saw much higher increases in rent of approximately 6.5% to USD 22.5 per square meter per month.

On the sales front, considering the trend of higher rental levels and lower borrowing costs, some domestic privately-run and self-employed businesses preferred to purchase rather than lease so as to meet the demand for medium to long-term investment or self-occupancy.

On the back of strong investment interest, average capital values had remained steady in both Pudong and Puxi at USD 2665 per square meter.

Major new projects completed in 2003 included Hong Kong New World Tower and Corporate Avenue Phase I at Huaihai Zhong Road, Raffles City near People's Square and Aurora Plaza in Central Lujiazui, Puodng. Notwithstanding the new supply, occupancy rates remained steady at 88.7%.

Source: Colliers International Topical Research Report, February 2004

Office Occupancy Costs 2002

City/ District	Global Rank*	Year 2002 Cost (USD psf p.a)	Annual Change(%)
Beijing	23	40.80	-0.20
Shanghai(Pudong)	39	32.30	-0.30
Shanghai(Puxi)	45	31.40	1.90
Shenzhen	49	29.00	1.80
Guandong	54	27.40	7.50
Tianjin	73	20.00	-10.30
Dalian	81	15.70	6.10

Source: Global Office Occupancy Costs 2003, DTZ Research
Note: *Number of surveyed cites was 92

WTO Impact on the Real Estate Industry

With China's entry to WTO in December 2001, its real estate market moved another step towards full opening. As the country's economic locomotive, Shanghai has enjoyed double-digit growth for more than a decade. With a favorable investment environment, location advantages, and international fame, it is likely to continue as a popular destination for foreign investors.

China's WTO accession has long-term repercussions on Shanghai's real estate industry in both positive and negative ways. It sets a specific timetable for the opening of the real estate market.

Immediately upon entry, all limitations were lifted on foreign-invested establishments in the real estate development sector, except for investment in high-end projects like high-class hotels, condominiums, and golf courses where only JVs are allowed; JVs and CJVs can be set up in real estate services, including property valuation, property management, and brokerage.

By December 2006, China must follow internationally accepted practices, such as national treatment, transparency, and market entry requirements. WOFEs will be allowed in all sectors of the real estate industry.

As WTO entry mandates lower import barriers, so an influx of real estate related products and technologies can be foreseen. This would greatly improve industry standards while increasing effective supply. The contribution to economic growth from technological improvements in

With World Expo 2010 coming up, this decade has good prospects: construction of exhibition halls may generate up to USD 3 billion in revenue, and related infrastructure and public services will add to the total. ... Following WTO entry, foreign investment flows to Shanghai have accelerated. In 2003, new contracts worth USD 11 billion were signed, up 23.5 % YoY. By end of 2003, the city had approved the establishment of 4,321 projects with total paid-up investment value of USD 5.85 billion.

developed countries is estimated at 60% and in China at 35%. But the figure is only 25.4% in China's real estate industry.

The situation is likely to change, however, with the introduction of new technologies, materials, equipment, and business concepts and philosophies. Foreign investment should boost technological advancement, such as the introduction and assimilation of new materials, design, intelligent technologies, and whole process planning. More competition would encourage innovation to improve product quality at controlled, if not lower, costs, while positively affecting supply of real properties.

Market Outlook

As China's economic locomotive, Shanghai has been developing quickly for over two decades, with GDP per capita approaching USD 5,000. Seen by itself, Shanghai is like a middle-level developed economy. During the 10th Five-Year Plan (2001-2005), Shanghai's annual GDP growth is forecast at 10%.

In the municipality's development plans, the real estate industry is one of the six "pillar industries" for the local economy. The goals are clearly set:

- An average annual growth rate of 14% for the industry's value added;
- Contribution of 7% or more to GDP by 2005 (already realized);
- Construction of new houses--more than 60 million m² floor area (likely to be achieved by mid-2004);
- Development of 20 large residential communities between the Inner and Outer Ring Roads.

The central government has positioned Shanghai as a center for international economic development, trade, finance, and shipping, and a modern cosmopolitan. In its "Economic and Social Development Fifteenth Five-Year Plan", Shanghai set its own goal to "become a better place for both domestic and overseas enterprises development and individual living".

The plan clearly spells out real estate development as a way to improve the living environment and residence standards and to enhance the overall competitiveness of the city.

In a new round of urban building, there will be comprehensive development on both banks of the Huangpu River, construction of tunnels and bridges, rail traffic systems, public transit interchanges and terminals, magnetic levitation (MAGLEV) transport, and large-scale ecology projects.

With World Expo 2010 coming up, this decade has good prospects for even better performance: construction of exhibition halls may generate up to USD 3 billion in revenue, and related infrastructure and public services will add to the total. For example, a more developed transportation network will greatly improve accessibility in Shanghai, with a positive impact on local real estate projects.

Following WTO entry, foreign investment flows to Shanghai have accelerated. In the first quarter of 2003, new contracts worth USD 3.39 billion were signed, up 59.2% year-on-year. By end-March 2003, the city had approved the establishment of 28,724 projects with total contractual foreign direct investment of USD 66.77 billion.

Although the SARS outbreak in 2003 temporarily delayed some new projects, Shanghai will remain an important center for FDI in the long term. With the entry of influential MNCs and a continual influx of foreign businessmen, the need for factories, offices, and accommodation keeps rising. Moreover, many Chinese returning from overseas and overseas Chinese from Hong Kong, Taiwan, and Macau who wish to retire in China, or to invest in property, find Shanghai a very attractive place.

TOURISM

Introduction

Tourism is one of the economic growth areas in Shanghai, and is crucially important for the city's continued economic expansion. In recent years, its contribution to the city's sum total investments and assets has increased significantly. In short, it has become an integral part of the city's rapid economic development.

The booming tourism industry has also created many job opportunities, although this figure is small in relation to the city's total employment figures. However, owing to its favorable indirect effects on job creation, the municipal government is according top priority to the industry's development.

Since the implementation of the 10th "Five-Year Plan" in 2001, the tourism industry has made impressive headway. Construction of the Shanghai Science Centre and the first phase of the new urban district Oriental Oasis

have been completed, large-scale festival activities were organized and many attractive tourist packages were launched.

At the end of 2003, the number of foreign tourist arrivals reached 3.2 million, down 14%; foreign exchange earnings went down 9.8% to USD 2 billion. The number of domestic tourists too had decreased 13% to 76 million, generating a total income of RMB 108 billion (USD 13 billion), a drop of 10.9%.

In spite of slower growth however, tourism had contributed 6% to the city's GDP. It has promoted development of related industries, expanded job opportunities, improved quality of life and made the city even more attractive internationally. In short, its contributions are direct and positive.

For 2004, tourist promotion in Shanghai is aimed at attracting more than 3.5 million tourists (including 2.5 million day tourists), and to achieve a total of USD 2.6 billion in foreign exchange earnings. As for domestic tourists, it hopes to attract about 95 million people, and generate earnings exceeding RMB 110 billion (USD 13.29 billion). In this way, total income of the tourism industry is expected to exceed RMB 130 billion (USD 15.71 billion), contributing about 6.3% to the city's GDP, and 20, 000 new jobs will be created.

Shanghai has also set its targets for 2005 – to attract 4 million foreign tourists, and generate foreign exchange earnings approaching USD 3.5 billion; as well as more than 100 million domestic tourists and additional domestic tourism earnings of RMB 13 billion (USD 1.57 billion). If these targets are realized, the overall economy should expand to the tune of RMB 51.1 billion (USD 6.17 billion), constituting 7% of the total GDP, and 50,000 new jobs for the industry would be created.

New Policies to Boost Tourism

The Shanghai government implemented the "Shanghai City Tourism Regulations" on 1st March 2004. It is known widely as the tourism industry's "Basic Laws" or the "First Law of Shanghai Tourism". Through innovative approaches, the series of new policies

aim to actively promote further development of tourism, opening up the tourist market to the world and at the same time, safeguarding the interests of tourists visiting the city. Some of the regulations are widely hailed by the country's tourism industry as ingenious and farsighted.

According to the Head of the Shanghai Tourism Policy Committee, Mr Yin Minfa, the basic objective of the new regulations is to create an open, trustworthy tourist market in Shanghai.

The new regulations affect practically every aspect of the city's tourism – food, accommodation, transport, sightseeing, shopping, information as well as investment. It has six chapters and 55 clauses. The new regulations stipulate that government servants may now approach private travel agencies to make travel arrangements; tourists from abroad may be serviced by agencies set up by foreign travel operators; government agencies in charge of tourism resources may relinquish their rights of management in return for adequate compensations after approval by the relevant authorities; major tourist attractions can now limit the number of visitors; companies offering tourist services online should possess certain acceptable

Forecast of Top 10 Travel Destinations in the World in 2020

S/No.	Country or Region	Number of Inbound Tourists (10, 000 persons)	Share in World Market (%)	Growth Rate from 1995 to 2020 (%)
1	China	13,710	8.6	8.0
2	USA	10,240	6.4	3.5
3	France	9,330	5.8	1.8
4	Spain	7,100	4.4	2.4
5	Hong Kong	5,930	3.7	7.3
6	Italy	5,290	3.3	2.2
7	UK	5,280	3.3	3.0
8	Mexico	4,890	3.1	3.6
9	Russia	4,710	2.9	6.7
10	Czech Republic	4,400	2.7	4.0
	Total	**70,800**	**44.2**	

Source: Forecast of World Travel Development in 2020, WTO

International Tourism Receipts and Visitor Arrivals in 2002

S/N	Region	International Tourism Receipts (million USD)	Visitor Arrivals (10, 000 persons)
1	Beijing	3114.54	310.38
2	Tianjin	342.38	50.6
3	Hebei	167.03	47.36
4	Shanxi	74.84	24.8
5	Inner Mongolia	149.35	43.94
6	Liaoning	550.21	92.94
7	Jilin	86.29	29.4
8	Heilongjiang	297.17	71.74
9	Shanghai	2275.45	272.53
10	Jiangsu	1052.05	222.63
11	Zhejiang	927.63	204.1
12	Anhui	123.82	45.91
13	Fujian	1100.22	184.82
14	Jiangxi	71.62	24.09
15	Shandong	472.49	97.68
16	Henan	145.49	41.01
17	Hubei	283.91	102.43
18	Hunan	311.08	56.62
19	Guangdong	5090.89	1525.88
20	Guangxi	321.44	136.34
21	Hainan	91.99	38.94
22	Chongqing	218.02	46.15
23	Sichuan	200.21	66.72
24	Guizhou	79.51	22.81
25	Yunnan	419.3	103.36
26	Tibet	51.66	14.23
27	Shaanxi	350.97	85.01
28	Gansu	543.1	23.68
29	Qinghai	9.99	4.35
30	Ningxia	1.61	0.6
31	Xinjiang	99.42	27.54

Source: China Economic Information Network Database

qualifications; and finally, travel agencies which fail to honor their contractual obligations must compensate tourists who suffered losses.

In addition, the new regulations now permit the commissioning of suitable enterprises to carry out promotional programs for tourism development and to set up consultant services networks. The regulations encourage the promotion of e-commerce in the tourism business and public participation in the formulation of tourist promotion programs. Market analysts say more than half of the new regulations are innovative and have far-reaching effects.

For the city's travel operators, the new regulations are both good as well as bad news. The wide-ranging policies ensure standardization in business practice, promote fair competition, and open up new areas for further business development. On the other hand, the new "open policy" means that local and foreign operators are now free to enter the Shanghai market and engage in open competition. Under these circumstances, existing travel operators in Shanghai are no longer shielded from external competition as in the past. Even in places where they had traditionally enjoyed preferential treatment as local operators, they now have to face stiff rivalry from competitors in other parts of China as well as other countries.

Indeed, the city's travel operators are now at a crossroads. They have to take advantage of the newly created opportunities for further business development, but at the same time, they have to upgrade their operations in the face of new challenges coming from perhaps more formidable competitors.

New Development Trends

Facilities for Business Travelers

Shanghai will strive to host at least 400 conventions and exhibitions by 2005, including 100 major international events. Presently it is actively preparing for EXPO 2010, and at the same time, working hard to expand the scale of various long-standing events, including established shows like

the China Trade Exhibition, Shanghai Trade Fair, Industrial and Commercial Exposition and Multi-national Purchasers Symposium etc.

Joint ventures and close cooperation between major international show organizers and Shanghai event organizers are being established, with the aim of organizing, and creating more favorable conditions for large-scale exhibitions and events, as well as to create "multi-national corporations" to compete with international players, and to set up enterprises capable of offering a wide range of professional services.

Shanghai has always been a frontrunner in organizing large international exhibitions and attracting exhibitors into the country. According to statistics, the exhibition trade generates substantial revenue for the city, with a ratio of about 1 to 9 to the total revenues collected. The forthcoming EXPO 2010 promises to bring in much greater economic benefits than ever before. It is estimated that potential income from direct sales of tickets, food and beverage, souvenirs etc. will generate a total income of about USD 1.09 billion.

Together with Nanjing, Changzhou, Hangzhou, NingBo, Yiwu, Shaoxing, Haining, Yongkang and other surrounding towns, Shanghai, the "Dragon Head" is poised to bring about unprecedented economic advantage to the region as a whole. The sprawling hinterland provides the city with huge market support for exhibitions and other related services. This has important implications for the long-term development of Shanghai's exhibition trade.

Historically, Shanghai possesses many cultural and demographic advantages that have made it the first choice for foreign exhibitors. Some of these foreign exhibitors have already established themselves firmly in the China market.

The metropolis' most important selling point is that many world-renowned exhibitions were first launched in the city. These exhibitions had large clientele bases and excellent track records, and their exhibitors occupied strong market positions. These factors had made Shanghai an ideal venue for exhibitions.

Currently, Shanghai has five large-scale exhibition centers with total area of more than 150,000 m². There are more than 300 luxury hotels with modern exhibition facilities, and over 100 companies offering exhibition-related services, which include event organization, management and marketing. They employ a large number of qualified professionals who are experienced in translation, sales, administration and public relations.

The city's impressive performance has contributed significantly to its success in clinching the rights to organize the EXPO 2010. In 2001, the exhibition trade earned a whopping RMB 1.8 billion (USD 220 million) in direct revenue, constituting 45% of the total national revenue of this sector. The successful organization of CeBIT Asia and APEC had  greatly boosted Shanghai's image as the city for world conventions and trade fairs. EXPO 2010 will therefore be a historic occasion for Shanghai to further strengthen its position as a world-class exhibition venue, thereby generating tremendous business opportunities for future industry expansion.

The continued growth of the exhibition industry will also enhance Shanghai's functional efficiency, particularly in the areas of regional economic exchange, trade showcasing, distribution services, the promotion of international and regional communications, technical cooperation, business development as well as personal and cultural exchanges. This will infuse the Yangtze River Delta Economic Zone with greater vitality.

Economists believe that the successful hosting of EXPO 2010 will create a favorable environment for the emergence of a so-called "Expo Economic Sphere" around the Yangtze River Delta region, and a potential integration of surrounding cities into an unified economic entity. In this way, cooperation between the various economic centers can be deepened further and coordination among them can become more

efficient, thus facilitating the expansion of tourist infrastructure for the north-eastern part of China.

Cultural Facilities

To promote Shanghai's comprehensive tourism resources – well known for their cultural and historical attributes – and at the same time publicize its famous brand names and rich social life, the city has embarked on a major project to expand and build more museums. The main emphasis will be placed on the construction of Zhi Dan Yuan Shrines and other similar historical sites. By 2005, the total number of museums will be increased from the present 64 to around 100. The city's more than 130 national and municipal-level cultural sites and more than 200 ancient homes of famous personalities will also be extensively refurbished to enhance their attractiveness.

Within three years, the historical town of Zhu Jia Jiao will be upgraded, old gardens rich in cultural significance will be expanded and more public parks will be built to give the urban areas ample greenery. Plans are also afoot to construct more public squares for social gatherings, and buildings along the coastal areas will be refurbished to enhance their aesthetic qualities as well as to make the city's skyline more enchanting. The ultimate objective is to attract more cultural, educational and technical conferences and seminars to the metropolis.

Shopping Facilities

The city's reputation as a shopping haven will be further strengthened. The famous Nanjing Dong Lu, Nanjing Xi Lu, Huai Hai Zhong Lu, Si Chuan Bei Lu, New Shanghai Commercial Town, Jia Bei Night Market, Yu Yuan Shopping District, Xu Jia Commercial Center and Five-Corner Shopping Plaza etc. will undergo a complete redevelopment.

Under the new construction plan, places such as the Xiao Lu Jia Jue, Xin Tian Di, Pu Jiang Coastal Area and the public areas around the Jing

An Temple will be refurbished to become a multi-purpose shopping district. There will also be between three and five mega shopping malls providing a wide range of services. A center for selling various kinds of souvenirs which is now under construction will be open sooner than originally scheduled. When  ready, it will become a unique tourist attraction, rivaling the famous Yu Yuan and Long Hua Handicraft Market, which are also being upgraded as part of the overall improvement program.

Holiday Facilities

For tourists intending to spend their holidays in Shanghai, the city is actively promoting the Se Shan-Ding Shan Lake District, Heng Sha Island Ecological Resort, Feng Yang Bay Holiday Resort, Chong Ming Forest Holiday District and the Nan Hui Seaside Holiday Resort. More new tourist attractions are also under construction. The Golden Hill Triple Island Ocean Eco-garden Protected District and Wan Mou Ecological Forest, for example, will be ready earlier than expected.

The well-known Shanghai Zoo is being expanded in a bold move to turn it into an "Animal World within a Garden City". New concepts in tourism have also been explored. The "Happy Farming Family" program, for example, is scheduled to be launched soon. Presently, there are 10 walking/ hiking trails open to intrepid tourists keen on ecological explorations. Three or four more will be added in the near future.

Industrial Tours

Leading corporations in the urban industry, such as Bao Gang, Da Zhong and GM, etc. will form the backbone of the "Urban Industrial Tour Programs". Under the program, visitors will be able to witness firsthand the operations of major industrial parks (such as the Shanghai International Automobile City, Shanghai Chemical Industrial Park, Caohejing High-tech Park etc.), Industrial Exhibition Hall (such as Industrial Arts Exhibition Museum) and the innovative Trade Museums, which will showcase a range of industrial products.

Cruising Tours

In the next three years, Shanghai will be launching cruising tours and other recreational activities along the sea coasts and rivers. It intends to provide such services at world-class standards. To achieve the objective, plans are afoot to develop the "Green Water and Golden Sand Lagoon". Cruising tours along rivers and lakes are being planned.

In line with this major project, other facilities such as the harbor cruise center at the Southern Coast, Cruise Service Station at Huang Pu River, and the International Passenger Centre at the northern coastal area will be built, albeit in stages. As for sea sports, facilities for activities such as yachting, canoeing, wind surfing etc. are in the pipeline. Recreational clubs for sea sports are currently under construction.

Festival Tours

Shanghai organizes annual celebrations such as the Shanghai Tourism Festival, International Cultural and Arts Festival as well as International Film and TV Festival etc., which have become part of the social calendar of the metropolitan city. These activities are very popular among foreign tourists. To build on its past successes, the city will stage more urban festivals. It intends to attract active public participation and to intensify international cultural exchanges, thereby further spreading Shanghai's cultural values and influences, both domestically and abroad.

Food Tours

To promote the development of its traditional food culture, more international food chains are invited to set up branches in Shanghai. They are encouraged to set up strategic networks to promote their brand names. Food Streets and Food Plazas are being built to make Shanghai a haven of delicacies.

In line with the efforts to promote tourism, more luxury hotels and guest houses will be operational by the year 2005. Tourist hotels (including guest houses and serviced apartments) will be increased from the present 300 to about 450. The number of guest rooms will be increased from 50,000 to 700,000. As for restaurants, besides those already in successful operation along Heng Shan Lu, Yan Dang Lu, Wu Jiang Lu and Huang He Lu, a further 20 food districts are planned and will offer both Chinese and Western cuisine.

Efficient transport systems are indispensable in the development of tourism. Efforts are being made to overcome severe traffic congestion by building more expressways. By 2005, the city's External Ring Road, Central Ring Line (at Pu Xi) and the Lu Pu Bridge, Da Lian Bridge, the motorway tunnel under the river linking Da Lian Lu to Fu Xing Lu and other highways will be ready to meet increasing demand.

Long distance transport stations will be built at strategic locations to provide convenient land transport services. Passenger information services and integrated traffic management systems will be upgraded and improved. A comprehensive transportation network for both inner city as well as suburban areas will all become a reality in the near future.

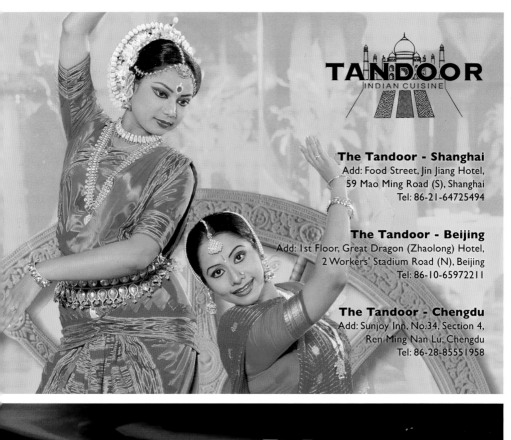

ENERGY

Overview

Shanghai is rapidly emerging as China's financial, commercial, and even logistics hub. Since the development of Pudong New District in the early 1990s, it has been undergoing many structural changes. The shift from traditional industry to commercial and services activities will have a profound impact on Shanghai's energy sector. Ensuring sustainable economic growth and improving the environment are tops on the agenda for Shanghai's energy sector.

Electricity Shortage

For more than a decade, Shanghai's GDP growth had been moving upwards by 10% annually. This fast growth has stretched Shanghai's energy sector. In 2003, Shanghai's electricity consumption surged to 74.8 TWhs (trillion-watt-hours), up 15.8% compared to 2002. During the same period, Shanghai, only generated 68.5 TWhs, up about 12.5%. As of mid-2003, Shanghai's power generation capacity was about 9820 MW while the peak load reached 13, 000 MW during the same period.

Shanghai used to enjoy the support from other provinces in the East China Grid, which includes Zhejiang, Jiangsu and Anhui. However, most of them are also facing serious power shortage now.

In 2003, 19 provinces in China had faced electrical blackouts. There are many reasons for this situation. SERC (State Electricity Regulatory Commission) however pointed out that the main reason was the overall lag in expansion of generation capacity due to inaccurate forecasts.

The lag in expansion of generation capacity may be explained by a situation of temporary power oversupply in China in the late 1990s. As a result, and in order to, at the same time, improve efficiency, the proposed construction of coal-fired plants in the coastal regions was postponed or cancelled.

As such, to avoid power failures, some companies were asked to shift production to nights and weekends. This has posed a serious threat to the sustainability of economic growth. At the same time, however, construction of power plants requires a huge amount of capital investment and will take two to four years to complete. The situation of shortage of power supply is thus expected to last for some time.

Since Shanghai is still in the developing phase, with industry still accounting for about 50% of GDP, and a surging residential consumption (up 27.8% in 2003, the fastest growth sector), it is plausible that Shanghai intends to keep its electricity consumption at a rate in tandem with GDP growth, about 10% annually in the next few years. It means the maximum load in Shanghai will surge up to 25, 000 MW in 2010.

Even if, according to plan, Shanghai receives 2880 MW from the Three Gorges Project after 2009, there is still a big gap to fill. Many big projects are under construction or in the process of assessment. Among them, the second phase of construction of the Waigaoqiao power plant is one of the biggest projects, which includes two 900 MW super critical units. It is also China's biggest unit so far.

China's thirst for energy also creates opportunities for foreign investors. SembCorp Utilities, a unit of Singapore conglomerate SembCorp Industries, will invest SGD 218 million (about USD 130 million) for a 30% stake in a joint venture firm, Shanghai Caojing Cogeneration Company. The co-generation plant, which produces both electricity and steam, will be located in the Shanghai Chemical Industrial Park.

This industrial park is one of the largest industrial investment projects in China during the period of "the 10th Five-Year Plan", and the total investment for Phase I of the project will be RMB 150 billion (USD 18.12 billion). It is the first special development park to be started, after the economic reforms and opening of China, which lays emphasis on developing crude oil processing and fine chemical products, and is one of the cornerstones of Shanghai's industry. The plant will have a capacity of 605 MW and 660 tons steam per hour, and will provide electricity and steam for the chemical industrial park.

Structural Changes for Cleaner Energy

As with most parts of China, coal plays a very important role in Shanghai. In 2000, Shanghai's total energy consumption was about 54.92 million tons standard coal. Of this figure, coal consumption accounted for 65.5%. Shanghai is China's largest coal consumer. This has created serious environmental problems.

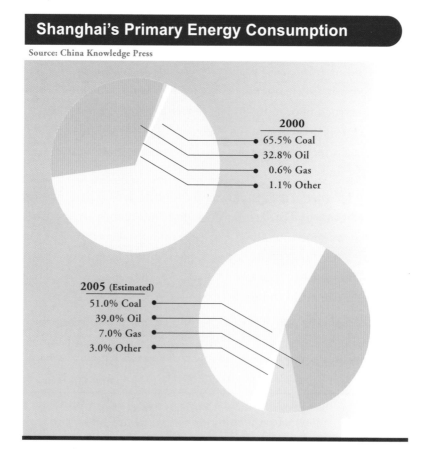

Shanghai's Primary Energy Consumption

Source: China Knowledge Press

2000
- 65.5% Coal
- 32.8% Oil
- 0.6% Gas
- 1.1% Other

2005 (Estimated)
- 51.0% Coal
- 39.0% Oil
- 7.0% Gas
- 3.0% Other

In order to solve these problems, the Shanghai government has adopted measures to improve its energy consumption mix. According to the 10th Five-Year Plan in Shanghai, coal consumption will be capped at 45 million tons, and the weighting of coal consumption will be decreased to 51% until 2005. Cleaner energy like natural gas, wind and solar energy will be encouraged.

Although oil is also treated as clean energy, due to the increasing pressure of supply in China, a flat increase is likely in the weighting of oil consumption in the future (even lower than the officially projected 39% in 2005).

Natural gas is a good alternative though. For developed countries, natural gas accounts for more than 20% of primary energy consumption while it is less than 1% in Shanghai in 2002.

Shanghai currently has two sources of natural gas. One is the Pinghu Natural Gas Field in East Sea, about 360 km offshore from Shanghai, which started to provide natural gas to Shanghai in 1999; the other is the Changjin gas field from northwest China's Shaanxi province, which started supplying natural gas from October last year. It is part of China's giant west-to-east pipeline project. The west end of the pipeline is Lunnan in Tarim Basin, and the east end is Shanghai. The 4,200 km long pipeline will pass through nine provinces and bring natural gas to the eastern part of China.

Since 1993, China has been an oil net import country. China surpassed Japan as the No.2 petroleum user after the U.S. in 2003. According to General Administration of Customs, China imported 81.87 million tons in the first 11 months of 2003, 28% higher than the same period in 2002. At the same time, China's oil production remained flat, up only 1.8% in 2003.

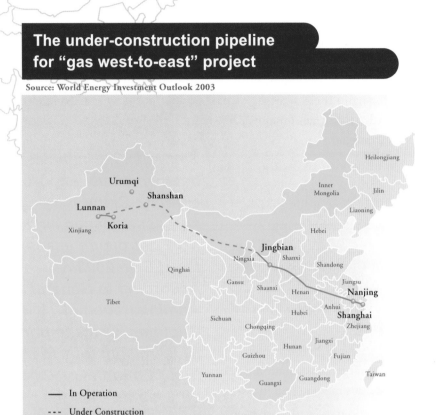

The under-construction pipeline for "gas west-to-east" project

Source: World Energy Investment Outlook 2003

— In Operation

- - - Under Construction

The total investment for this project is estimated at USD 16.91 billion (including city pipeline networks and other facilities). The whole project is scheduled for completion by 2005.

At the initial stage, the pipeline will provide 12 billion cubic meters (BCM). According to plan, 0.43 BCM natural gas will be provided to Shanghai in 2004, and the value will be increased to 3 BCM in 2005, and will be further increased to 7 BCM by 2010.

Furthermore, to diversify gas supply, Shanghai plans to follow the examples of the Guangdong, Fujian and Zhejiang provinces, and implement a liquefied natural gas (LNG) project to import LNG from foreign countries.

Shanghai will leverage on the new gas sources to restructure its energy consumption mix. Before Pinghu Natural Gas Field came into operation, Shanghai's gas was generated by coal processing. With ample supply of natural gas, natural gas will replace coal gas as fired gas in Shanghai by 2010, as part of the government's plan to promote the use of clean energy. A total of 600,000 to 1 million households will use natural gas instead of coal in the next few years.

In fact, households will be the smallest consumers of natural gas. The biggest users will be power plants. More than 50% of natural gas will be used for power generation in the future. Currently over 90% of power plants are coal-fired, which will pose serious problems to environment improvement. Shanghai has decided to keep the capacity of coal-fired plants below 12,000 MW. Gas-fired units will become the main new generation source in the future. Besides Caojing Power Plant mentioned above, Huaneng Group, one of the big five in China's power sector, has invested capital for the building of a 3 x 300 MW gas-fired plant in Shanghai. It is scheduled to be in operation in 2006.

Compared with coal-fired units, gas-fired units will cause fewer pollution problems. The construction period is shorter and more flexible.

However, gas price may be an issue. According to State Development Planning Commission (SDPC), the price of gas from the west-to-east pipeline in Shanghai will be RMB 1.32/CM. It is lower than Pinghu Natural Gas Field (RMB 1.45/CM) or the proposed LNG price (RMB 1.60/CM). For power generation, the price will be RMB 1.12-1.30/CM.

Nontheless, it is still higher than the expectations of power producers. According to Huaneng, the acceptable price is about RMB 0.9-1.0/CM to keep its competitiveness. The government may adopt new laws and policies to solve this disparity. For potential investors, they may need to pay closer attention to the issue in the next few years.

Shanghai will be the first city in China to adopt "Green Electricity Scheme", mainly targeting large non-household consumers. It is believed that it will be implemented some time this year. The plan will focus on wind and solar power. The Shanghai government will encourage businesses to buy green electricity—energy produced from renewable resources such as wind and solar power.

A 34 MW windmill and a 10 kilowatt (kW) solar power generator have been established along the coastal area in Shanghai's southern suburbs. In addition, a 200 MW wind power project, financed by the World Bank, is under construction. The project, scheduled to supply power to Shanghai by the end of 2004, comprises a 140 MW wind power plant in Nanhui District and a 60MW windmill in Chongming Island. The total investment is about RMB 200 million (USD 24.16 million), and it will be the largest wind power plant in China. It is expected that wind power will account for 3% of total electricity consumption in Shanghai by 2015.

Although green electricity is only a small part of electricity supply, it will certainly improve the public awareness of sustainable development and environmental protection, because the economic cost for green electricity will be higher than traditional power plants. Some special mechanism will be adopted to encourage the purchase of green electricity.

To produce equipment for windmills or solar power plants locally will reduce the cost dramatically. At the same time, the investment size for green electricity is much smaller than traditional power plants and is encouraged by the government. It certainly will create many investment opportunities in the future, especially in cities like Shanghai, Beijing etc. (Due to pollution problems, the Chinese government encourages the building of coal-fired power plants that are above 300MW/unit. For 300MW coal-fired unit, the investment will be somewhere between RMB 900 to 1200 million).

Major Players

For power supply, there are three major players in Shanghai. They are Shanghai Electric Power Ltd. Co., Shenergy Company Ltd. and Huaneng Group. They are all publicly listed companies.

Shanghai Electric is the biggest electricity producer in Shanghai. It was listed on Shanghai Stock Exchange in Oct 2003. Its total generation capacity is about 30% of Shanghai's total capacity. Its parent company is a unit of China Power Investment, one of the big five producers in China. The total capacity of China Power Investment is about 30,150 MW, or 22,220 MW on equity basis. With the support of China Power Investment, Shanghai Electric will strength its position in Shanghai's energy market.

Shenergy Ltd. Co. is the energy development and construction arm of Shanghai municipal government. Its business scope includes power generation, and supply of oil and gas. By the end of 2002, its accumulative capacity was about 2920 MW, or 1970 MW on equity basis. It constituted about 18% of Shanghai's total capacity.

Shenergy has 40% interest in Pinghu Natural Gas Field. In 2002, 438.9 k tons crude oil and 430 million CM natural gas were sold. Besides this, Shenergy has 60% shares in the newly founded company – Shanghai Gas Network Co., which is responsible for gas pipeline network construction and management in Shanghai.

Another big player is the Huaneng Group, one of the big five in China's power sector. Huaneng is also Asia's biggest Independent Power Producer (IPP). The total capacity is 36,270 MW, or 19,380 MW on equity basis. It is listed on the Shanghai, Hong Kong and New York Stock Exchanges. Huaneng now owns two power plants in Shanghai – Shidongkou Power Plant and Shidongkou Power Plant (second phase), with total capacity of 2400 MW. A 3 x 300 MW gas-fired power plant is under construction and is expected to be completed by 2006.

The issue of energy supply will remain one of the biggest challenges for Shanghai. But given Shanghai's status in China, the government will solve this problem one way or another. Along the way, clean energy presents enormous investment opportunities.

FURNITURE

Introduction

Driven by the development of Pudong, urban construction in Shanghai is in full swing. The Shanghai furniture market has also been showing unprecedented prosperity. In the last ten years, due to improved living standards of Shanghai citizens and their better housing conditions, there has been a quick rise in demand for furniture.

A rough estimate shows the development rate has moved upwards progressively, averaging more than 20% each year, from RMB 700 million (USD 84.57 billion) in 1990 to RMB 14 billion (USD 1.69 billion) in 2002. The demand for furniture had increased nearly 15 times.

In the past 10 years, the furniture industry in Shanghai has gone from the stage of mechanism reform to a mature market; from importing western furniture to exporting home-made furniture.

Furniture Market

An essential change has taken place in the economic structure in Shanghai's furniture industry. The state-owned economic structure has been done away with. Instead, various economic elements such as joint-venture, sole proprietorship, collective-owned, civilian-run, individual-run and the like, have sprung into existence.

The importing of western furniture to Shanghai in great

quantities has promoted the local furniture sales market tremendously. At present, the furniture market in Shanghai is an industry platform from which the country may propel itself into the world market; at the same time, the rest of the world are also seeking Chinese products. As the furniture market moves to conform to international regulations, it will become increasingly mature in the fiercely competitive international market.

In the past few years, the number of furniture enterprises in Shanghai has grown from slightly more than 200 to 2500 – of which over 1900 are furniture manufacturers; the others are commercial enterprises.

The furniture market comprises five big categories and market share.

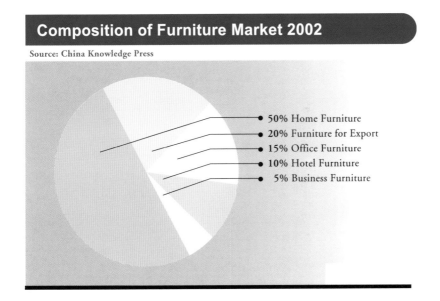

Composition of Furniture Market 2002

Source: China Knowledge Press

- 50% Home Furniture
- 20% Furniture for Export
- 15% Office Furniture
- 10% Hotel Furniture
- 5% Business Furniture

There exists unlimited business opportunities in the market as there are over 250,000 families moving into new or renovated houses annually.

Rapid Development of Joint Venture (JV) Enterprises

With the economic reforms and opening of the China market, overseas furniture manufacturers are turning their attention to this huge market, and channeling their investments into China's furniture industry.

According to statistics, there are more than 500 JV enterprises from America, Germany, Italy, France, Denmark, Japan, Korea and other countries and regions, with a total investment of USD 500 million. In view of its favourable investment environment, enormous market potential, advanced transport system and convenient port facilities, Shanghai is widely considered as a strategic and ideal location.

Shanghai Furniture Sales 2002

Source: China National Furniture Association, 2003

- 44% Home Furniture
- 13% Office Furniture
- 9% Hotel Furniture
- 9% Business Furniture
- 4% Others
- 7% Sales to Other Regions
- 14% Sales to Overseas

At present, among the JV furniture enterprises, Hong Kong and Taiwan enterprises contribute 60% of furniture production, and enjoy the biggest share of the office furniture market. Their extensive reach in furniture production is a result of furniture demand arising from 10 million m^2 of new office building in Shanghai, 40% more than Hong Kong's 6 million m^2

office building and hence a higher demand for furniture in Shanghai than Hong Kong.

Numerous buildings under construction reflect a great potential demand for third generation middle and high class office furniture of international standards. Take the Hong Kong Lamex Group as an example, its office furniture sales is flourishing and set to increase further. Its annual sales in Shanghai alone reaches over RMB 300 million (USD 36.25 million).

Global Furniture Manufacturers in Shanghai

Attracted to the furniture market in Shanghai, furniture transnational companies are emerging one after another. Among them is the American "Universal Furniture Group", one of the three biggest furniture manufacturers in the world. It has a production base of 550,000 m² in the Asia-Pacific region with assets of USD 5 billion. In 1993, Universal Furniture Group entered China and two years later, set up a base in Shanghai in 1995 and launched an exclusive retail store.

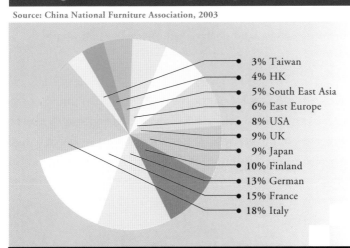

Shanghai Furniture Import by Country/Region

Source: China National Furniture Association, 2003

- 3% Taiwan
- 4% HK
- 5% South East Asia
- 6% East Europe
- 8% USA
- 9% UK
- 9% Japan
- 10% Finland
- 13% German
- 15% France
- 18% Italy

Likewise, Italian furniture manufacturer, the Milan-listed Arquarti Group opened a home furnishings retail center in Shanghai in 1997. Optimistic about Shanghai's future, the Group set up a factory in Jiading, in the suburbs of Shanghai in 1999.

The Swedish company Ikea Group, the biggest retailer of household furniture and

accessories in the world, started operations in Shanghai at the beginning of 1998. The Ikea Shanghai bazaar takes up an area of 8,000 m², selling more than 4,000 kinds of furniture and household items.

Trendy Furniture Products

The onset of the more open economy has led to a booming furniture industry, with more and bigger manufacturers offering a wide variety of dazzling styles.

At present, furniture styles and designs which are in fashion are:

Danish Style

The structure is simple and straightforward in style. The lines are sleek and smooth. Lines embodying a North European style appear to find favor with the younger set of buyers who prefer a more relaxed decor. Another favorite is the homemade deductive products, with basic material fiberboards and surfaces that are covered with paper or wood grain plastic plate. As the price is rather reasonable, this kind of furniture enjoys a measure of popularity.

Italian Style

The Italian style is typically the fashion leader because of the use of new materials and new technology. This style is replicated in many Guangdong-made furniture products sold in Shanghai. Characteristic of these products are the strong artistic quality and fine carving. The paint used is similar to that used for the piano, so elegant that it is well received by the middle-aged and older generation.

Spanish Style

It occupies a niche in the Shanghai furniture market because of its intrinsic cultural content. The furniture is made of genuine wood, generating a sense of warmth and comfort. At the Spanish Furniture Expo held in Shanghai in 2003, it was apparent that Spanish-styled furniture was very well-received by the Shanghai people.

American Style

"Huan Mei" furniture, which embodies the American style, enjoys a market share of 40%. The furniture is made of solid wood with strong decorations showing an air of luxury. It finds favor among the middle-class families.

Japanese Style

Famous for its simple structures, the Japanese style represents excellent quality and special stylistics. Typically, there are fewer pieces in a set of furniture. The Japanese style appears to suit the physical living conditions and lifestyle of the Shanghai people. There are more than 100 manufacturers replicating Japanese-style furniture, and their sales are expected to rise.

Shanghai Style

A style influenced by western furniture design during the 1930s, this kind of furniture is at present being made by the Shanghai Furniture Factory. It is made with plywood covered with precious wood vein. The style is traditional Chinese, combined with western design, which has been fashionable for more than 50 years, and it represents the kind of furniture found in Shanghai in the past.

Furniture Export

Shanghai furniture export has a long history. For 54 years from 1949 to 2003, the furniture export of Shanghai earned nearly USD 100 million. The export value was USD 11 million in 1990 and USD 394 million in 2002, a jump of 36 times in the 12-year period.

In recent years, the exports of foreign-invested enterprises have gained greater influence. Products made by some foreign-invested enterprises are all for the purposes of export. Sino-American joint-venture, Shanghai "Sen Hai" Furniture Co. Ltd., for example, specializes in making solid wood wardrobes and cabinets, and exports to America.

Each month the lowest production output is 60 containers and the highest output reaches more than 100 containers. The export value amounted to RMB 50 million (USD 6.04 million) in 2002.

Some foreign-invested enterprises do business both at home and abroad. Aurora Co. Ltd. of Taiwan, making full use of cheap manpower resources, low rent of land, and local raw materials, had reached, in 2002, total sales value of RMB 20 billion (USD 2.42 billion) in Shanghai and export value of RMB 30 million (USD 3.62 million).

Furniture Expos

Noting that Shanghai, which lies at a key point in the Yangtze River Delta is a highly important site, members of the China National Furniture Association (CNFA) believe its favorable geographical position and its international prestige could be used to lead the furniture industry towards a bigger market and a more promising future.

Shanghai Furniture Export 1998 - 2002

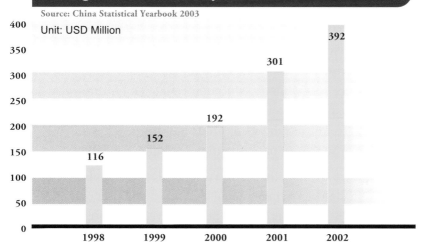

Source: China Statistical Yearbook 2003

Unit: USD Million

Year	Value
1998	116
1999	152
2000	192
2001	301
2002	392

Each year, the China International Furniture Exposition is held in Shanghai, the purpose of which, on the one hand, is to bring in the most fashionable furniture from other countries to meet the demand of some "white-collar" workers and foreigners who need imported furniture; and on the other, to stimulate the development of new furniture products at home. Finally, it will also drive China's furniture export, thereby increasing the Chinese furniture industry's competitiveness in the international market.

Each year there are two or three expositions held in Shanghai. The exposition jointly sponsored by CNFA and Shanghai CMP Int'l Exhibition Co., Ltd. is the largest in Asia, and takes up three exhibition halls in Shanghai. It is a professional furniture show and has "export-directed" strategies as its focus. At each show, there are overseas exhibitors from over 20 countries, over 50,000 domestic visitors, and several thousand overseas visitors. Exhibition area has increased from 3,000 m² in 1994 to 80,000 m² today. This furniture show is working towards arriving at European and American professional furniture exhibition standards in the near future.

EDUCATION

Introduction

The Shanghai education system comprises primary school, middle school, college and university education. The compulsory nine years of education consists of a six-year primary education course and a three-year junior middle school education course. Thereafter, students may choose to go to vocational or technical schools in order to acquire skills for jobs, or to continue senior schooling in preparation for higher education.

As at 2002, there are more than 3,000 preschool and compulsory education schools in Shanghai. Of them, about 850 are middle schools, 1,200 are primary schools and 930 are kindergartens. Over 760,000 middle school students and 871,000 primary school students are taught by 76,000 and 64,000 teaching staff respectively. There are 158 vocational technology schools catering to 232,700 students. There are 41 institutions of higher learning that offer 3-year-diploma programs and 4-year-undergraduate programs to 200,000 students. There are also 138 adult senior and higher education institutions, with total enrollment of 176,700 students.

Basic Education in Shanghai

Shanghai has the country's most developed basic education system. It is the first city in China that had the 9-year compulsory education implemented. Administration of schools offering basic education is delegated to the local government. Shanghai has recently achieved the following:

Standardized School Project

The Project was launched in order to standardize processes in the areas of administration, teaching staff, capital construction, facilities etc. among urban and rural schools. By 1999, 379 rural schools have been successfully inducted into the project.

Modern Boarding High School

More than 13 modern boarding high schools were set up by 2002. There are over 400 classes catering to 20,000 students. Total investment in these schools is more than RMB 2 billion (USD 240 million).

Public-run Schools

In accordance with the national policy 'Active Encouragement, Great Support, Correct Guidance and Powerful Management', public-run basic education has developed quickly. There are altogether 159 public-run primary and middle schools, accounting for 7.1% of total schools. Of them, there are 130 middle schools and 29 primary schools. 74,440 students attend these public-run schools, or 4.4% of Shanghai's total number of students.

Competence-oriented Education

Much attention has been paid to developing both the compulsory curriculum (Chinese, Mathematics and English) and extra-curricular activities. Hobby groups pertaining to sports, IT, environment protection, arts, and painting have been set up to enrich students' school life.

Special Education

Special education for the handicapped or mentally retarded children is an integral part of the city's preschool and elementary education program. It is available not only in schools exclusively for the handicapped, but also in many ordinary schools. Nearly all the visually-handicapped are enrolled for compulsory education every year. However, only 70% of these students will eventually attend high school. Likewise, almost all the hearing-impaired children receive compulsory education in Shanghai, but their numbers drop to around 63% in the enrollment for high schools.

The Education Market

Education providers are undoubtedly encouraged by the nine-fold jump in expenditure across the Shanghai education sector that took place between 1992 and 2002. Over the decade, annual consumer expenditure rose from RMB 1 billion (USD 120 million) to RMB 23 billion (USD 2.78 billion).

This large increase indicates the growing belief in Shanghai that the education sector presents good investment opportunities. Actual expenditure in Shanghai's higher education programs in 2002 was RMB 3 billion (USD 366 million). University tuition fees range between RMB 5,000 (USD 600) and RMB 30,000 (USD 3,620).

Only 32% of the 343,000 high-school graduates in 2002 enrolled in regular higher education institutes in Shanghai, and about 3% of students headed overseas to study. According to a survey conducted at 10 prestigious universities in Shanghai, 75% of students intended to go abroad, due to the weaknesses in the domestic higher education system. As travel restrictions are eased, higher numbers of Chinese students are expected to pursue overseas education.

Aetna School of Management

Aetna School of Management (ASM) is the business school of Shanghai Jiaotong University. Restored in 1984, the school had its name changed in appreciation of the USD 10 million donation from Aetna Insurance in 1998. ASM now has 1, 200 registered MBA students and recently started EMBA enrollment in December 2002.

A two-year full-time IMBA program with English as the instruction medium at ASM costs RMB 80,000 (USD 9,670). And full-time or part-time MBA program is priced at RMB 60,000 (USD 7,250). The 20-month-long part-time EMBA program costs RMB 218,000 (USD 26,340).

As Shanghai Jiaotong University has extensive cooperation and exchange programs with many world-renowned universities, ASM also offers a wide range of options like UBC-MBA of Canada, NTU-MBA of Singapore, City University MBA of Hong Kong, China-Germany International MBA (IMBA), and Rutgers-EMBA, etc.

Yet, even as demand for foreign education and foreign degree programs is rising, a lack of funding is an obstacle for most Shanghai high-school graduates. This reality, coupled with the weaknesses in the domestic higher-education system, present an opportunity for investors to penetrate the Shanghai education market, particularly in providing foreign higher learning.

China Europe International Business School (CEIBS)

Widely recognized as a leading business school in China, CEIBS has a world class faculty, excellent teaching quality, westernized management, international exposure, extensive program size and coverage, authenticity and methodology. In 2002, its MBA and EMBA programs were ranked the 3rd and 2nd in Asia, or among the world's top 100 and top 50, respectively, by the Financial Times. Its Executive Education Program is also ranked the 1st in Asia, making it the only Asian school ranked among the world's top 50 by the Financial Times.

Located in Pudong, CEIBS sees two classes of MBA students and eight classes of EMBA students (including three in Beijing) a year. In 2002, it trained over 5, 000 senior executives for companies operating in and outside China, in both its open programs and specific programs customized for client companies.

Tuition fees are by no means inexpensive – RMB 120,000 (USD 14,500) for a 17-month full-time MBA course and RMB 238,000 (USD 28,760) for a 23-month part-time bilingual EMBA program –, and entry requirements are stringent. MBA candidates must have passed GMAT and an exam designed by CEIBS before they can be considered for an interview. In addition, proficiency in English is necessary as all courses are taught in English. As a result, the ratio of enrollment to applicants remains at 1: 6 for MBA and 1: 4 for EMBA.

Though the majority of students are those who wish to upgrade and broaden their management knowledge and expertise for a better career, some are sponsored by their foreign employers in China. Among the 127 new MBA students in 2002, there were 18 overseas students from the US, Korea, Singapore, Taiwan, Israel and Mexico. More than half of the EMBA students are general managers, presidents or CEOs from local or foreign-invested companies.

Short-term executive education programs are also available all year round, covering topics in general management, marketing strategy, leadership, advanced financial management, supply chain and entrepreneurship. There is also a multi-module course tailored for expatriates in China.

According to a survey conducted by the State Bureau of Statistics, almost half of the respondents in Shanghai think that investment in education is an important family expense. Shanghai with over 250,000 high school students in 2002, has a market potential estimated at USD 23.9 million.

Business Schools in Shanghai

Due to the expanding community of business executives in the area, many Shanghai-based universities have been actively offering MBA or Executive MBA (EMBA) programs. These include the national "key universities" of Shanghai, namely, Jiaotong, Fudan and Tongji, and other universities and institutes.

International Exchange and Cooperation

With the continuing globalization of knowledge, Shanghai is endeavoring to become an international metropolis. International exchange and cooperation in the field of education plays an indispensable role in the world. In this manner, the rest of the world acquaints itself with Shanghai, and vice versa.

Culture and education contacts serve as a bridge to deepen understanding and friendship. By striking up alliances with governments and schools in different countries and regions Shanghai has built an extensive international education exchange network. This provides a platform for schools both at home and abroad to carry out their education exchange. These exchanges have made it easy for many international students to study in Shanghai and for many Shanghai students to study abroad.

At present, there are 13,000 international students from more than 100 countries and regions studying in 24 universities in Shanghai. At the same time, 71 primary and middle schools have begun to receive international students. As of 2004, 143 different levels of cooperative education programs have been set up. The introduction of first-class education resources from abroad has been most helpful in further improving the education structure of Shanghai and paving the way for the internationalization of Shanghai education.

AUTOMOTIVE PARTS

Introduction

Automobile manufacturing is the most important industry in Shanghai. In Jan-Aug 2003, its gross output value increased by 60.5% and recorded the fastest growth among the six key industries. Shanghai's automobile output volume had always ranked first in China, but in recent years, its market has decreased. In the first half year of 2003, the market share of Shanghai's car industry was 30.4%.

With an estimated value of RMB 175 billion (USD 21.14 billion) in 2002, China's automotive parts industry is large and poised for further growth, buoyed by the rising fortunes of automobile manufacturers here. Largely driven by four major multinational automotive parts companies (Delphi, Bosch, Visteon and Denso), the industry comprised 2813 automotive parts manufacturers in July 2002. In the 2000-2002 period, the auto parts industry's output leaped in value from RMB 106.93 billion (USD

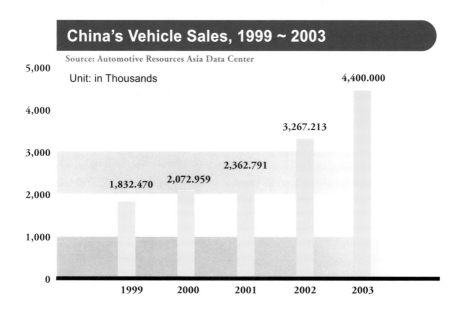

China's Vehicle Sales, 1999 ~ 2003

Source: Automotive Resources Asia Data Center

Unit: in Thousands

Year	Sales
1999	1,832.470
2000	2,072.959
2001	2,362.791
2002	3,267.213
2003	4,400.000

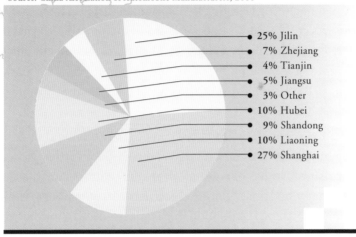

Auto Parts Production Facilities, Geographical Distribution

Source: China Association of Automobile Manufacturers, 2000

- 25% Jilin
- 7% Zhejiang
- 4% Tianjin
- 5% Jiangsu
- 3% Other
- 10% Hubei
- 9% Shandong
- 10% Liaoning
- 27% Shanghai

12.92 billion) to RMB 174.634 billion (USD 21.1 billion). At the same time, exports of auto parts jumped from USD 1.2 billion to USD 2.264 billion.

In 2003, Shanghai's auto parts export volume was worth USD 443 million and import volume was worth USD 124 million. Together with Tianjin, and the provinces of Liaoning, Jiangsu, Jilin, Zhejiang, Shandong and Hubei, total sales of auto parts have exceeded USD 100 million annually.

To become a leading center for auto parts production, it is vital to rectify some of the weaknesses of domestic auto parts companies – by developing more sophisticated production techniques. Local companies would benefit from working more closely with their foreign counterparts, particularly in research and development and quality control. Examples of Sino-foreign joint ventures include Shanghai Huizhong Automotive Manufacturing Co. Ltd., Shanghai Automotive Co. Ltd., United Automotive Electronic Systems Co. Ltd., and Shanghai Yanfeng Johnson Controls Seating Co. Ltd.

The 10th Five-Year Plan

By 2005, the auto parts industry will constitute 25% of the total value of car production. Under China's 10th Five-Year Plan (2001-2005), domestic firms are encouraged to undertake joint ventures with foreign counterparts in order to raise production efficiency by adopting more advanced technologies.

One of the Plan's principal sector goals is to develop five to ten domestic auto parts firms with world-class R&D capabilities and competitiveness. These firms should gain 60% of the domestic market, with 30% earmarked for export. The Plan commits China to raise production of luxury car parts. It also mandates the gradual elimination of CFC-12 in vehicle air-conditioning systems.

The Plan aims at establishing a few world-class automotive parts research centers by 2005. The auto parts industry is expected to have a share of 15-20% in all new joint ventures; on the domestic side, it is expected to contribute 30-40% to the Chinese automotive parts industry. Through better economies of scale, the industry should be able to lower production costs by 20%. Product quality must attain international standards by 2005, as directed in the Plan, and domestic companies should make 40% of auto parts used in mainstream vehicles. If this target is met, China would achieve 60-70% of the Plan's main goals. Export revenues from auto parts should account for 20% of domestic sales by 2005.

In order to boost the industry's overall competitiveness, the government is supporting the development of high-value and high-tech parts such as electronic fuel-injection systems, steering and air-conditioning systems, airbags, gearboxes and converters. China will implement measures to strengthen competitiveness in the production of steering wheels, cables, seats and bumpers. The Plan calls for reduced production of low technology items like fuel processors as China wants to focus on the production of high technology items such as electronic fuel-injection and automatic transmissions systems. This policy is in keeping with China's aspirations

In 2004, China's vehicle and components import quota is expected to reach USD 10.5 billion, up 15% from the preceding year. Total vehicle output in China will reach 5.1 to 5.34 million units this year, including 2.5 to 2.62 million passenger cars.

Industry insiders said that with overseas capital flowing into China's auto market, the industry is in need of new policies to replace rules enacted in 1994 in order to better guide the development of the sector. In view of this, the National Development and Reform Commission released a draft policy for suggestions last year. New rules are expected to be put into effect soon.

The most obvious change in policy, according to industry insiders, is the stipulation that the largest shareholder of a joint venture must now be Chinese.

In the 2003 draft, the government predicted that by 2010, 50 percent of China's market would comprise Chinese-made vehicles, using only Chinese designs, brands and spare parts. However, this ambitious target may be dropped from the policy, as it has aroused discontent from overseas automakers, industry insiders said.

Industry sources predict that car imports would grow by just 15%, after accelerating by 34.6% in 2003, when the nation imported 172,683 vehicles, including 103,017 passenger cars. This slowdown in growth is mainly due to customers holding out until expected price cuts in 2005 before they start to snap up new cars.

Price cuts are expected due to the cancellation of quotas and further import tariff cuts as part of China's commitments to the World Trade Organization (WTO). Tariffs will fall to 30% next year from the current rate of between 34.2 and 37.6%, to 28% at the beginning of 2006, and finally to 25% in July that year.

Source: China Daily, 1st February 2004

to move from a low-tech assembly environment to a high-tech manufacturing culture driven by constant innovation.

Impact of WTO on the Industry

Post-WTO accession, China will reduce auto parts tariffs (by 1st July 2006) and remove all import quotas on auto parts (by 2005). These changes are expected to lead to a 15% growth of the industry annually, in conjunction with the auto industry's rapid development.

China has also pledged to gradually remove all sales and retailing restrictions of foreign companies. This would aid the establishment of more integrated distribution, retailing ad import/export networks.

Prior to China's WTO membership, foreign financial institutions were only allowed to do RMB business in certain cities and provinces in China (see Banking and Finance). By end-2006, however, there will no longer be any geographic restrictions on foreign financial institutions participating in RMB business. They may also provide direct services to Chinese firms. Foreign banks licensed for RMB business in a particular region may also service clients in other regions, including credit financing for automobile purchases.

More specifically, policy changes with regards to the auto parts industry are as follows:

Tariffs Tariffs on auto parts will be lower than on completed vehicles. By 1st July 2006, tariffs on all auto parts and related items will be reduced from 25% to 10%.

Import Quotas Import quotas on automotives (including auto parts) will be removed by 2005. The government will progressively increase the amount of imported automotives by 15% before end-2004. In 2002, the total value of imported cars was USD 8 billion, a jump of USD 2 billion from 2000. This increase is indicative of the government's resolve in opening up the domestic automotive market.

Approval of Foreign Investment Approval of foreign investment was broadened to include the provincial administrative level. The approval limit was USD 60 million at end-2002. By end-2004, the approval limit will be raised to USD 100 million; and by end-2006, to USD 150 million. There will be no limits on foreign investment after 2006.

Retail Starting in 2002, retail auto outlets were permitted to enter into joint ventures with foreign investors. If the number of outlets in a particular chain exceeds 30, the foreign party may not hold a controlling interest.

This condition will, however, be rescinded in 2006. Foreign non-financial institutions may provide auto financing credit facilities.

Other changes At end-2003, the government removed restrictions on the type and make of automobiles that manufacturers can produce. It has also changed the rules to allow foreign investors to hold more than 50% stake in joint ventures dealing in auto engine manufacturing.

Foreign Investment

At an early stage, the auto parts industry attracted foreign investment, which grew to very high levels. The formation of the Beijing Jeep Corporation in 1983 marked the beginning of this era.

In 2003, there were 466 foreign investors in the industry – 102 auto manufacturers, 350 auto parts makers, and 14 others. In all, these companies had invested USD 20.4 billion to develop China's automotive industry – total investment by automakers was USD 11.04 billion, and auto parts companies, USD 9.04 billion. On the whole, foreign investors have concentrated their investments in large cities and China's eastern and northern provinces.

Distribution of Foreign Investment 2003

Amount	Location
US$ 3 billion and above	Shanghai
US$ 2 - 3 billion	Liaoning, Jilin
US$ 1 - 2 billion	Hubei, Guangdong, Beijing, Jiangsu, Tianjin, Shandong
US$ 500 million - 1 billion	Chongqing, Heilongjiang, Hunan

Source: China Knowledge Press

Foreign Investors

The main foreign investors in China's automotive parts industry in 2003 were Delphi, Bosch, Visteon and Denso.

Denso Corp

Denso Corp is the largest automotive parts subsidiary under Japan's Toyota Corp. It was established in 1949 and its capital investment has since increased to about USD 1.4 billion. It supplies automotive air conditioning, engineering and related components to Toyota, Honda and Isuzu. Denso common stock is traded on the Tokyo, Osaka and Nagoya stock exchanges.

In a move that underscores its commitment to China, Denso, besides already operating eight production companies in China, established a new wholly-owned holding company which will function as a regional headquarters in China in February 2003.

Seven months later, Denso announced the establishment of a JV with Shanghai Pudong EV Fuel Injection Co. Ltd and Shanghai Dong Song International Trading Co. Ltd. to manufacture fuel injection pumps for diesel vehicles. Denso has invested USD 4.6 million in Shanghai DV Fuel Injection Co. Ltd (owned by its partners).

In October 2003, Shanghai DV Fuel Injection Co. Ltd was renamed Shanghai Denso Fuel Injection Co Ltd. It will produce fuel injection pumps for diesel vehicles made by Chinese companies. As China tightens its emissions regulations, Denso plans future expansion to the common rail system components production business.

Yanfeng Visteon Automotive Trim System Co.

The Yanfeng Visteon Automotive Trim System Co. is a 50/50 joint venture between Visteon Corporation of the US and Shanghai Automotive Co. Established in 1994, the company has total investments of USD 223 million.

One of the largest automotive suppliers in the world, Visteon was ranked 114 among the Fortune 500 companies in 2002. It has 75,000 employees in 25 countries and a global sales revenue of USD 18.4 billion in 2002. The company has 84 production facilities worldwide and 25 global sales and services offices.

Domestic Companies (including Joint Ventures)

The main Chinese automotive parts companies are Shanghai Huizhong Automotive Manufacturing Co. Ltd., Shanghai Automotive Co. Ltd., Wanxiang Qianchao Co. Ltd., Jiangyin Mould & Plastic Group Co. Ltd., United Automotive Electronic Systems Co. Ltd., Shanghai Yanfeng Johnson Controls Seating Co. Ltd., Shanghai Ek Chor General Machinery Co. Ltd., and Fuyao Glass Co. Ltd.

Visteon moves in on China's big market

Visteon, the car parts producer, is to move its Asian regional headquarters from Tokyo to Shanghai as it tries to take advantage of the explosive growth in demand for vehicles in China. The US company, spun off from Ford three years ago, is trying to streamline internal procedures to speed up investment in China, the world's fastest growing car market.

The location of the headquarters is symbolic of the heavy investment in China's automotive industry, where every big car maker is racing to build factories. Car sales passed one million last year. Volkswagen, the market leader, said that its local partners expected another 50% growth in the next three years to 1.5 million units plus one million in light truck sales.

"China is where the growth is happening and we felt that it was strategically important to have our HQ there, " said Visteon, which has five joint venture plants in China. The factories – in Nanchang, Changchun, Beijing and Shanghai – supply within the country and have no exports. Last year, they had a revenue of USD 550 million, against USD 350 million from Japan.

Source: (excerpt) Financial Times, 24th June 2003

Shanghai Huizhong Automotive Manufacturing Co. Ltd.

Established in 1992, it currently has more than 8,000 employees and five manufacturing plants in China:

• Shanghai Automobile Axle Plant
• Shanghai Automotive Chassis Plant
• Shanghai Heavy Duty Truck Plant
• Shanghai Internal Combustion Engine Components Plant
• Shanghai Tractor Chassis Plant

Its China sales revenue was RMB 3 billion (USD 360 million) in 2002, and the company had fixed assets of RMB 1.58 billion (USD 190 million). For two consecutive years, (2000 – 2001), it ranked 14 on the list of Shanghai's top 500 industrial companies. Its products have attained international ISO-9001, QS-9000, and VDA 6.1 quality assurance certifications.

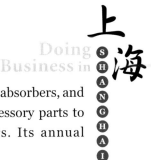

The company produces front suspensions, rear axles, shock absorbers, and low rocker-arm assemblies. It is the main supplier of accessory parts to shanghai Volkswagen and Shanghai General Motors. Its annual manufacturing capacity is 300, 000 sets of auto parts.

Shanghai Automotive Co. Ltd.

Established in August 1997, it is the listed unit of China's top car maker Shanghai Automotive Industry Corp (SAIC). It was listed on the Shanghai Stock Exchange in November 1997.

In 1999, it was voted as one of the top 50 listed companies with the greatest development potential. The company has AAA-rated production techniques and facilities and has achieved ISO 14001, QS 9000 and VDA 6.1 certification.

The company has production facilities for gears and automotive springs. It has formed a number of JV arrangements: with Shanghai GM, Shanghai Ek Chor general Machinery Co. Ltd., Shanghai GKN Drive Shaft Co., Shanghai Xiao Xi Deng Co., and ZF Shanghai Steering Co. Ltd.

Future Developments

In order to achieve its aim of becoming a world leader in auto production, China is planning and indeed, is on-course, in the development of an excellent auto parts industry. It intends to make auto components inexpensive, while meeting international standards. Once domestic auto parts companies reach a certain size and financial standing, China's policies would encourage mergers and acquisitions in the industry. This would enlarge companies' size, making them similar to MNC competitors like Delphi, Bosch, Visteon and Denso.

Domestic companies are developing more sophisticated production techniques. For example, in an attempt to reduce their capital costs, Fulin and Fushi Machinery Groups plan to share engines and gearboxes in their new vehicles.

If China manages to harness new foreign technology effectively, it would not be long before it arrives at its overall goal: to develop a world-class auto components network. With a proper modern auto parts industry, China would be well on its way to becoming the world's largest car market outside the US.

In this decade, China will try to shed its image as a low-tech assembler and move to production of high value-added auto components – ABS, GPS systems for electronic fuel injection, airbags and central locking.

China is endeavoring to produce interchangeable auto components, e.g. parts meant for a Mercedes luxury car can also be used in a Citron or Opel. This would facilitate mass production while reducing production

Chinese Automakers' Profits Grow

China's major automakers doubled their profits in the year's first half, despite hot price wars and increasing vehicle imports.

The nation's 14 biggest State-owned automakers reported a combined RMB 17.99 billion (USD 2.17 billion) in profits during the period, up 100 per cent from a year earlier, indicate State Assets Regulatory and Administration Commission figures.

The top three companies - First Automotive Works Corp (FAW), Dongfeng Motor Corp and Shanghai Automotive Industry Corp (SAIC) - accounted for nearly all of the profits. The three firms earned a combined RMB 16.75 billion (USD 2.02 billion) in profits during the year's first six months

up 96.8 per cent from the same period last year. ...

Meanwhile, more vehicles were imported into China. Sales of Chinese-made vehicles reached 2.03 million units during the year's first half, rising 31.99 per cent from a year earlier. Sales of passenger cars climbed 82.44 per cent, year-on-year, to 842,800 units.

Prices of Chinese-made vehicles are much higher compared with foreign vehicles, even though prices in China have been falling, especially since the nation's 2001 entry into the World Trade Organization (WTO).

Chinese automakers' profit margins are also higher compared with their overseas counterparts. Domestic automakers'

average profit margin was 30-35 per cent, compared with around 5 per cent of developed countries' vehicle makers, said Liu Shijin, an industry analyst with the State Council's Development Research Centre.

"Car prices in China will decline to levels in keeping with the world's market within the next six years, as a result of the nation's tariff cuts and increases in domestic automakers' economies of scale," said Zhang Xiaoyu, president of the China Association of Automobile Manufacturers.

Tariffs on vehicle imports will decrease to 25% by mid-2006, from 38.2 - 43% at present, in accordance with China's WTO commitments. ...

Meanwhile, vehicle imports to China grew strongly, but still accounted for a tiny proportion of the domestic market. Imports surged 73.6% year-on-year, to 90,600 units during the year's first half. ... Passenger cars accounted for 59% , or 53,440 units, of the imports; and SUVs, 26%. Vehicles from Japan, Germany, South Korea, the United States and Sweden, accounted for 90% of the imports. ...

Imports of 2.5-litre and larger passenger cars and SUVs reached 32,300 units in the year's first half, indicate statistics from the trading centre. The average price stood at US$27,088 during the first half of this year, up from around US$23,000 during the corresponding period last year, indicate statistics.

Source: (excerpt) www.ccpitinvest.org, 14th August

costs. Non-polluting auto components are also in the works – solar and electric engines for example.

The industry is taking steps to ensure that domestic auto parts meet the rigorous standards of international accreditation bodies like the International Organization for Standardization (ISO). Currently only a handful of the larger companies have attained ISO 9000 or QS 9000 accreditation – Shanghai Automotive, Wanxiang Group, United Automotive Electronic Systems, Shanghai Ek Chor General Machinery and Fuyao Glass. Some of these larger companies which have attained both are now considering the more advanced ISO/TS 16949:2002 system.

Domestic auto parts companies also have ambitions to turn their products into well-known international brands along the lines of Delphi, Bosch and others. Such a brand name helps to assure quality and reliability. China currently has very few such brand names. Fuyao Glass may be the best known brand in the auto parts industry, with a substantial market share in China, North America, Europe and Japan.

If China manages to harness new foreign technology effectively, it would not be long before it arrives at its overall goal: to develop a world-class auto components network. With a proper modern auto parts industry, China would be well on its way to becoming the world's largest car market outside the US.

AUTOMOBILE TIRES

Introduction

The remarkable progress of China's automotive industry has culminated in the development of a significant tire subsector. Following China's accession to the WTO in 2001, growth rates for both sectors accelerated.

To fulfill China's aim of becoming the main base of operations for leading foreign auto companies, a world-class tire industry would have to be developed. In so doing, the country would become more attractive to leading automakers. Ready access to high quality tires would enable these companies to streamline their supply chains and purchasing operations while avoiding costly tire imports.

With an estimated value of nearly USD 6 billion in 2002, and buoyed by the rising fortunes of automobile manufacturers in the country, China's tire industry is large and poised for further growth. This industry is still largely driven by a few multinational tire companies, including Michelin, Bridgestone, Goodyear and Yokohama, and their joint venture partners. Michelin alone accounts for 30% of the replacement tire market.

To become a leading player in the global tire industry, domestic tire companies would need to rectify their weaknesses as well as develop more sophisticated production techniques, and better-quality products. Moving in this direction, China has taken steps to produce products that are higher up the value chain. For instance, the country is now encouraging the production of radial tires by promising the waiver of the 10% excise tax for radial tire products. Many domestic companies are also forming strategic alliances with multinationals to acquire greater expertise in production, distribution and marketing.

Foreign Businesses Eye Chinese Tire Market

Encouraged by rapid growth of the automotive industry, the production, sales and profitability of China's tire industry have kept on rising.

China now has more than 325 tire manufacturers. Their output of outer tires increased 9.4 per cent in 2002, related sales revenue went up 13.3% and their total profits surged 312%.

Sales of reinforced heavy-weight radial ply tire surged 55.1% in 2002, volume of tires delivered for export went up 7.8% and the sales rate rose 2.09 percentage points.

Based on a forecast that China's annual car sales will exceed 3 million units in five years, domestic annual demand for tires is estimated to reach 15 million pieces, posing a rosy picture for the whole tire manufacturing sector.

At present, production of tires in the world is becoming more and more concentrated. Sales of the top three giants in the world, Michelin, Bridgestone and Goodyear, which accounted for 54% in 1997, jumped to 61% in 2002 and are expected to reach 70% by 2005.

China's huge potential tire market, and low cost on labor force and construction of infrastructure facilities have attracted the eyeball (sic) of multinational companies. All the top ten tire makers in the world, except for the German Continental Company, have now entered China market...

Among the designated tire production enterprises in China, more than one third involve (sic) foreign participation. In particular, the present development trend in the sector has turned from launching joint ventures in the past to merger and acquisitions by foreign firms and wholly foreign owned companies.

Foreign-funded and foreign-controlled tire enterprises in China are growing fast in output and market share by relying on their advantages in technology, fund and brand-name products, with their output exceeding 50% of the total in the country. ...

The average annual tire output of China's 325 factories in 2003 is 410,000 pieces, considerably behind the 2.7 million of foreign tire enterprises.

In 2002, the average annual output of tire factories in the United States is 5.4 million, that of Japan is 7.1 million and that of the Republic of Korea is 11 million. Investment in advertising by tire enterprises increased 349% in 2002. Michelin injects about RMB 60 million (USD 7.25 million) in advertising in China each year, and Bridgestone has quadrupled its expenditure on advertising in China since 2000.

Source: (excerpt) AsiaPulse, 4th December 2003

Strong Demand for Radial Tires

Production of radial tires looks set to be the fastest growing segment within the tire industry. By 2005, demand for radial tires is expected to rise to 5.67 million annually. China's annual radial tire market is expected to double within the next five years from its current production of 30 million units. This steep increase would not be possible without simultaneous increases in quality and international competitiveness. These fundamental changes were driven largely by foreign tire multinationals and their joint venture partners.

Invented by Michelin in 1949, radial tires are now their bestselling product in China. Despite costing three times more than the standard tire, radial tires are in high demand. As explained by a local truck tire dealer, Chinese haulers typically overload their trucks, placing 20 tons of goods on trucks designed and built to carry only five tons. After a few trips, while the standard tires will burst, the more robust and hardy radial tires remain sturdy enough to take the load.

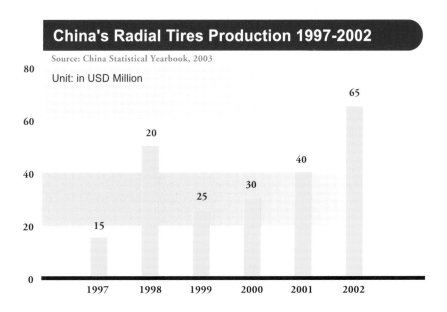

China's Radial Tires Production 1997-2002

Source: China Statistical Yearbook, 2003

Unit: in USD Million

Year	Value
1997	15
1998	20
1999	25
2000	30
2001	40
2002	65

In addition, radial tires eliminate the huge problem of squirm by conforming to the road without distortion or deflection. Radial tires have at least twice the tread life of bias-ply tires, and fuel consumption for automobiles decline due to lessened tire friction.

The Chinese government is now encouraging the production of radial tires to boost the overall competitiveness of the domestic tire industry. From 1997 to 2002, the production of radial tires had risen from 15 million units to 65 million units – an astounding increase of more than 333%.

WTO Impact on Foreign Investment

Agreement on Trade-Related Investment Measures (TRIMS)

Under the WTO, China is now subject to a whole list of trade agreements. An important one is the Agreement on Trade-Related Investment Measures (TRIMS) which addresses investment measures that have "trade-distorting" effects. Its scope is limited to trade in goods, not services.

Under the TRIMs, WTO members must accord national treatment to other members and may not maintain quantitative restrictions in their investment rules. A look at the TRIMs agreement provides a few examples in connection with requirements on local content, export performance, and foreign exchange.

1. Before joining WTO, China had the same tariff rate for auto parts imported for vehicle assembly (knocked-down vehicles) and for completed (built-up) vehicles, if the imported content exceeded 40% of the assembled vehicle (by number of auto parts). Chinese regulators are redrafting the rules to meet TRIM provisions that prohibit localization policies. At the same time, they want to maintain a threshold beyond which the imported content of knocked-down vehicles will be assessed at the built-up rate.

2. TRIMs prohibits quantitative restrictions when investment measures require an enterprise to use its own foreign exchange reserves to import products.

3. Under TRIMs, local and foreign enterprises will be given equal status. The Most Favored Nation status granted to foreign enterprises will be revoked. These foreign enterprises will no longer receive 10-year tax exemptions or have direct access to foreign banks.

4. China's WTO commitments did not include a timetable for the elimination of equity controls in auto assembly facilities. The government is likely to limit foreign equity ownership to no more than 50% for some time.

Foreign Auto Imports (including Tires)

China also promised to revise tariffs on automobiles, for instance to reduce taxes on luxury cars from current rates of 70% to 80% by July 2006. Since 1st January 2002, the tariff on cars with engine capacity less than 3 liters was lowered from 70% to 43.8%, with a further annual reduction of 4-5%. For cars with engine capacity above 3 liters, tariffs were lowered from 80% to 50.7% in 2002, with subsequent annual reductions of 6%.

By 2006, tariffs on passenger cars will be reduced 20% to 40%, declining 4% to 8% annually. On imported commercial vehicles, the tariffs will be reduced 10% to 20%, declining annually at 2-4%.

Since 2002, auto retail outlets were permitted to enter joint ventures with foreign investors. If the number of outlets in a particular chain exceeds 30, the foreign party may not hold a controlling interest (this condition will be revoked in 2006). China is trying to remove JV restrictions on auto engines – currently foreign parties may not own more than 50%.

Once local car manufacturers attain a substantial production volume, the government will revoke their special privileges. In 2003, restrictions were removed on the type and make of cars which manufacturers can produce.

The government's pledge of lower tariffs covers passenger vehicles, trucks, vans, motorcycles and automotive parts. The table below shows tariff reductions on vehicles and other automotive products.

Table of Tariff Reductions on Automotive Products

Items	Current Rates (%)	Future Rates (%)	Year Due
Luxury Vehicles	70%-80%	25%	July 2006
Passenger Vehicles	45%-60%	20%-25%	1ˢᵗ January 2005
Commercial Vehicles	40%-50%	20%-25%	1ˢᵗ January 2005
Motorcycles	48%-50%	30%-45%	2004
Motorcycle Parts	30%	-	-
Automobile Parts	25%	10%	1ˢᵗ July 2006

Source: Fudan University, School of Economics, China Center for Economic Studies

Table of Tariff Reductions on Tire Products

Tires and Related Products	Current Rates (%)	Future Rates (%)	Year Due
New Tires	30%	10%	2006
Retreaded Tires	25%	20%	2006
Used Tires	34%	25%	2006
Inner Tubes	18.5%	15%	2006

Source: Fudan University, School of Economics, China Center for Economic Studies

For tires and related products, the following tariff cuts will be imposed by 2006.

On top of the tariff reductions, the Chinese Central Government has promised to waive the 10% excise tax for radial tire products, which has been earmarked by the state as a key driver of the domestic tire industry. The State has also pledged to waive the import license and quotas for new pneumatic tires, inner tubes, retreaded, used and solid/cushion tires of motorcars, buses and lorries, and automobiles.

Foreign Investors

The main foreign investors in China's tire industry in 2003 are Michelin, Bridgestone, Goodyear and Yokohama. A brief profile of the joint venture between French-based Michelin and China's Shanghai Tire and Rubber Co. Ltd. is given below.

Shanghai Michelin Warrior Tire Co.

World tire giant Michelin formed a joint venture with China's Shanghai Tire and Rubber Co., Ltd in 2001, after 30 months of negotiations. Michelin is one of the world's largest tire companies and has its headquarters in Clermont-Ferrand (France). It has more than 70 manufacturing locations in 18 countries and in 2002, its global sales amounted to 15.6 billion Euros.

In China, Michelin supplies major foreign automakers - including Germany's Volkswagen, US-based General Motors, France's PSA Peugoet Citroen and Japan's Honda and Toyota. Currently, Michelin controls about 10 per cent of China's radial tire market.

Michelin's joint venture with China's Shanghai Tire and Rubber Co. Ltd, named the Shanghai Michelin Warrior Tire Co., was started with an initial investment of USD 200 million, with Michelin taking 70% of the stakes and the Shanghai Tire and Rubber Co. the other 30%. This company is expected to have an annual production of eight million radial tires for sedans and 15,000 tons of wire for tires by the year 2010.

Michelin to Spend Millions More in China

Tire giant Michelin plans to pour several hundred million dollars more into China's fast-revving auto market over the next decade to outfit cars and trucks, a top company executive said on Thursday.

"There is no doubt in the next five to 10 years, we will invest several hundred million US dollars more," Michelin's Asia-Pacific president Jean-Marc Francois told Reuters.

The money would be invested in Michelin's current joint ventures in Shanghai and Shenyang, in building new factories around China and in advertising the Michelin brand, he said.

Some of the money could also be earmarked for other potential opportunities, he added.

The French-based company has already invested several hundred million dollars in China, including teaming up with China's top tire maker, Shanghai Tire and Rubber Co.

Source: (exerpt) Reuters, 6th November 2003

The Chinese partner's trademark brand, Warrior, which enjoys a high degree of popularity in the domestic market, has been preserved as one of the key products of the joint venture. This joint venture launched a new product - the New Warrior R28 tire in 2003.

Confident of Michelin's dominant position in the Chinese tire industry, and with hopes that this will lead to a domination of the Asia tire market, Herve Coyco, head of Michelin's car and light truck tire division had said, " Whoever is No. 1 in China and can hold on to that will be No.1 in Asia in 30 years".

Domestic Companies (including Joint Ventures)

The main domestic companies in the tire industry include the Shandong Chengshan Tire Co. Ltd., Shanghai Tire and Rubber Company, Triangle Tire Co. Ltd., Hangzhou Zhongce Rubber Co. Ltd., Qingdao Rubber Group Co. Ltd., Yinchuan C.S.I (Great Wall) Rubber Co. Ltd., Longkou Xinglong Tire Co., Ltd., Shandong Luhe Group Co. Ltd. and Guizhou Tire Co. Ltd. The following is a brief profile of one such Shanghai-based tire company.

Shanghai Tire and Rubber Company

The Shanghai Tire and Rubber Company was established on 16th June 1990, through the merger of Shanghai Ta Chung Hua Rubber Factory and Shanghai Tsen Tai Rubber Factory.

The company boasts a strong technological team with a state-level research and development center with 150 intermediate and advanced technical staff engaged in research and development. The Double Coin heavy radial tire factory with state-of-the-art technology and huge production capacity was established in the early 190s in the Min Hang development zone. The output of all-steel radial truck tires reached 1.3 million units per year. The company's range of tires includes the Double Coin All Steel Radials, the Double Coin Bias Truck Tire and the Warrior Bias Truck Tire.

The radial tires have been certified by the US Department of Transportation (DOT), the Economic Committee of Europe (ECE) and the INMERTO of Brazil. In addition, the company has also been certified by ISO 9002 quality control system. To cement its position as one of China's leading tire manufacturers, the company formed a joint-venture with Michelin.

With all the signs looking up for the automobile industry, the future looks bright for the tire industry... it is forecasted that in 2005, China's new tire and replacement tire market will have 26% more demand than in 2002.

Future Developments

If the Chinese economy continues to maintain her robust growth, the domestic automobile industry would be able to sustain its current momentum. In this favorable scenario, it is likely that the tire industry would continue on its existing growth path. David Thursfield, head of international business at Ford Motors, says the company's China operations are highly profitable due to strong demand and high prices. This bodes well for China's expanding automobile industry.

Frederick Henderson, the Asia-Pacific president for General Motors, said that in five years' time, China would become Asia's largest automotive market, pushing ahead of Japan. The CEO of Delphi Automotives (the world's largest auto parts manufacturer) J. T. Battenberg III had stated,

"Almost all the automakers in the world have come to China to set up manufacturing bases, so there is no doubt that Delphi will make its major battlefield here".

These examples allay any fear of overcapacity for the time being.

In fact, most automotive manufacturers expect China's demand for cars to grow at 15-20% for the rest of the decade, creating a market that Volkswagen CEO Bernd Pischetsrieder asserts is on track to become the second largest in the world after the United States. With all the signs looking up for the automobile industry, the future looks bright for the tire industry, as it is directly dependent on the good performance of its parent industry. It is forecasted that in 2005 China's new tire and replacement tire market will have 26% more demand than the 126 million units of tires in demand in 2002.

RETAIL

Introduction

China is leaving behind an era of protectionism and is playing more and more by international rules and regulations in its trade and investment activities. A direct result, one that can already be seen and measured, is greater access by importers and foreign firms to the burgeoning urban consumer market. Gone are the days of rationing the most basic daily necessities. In a growing national market with rising disposable income, Shanghai is the jewel in the consumer crown.

In 2002, total consumer retail sales in China was USD 454.23 billion. Of this national total, Shanghai's contribution was USD 22.49 billion, or 5%. Recently IKEA opened another megastore in Shanghai. This 33,000 m² outlet is its largest in Asia. Other international retail giants also have a presence in Shanghai – B&Q, Walmart, 7-Eleven, Carrefour, Makro, Lawson, Auchan, and others. It is fair to say that this port city is the frontline battlefield for domestic and international retail operations.

Chinese companies, such as Hualian, Guomei, Jinjiang and Sanlian are learning fast and gaining market share. China's entry to the World Trade Organization (WTO) in November 2001 has brought changes to key sectors, including retailing, wholesaling, and distribution. Excellent overall growth rates, starting from a relatively low development base, mean that there is room in this fast-growing industry for foreign companies and domestic firms.

Gross Domestic Product

Between 1978 and 2001, Shanghai's economy grew 13.4% annually. In 2001, the growth rate dropped to 8.7%. In 2003, Shanghai's GDP was RMB 625 billion (USD 75 billion). Going forward, the city's GDP is expected to register double digits again by 2010.

Urban Disposable Income

Shanghai consumers have the highest urban disposable income, compared to other regions in China. This suggests a potentially lucrative market for retailers.

City	RMB	USD	City	RMB	USD
Shanghai	13,249	1,600	Beijing	12,463	1,505
Zhejiang	11,715	1,415	Guangdong	11,137	1,345
Tianjin	9,337	1,128	Fujian	9,189	1,110
Jiangsu	8,177	987	Hunan	6,958	840
Jilin	6,260	756	Henan	6,245	754
Shanxi	6,234	753	Gansu	6,151	743

Source: China Statistical Yearbook 2003

Price Levels

In the early 1990s, Shanghai, like the rest of China, achieved high GDP growth despite high inflation rates. Inflation peaked at 24% in 1994, tapering off by 1997. With the onset of the Asian financial crisis and with new technological advancements, China started an era of deflation.

With China's entry into the WTO, a twofold impact on price levels is expected. With the opening up of more sectors and the relaxation of existing rules, firms previously hampered by regulatory hurdles will be prompted to invest. Increased demand for local skilled professionals will drive up wages and production costs. Whether there is room for price increases depends on the success of the manufacturers or distributors in passing on their increased costs to consumers. Given the keen competition among retailers, consumers should continue to enjoy better quality at stable price levels.

Consumer Price Index, 1994 - 2003

Source: China Knowledge Press

Preceding Year = 100

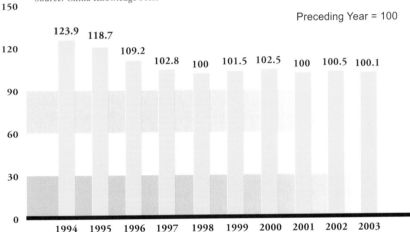

Retail Price Index, 1996 - 2003

Source: China Knowledge Press

Base Year = 1995

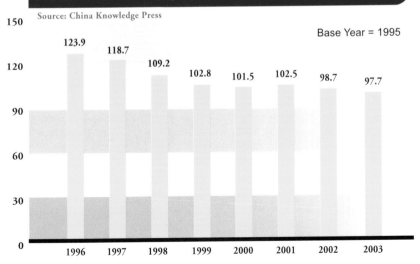

China Embraces Franchising

[Century 21 Real Estate], the big US franchiser of real estate brokerages, owned by New York-based Cendant, is cashing in on a boom in home ownership, economic growth and franchising in China. It expects its China franchises to double to about 600 this year, putting China in line to become its second-largest overseas market, after France.

"China is our fastest-growing market right now," says Van Davies, president and chief executive officer of Century 21 Real Estate. By contrast, he says, "we have a very mature real estate market in America."

Another Cendant brand – Coldwell Banker – is also off to a good start in China. That chain is growing in Shanghai and nearby provinces. Sinyi Real Estate, one of Taiwan's largest real estate brokerage chains, has been Cendant's master franchise partner for the last five years.

"The brand is known better than our own, and it's positioned toward the middle to high end, which is where we wanted to be," says Andy Liu, a Sinyi executive in Shanghai. Sinyi wants to increase the number of Coldwell Banker shops in China to 1,200 in 2012 from about 55 today.

The Cendant units' growth is part of a boom in franchising in China. The number of franchise outlets soared to about 87, 000 at the end of last year, from about 15, 000 at the end of 2000, according to the China Chain Store & Franchise Association, an industry group. ...

The franchising model, which allows people with limited capital to enter an established business, is well suited to a developing economy. "The Chinese entrepreneurs are ready for it," says Bill Hunt, president of Century 21 China Real Estate, the master franchiser for the chain in China. ...

For those franchisers that can navigate China's ways, the prizes can be big. China's GDP expanded by 9.1% last year, the best among the world's biggest economies. Despite a slowdown in 2003's second quarter due to the SARS outbreak, retail spending grew by 9% for the year and will gain by 12% to 15% this year, according to a report by Taipei-based SinoPac Securities. Government encouragement of urban migration among China's still mostly rural populace will stoke growth among successful retail chains – many of them franchised – for decades, economists say. ...

[But] intellectual property protection can be spotty, for franchises and retailers alike. Earlier this year, Starbucks filed a trademark-infringement lawsuit against a Shanghai coffee chain. But lawyers and industry executives say things are moving in the right direction. "We have a close relationship with the government, to make sure that they understand what franchising is about and the necessity to protect our brand, " Hunt says.

Source: (exerpt) www.forbes.com, 19th February 2004

Sector Overview

Food and Beverage

According to a survey done by the China General Chamber of Commerce (CGCC), the China Cuisine Association (CCA) and the China National Commercial Information Center (CNICC), revenue in the food and beverage sector in 2002 reached RMB 509.2 billion (USD 61.52 billion), a 16.6% increase over 2001.

The number of chain store enterprises in the top 100 increased from 79 companies in 2001 to 87 companies in 2002. Annual sales of these 87 enterprises accounted for 94% of the total sales generated by the top 100. Of the 100 enterprises, 26 are based in Shanghai, an increase of 6 from 2001 to 2002. Some companies (such as Parkson) have multiple listings as their subsidiaries were also included in the ranking.

The F&B sector is moving towards more individualist and theme-oriented consumerism. Purchasing decisions are based on more than just price comparison. Consumers increasingly are willing to pay for qualitative factors like brand, service, culture, and atmosphere.

Top Three F&B Operators

Rank / Company Name	2001 Turnover in China		2002 Turnover in China		No. of Outlets
	RMB billion	USD million	RMB billion	USD million	
1 Parkson	5.49	660	7.16	870	897
2 Neimonggu Xuaifeiyang	1.51	180	2.52	300	606
3 Shanghai New Asia Group	1.2	140	1.33	160	N/A

Source: CGCC, CCA, CNCIC

The parent company of Parkson is US-based franchiser Tricon Global Restaurants, which owns a number of franchise names worldwide – Kentucky Fried Chicken, Pizza Hut, Taco Bell, A&W and Long John Silver.

Fashion

Shanghai is rightfully the nation's fashion capital, with relatively high consumption. International brands available in Shanghai jumped from 170 in 1997 to 370 in 2002. These include renowned brands such as Chanel, Fendi, Escada, Hugo Boss and Ferragamo.

Hong Kong retailers also enjoy brisk business in China, whether they are franchised outlets or wholly-owned stores. Many retailers had their manufacturing bases shifted to China in the 1990s, so they are well-positioned to take advantage of China's post-WTO liberalization policies which allow distribution of their locally-made products.

With lower costs and pricing, it is not surprising that Hong Kong labels like Baleno, Bossini, and Giordano are familiar brands in Shanghai. These brands are getting a good return on their China investments.

Like other Asian consumers, Shanghainese are brand- and price-conscious. Sub-RMB 500 women's clothing constitutes an 80% market share and

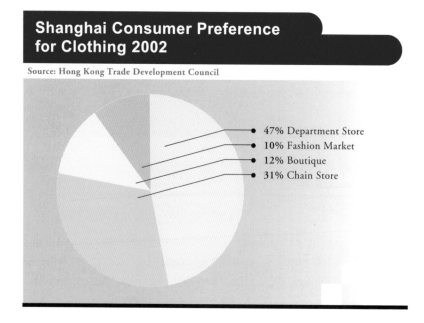

Shanghai Consumer Preference for Clothing 2002

Source: Hong Kong Trade Development Council

- 47% Department Store
- 10% Fashion Market
- 12% Boutique
- 31% Chain Store

sub-RMB 100 men's clothing takes up a 40% market share. For casual wear, consumers typically spend less than RMB 200. In addition, there are many small boutiques selling unique designs by local designers. Highly ubiquitous though are the products of local companies that specialize in changing tiny details in the designs of foreign brands and then re-branding them as their own.

Cosmetics

Like fashion, cosmetics has a somewhat fragmented market with no dominant players. Consumers can be fickle and companies need to continuously market new products or brands. If companies are insensitive to changing trends, they may risk being displaced by discerning new entrants. This industry has the advantage of low barriers to entry and exit.

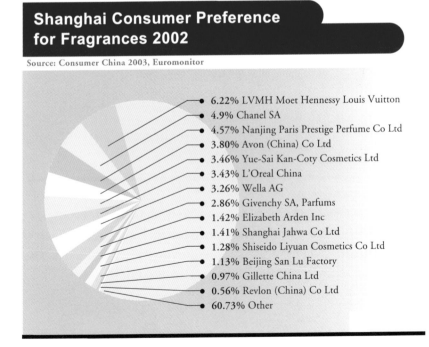

Shanghai Consumer Preference for Fragrances 2002

Source: Consumer China 2003, Euromonitor

- 6.22% LVMH Moet Hennessy Louis Vuitton
- 4.9% Chanel SA
- 4.57% Nanjing Paris Prestige Perfume Co Ltd
- 3.80% Avon (China) Co Ltd
- 3.46% Yue-Sai Kan-Coty Cosmetics Ltd
- 3.43% L'Oreal China
- 3.26% Wella AG
- 2.86% Givenchy SA, Parfums
- 1.42% Elizabeth Arden Inc
- 1.41% Shanghai Jahwa Co Ltd
- 1.28% Shiseido Liyuan Cosmetics Co Ltd
- 1.13% Beijing San Lu Factory
- 0.97% Gillette China Ltd
- 0.56% Revlon (China) Co Ltd
- 60.73% Other

Consumers, particular older ones, are not eager to use new foreign products. A study by AC Nielsen-SRG in the 1990s had shown Chinese women's reluctance to try foreign skin moisturizers. For example, despite strong promotional efforts, Unilever's Pond's and Vaseline creams and Procter and Gamble's Oil of Olay continued to lag behind dominant local brands Da Bao, Phoenix, and Eesli. This situation may be changing, however, as the younger generation is more open-minded.

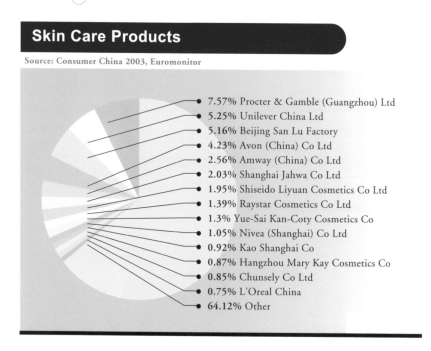

Skin Care Products

Source: Consumer China 2003, Euromonitor

- 7.57% Procter & Gamble (Guangzhou) Ltd
- 5.25% Unilever China Ltd
- 5.16% Beijing San Lu Factory
- 4.23% Avon (China) Co Ltd
- 2.56% Amway (China) Co Ltd
- 2.03% Shanghai Jahwa Co Ltd
- 1.95% Shiseido Liyuan Cosmetics Co Ltd
- 1.39% Raystar Cosmetics Co Ltd
- 1.3% Yue-Sai Kan-Coty Cosmetics Co
- 1.05% Nivea (Shanghai) Co Ltd
- 0.92% Kao Shanghai Co
- 0.87% Hangzhou Mary Kay Cosmetics Co
- 0.85% Chunsely Co Ltd
- 0.75% L'Oreal China
- 64.12% Other

Market penetration rates are not high and Shanghai presents good opportunities for new entrants. Skin care products targeting babies, the elderly and men also should present significant market opportunities. These market segments are currently still only in the nascent stages.

Top 15 Chain Stores in China by Sales, 2002

Ranking / Name	Sales in billion RMB	USD	Sales Growth (%)YoY	No. of Stores 2002	Ranking 2001
1 Huailian Supermarket	21.5	2.6	52.5	1541	-
2 Lianhua Supermarket	18.3	2.21	30.3	1921	1
3 Dalian Shopping Center	12.8	1.55	70.5	51	-
4 Beijing Guomei Home Appliance	10.9	1.32	70.4	107	6
5 Beijing Huailian Group	10.3	1.24	29	54	3
6 Shanghai Nong Gong Sang	8.65	1.05	15.7	702	4
7 Huarun Wanjia	8.59	1.04	37.5	456	11
8 Parkson (China) Investment	7.3	0.88	32.5	902	7
9 Suguo Supermarket	7.0	0.85	32.9	940	8
10 Suning Electrical	6.1	0.74	52.1	134	12

Source: Chain Store & Franchise World

Chain Stores

Shanghai has the highest penetration of chain stores in China, with more than 30% of total retail sales in 2002 transacted through chain stores. China's first retail license for a Sino-foreign retail JV was issued to Yaohan in 1992. Since then, retail and chain store development has proceeded at a rapid pace.

China's WTO Commitments – Retail Industry

In 1992, only two Sino-foreign joint ventures were allowed in six selected cities and five economic zones. Seven years later, majority control of JVs by foreign partners and foreign investment in distribution companies were allowed. By end-2004, most restrictions will be relaxed, including those pertaining to geographical spread, foreign ownership, number of stores and forms of establishment.

New Regulations

In 2001 — the year leading up to WTO membership — and 2002, China witnessed a high number of store openings. This had led to increased competition among local and foreign retailers, especially in Shanghai, where competitive stores are located in close proximity.

In order to curb excessive retail competition, tighter rules were issued on 11th February 2003. Under these new measures, domestic and foreign retailers planning new outlets must present their proposals at a public hearing attended by competitors and government officials.

Local governments were also required to draw up plans for the development of retail space in provinces and cities. This new rule gives cities until the end of 2004 to submit such plans, so implementation may not be immediate. The speed of implementation may vary among cities according to the relative level of competition.

Post-WTO Changes in the Retail Industry

Pre-WTO	JVs allowed only in Beijing, Shanghai, Tianjin, Guangzhou, Dalian, Qingdao, Shenzhen, Xiamen, Shantou, Zhuhai and Hainan.
Upon accession to WTO	Zhengzhou and Wuhan also open to JV retailing enterprises.
Within 2 years – by November 2003	Foreign majority control allowed, and all provincial capitals open to JV retailing enterprises. No restriction on range of products, except: • books, newspaper and magazines (within 1 year), and, • pharmaceuticals, pesticides, mulching film, and processed oil (within 3 years).
Within 3 years – by November 2004	All restrictions lifted except: • retailing of chemical fertilizer (within 3 years); • chain stores with more than 30 outlets which sell products of different types and brands from multiple suppliers; • stores of more than 20, 000m^2; and, • foreign majority ownership for distribution of motor vehicles. Foreign chain store operators will have freedom of choice of partner.
Within 5 years – by November 2006	• Retailing of chemical fertilizer allowed; • Foreign majority ownership for motor vehicle distribution, processed oil and crude oil allowed; and, equity limits totally eliminated.

Surviving in Shanghai's business climate would involve adapting to the constantly changing business environment, finding new ways to create value, and making necessary improvements to products and services.

This new procedure would, however, likely slow down store openings and would create a business environment conducive to mergers and acquisitions of retail operations.

Future Developments

Open to foreign retailing for more than ten years, Shanghai remains China's most competitive market, and now has international retailing veterans. In the light of this vigorous competitive environment, there appear four paths to a new sustainable business. These are in the areas of, namely, cost leadership and/or value perception, product differentiation (offering better quality or unique products), building rapport with customers and suppliers and finally, efficient logistics management.

Their expertise, new store concepts and management techniques had given foreign retailers the initial competitive edge. But domestic retailers are increasingly quick at learning from their foreign counterparts in terms of store layout, design and concepts. Intense competition will force the closure of similar stores selling identical or incoherent product mixes. Surviving in Shanghai's business climate would involve adapting to the constantly changing business environment, finding new ways to create value, and making necessary improvements to products and services.

Introduction to Huangpu District

Facing Huangpu River in the south and east and Suzhou Creek in the north, Huangpu District is located in the center of the city. The district occupies an area of 12.47 km^2 and has 650 thousand permanent residents. Boasting prosperous commerce, convenient communications, well-developed information infrastructure, centralized culture and entertainment, as well as an outstanding talent pool, Huangpu District is a unique and attractive central district with integrated functions of administration, commerce, tourism and culture. Several world-famous scenic spots and commercial areas are located here, including the Bund, 'Old Town' Yu Garden, and the 'No. 1 Commercial Street in China', Nanjing Road.

As a key part of Shanghai's Commercial Center and Central Business District, Huangpu District has defined a strategic plan centering on five industries and five areas. The five industries are the modern service industry, real estate industry, commercial industry, tourist industry, as well as cultural and entertainment industry. The five areas are the Bund and riverside area, Nanjing Road Commercial Area, People's Square and neighboring area, old town historical area, and modern residential area.

The Huangpu District government has launched five customized service plans for companies. The 'Settle Down in Huangpu' plan provides more convenience for companies to locate in Huangpu. 'Welcome Home' plan provides services for companies to register in Huangpu. 'Well-being' plan serves companies which are already located in Huangpu. The VIP plan provides privileged services to top executives of leading companies. Finally, the 'Incentive' plan provides incentives to real estate agencies and consulting companies.

With superior fiscal capacity, investment policy and geographic location, Huangpu creates a favorable environment for foreign investors. In Huangpu there are over 1, 000 foreign invested companies from more than 30 countries and districts, including 37 companies listed in Fortune 500, such as Emerson, Nokia, HSBC Data, McKinsey, and HP etc.

The main responsibilities of the Huangpu Foreign Economic Commission include introducing foreign multinational companies, especially those Fortune 500 companies, to Huangpu; examining and approving the establishment of foreign invested companies; providing services for established foreign invested companies; supervising foreign trading matters, as well as defining long-term plans and developing strategies for foreign economic development according to the overall economic plan of Huangpu District.

Introduction to the Waitanyuan Project

Located at the intersection of Suzhou Creek and Huangpu River, Waitanyuan occupies an area of 17.06 hectares. It faces the Huangpu River in the east, Suzhou Creek in the north, Middle Sichuan Road in the west, and Dianchi Road in the south. Waitanyuan is not only the origin of modern Shanghai, where modern industries of finance and trade had come into being, developed and prospered, but also the origin of the 'Exhibition o World's Architecture'. 14 buildings have been classified as having 'The Ex cellent Architecture of Modern Times in Shanghai'. Used as foreign bank ing offices and departments, most of them were built between 1920 and 1936, and are artistically decorated with a neoclassic flavor. Besides these buildings, there are blocks of historical local and foreign buildings of varied styles, reflecting the core of Bund culture and history.

As a key project in the comprehensive development of Huangpu Riv er's riverbanks, the Waitanyuan project will integrate the development of the Suzhou Creek, the greenbelt, historical and cultural feature areas, as well as the reconstruction of old areas.

The Waitanyuan project attracts various developers locally and abroad After rounds of negotiation, Shanghai New Huangpu Group, developer of this project in the beginning stages, finally signed a cooperative agreement with the Rockefeller Group from the U.S on May 7th 2004, a milestone in the development of the Waitanyuan project.

The project will be divided into three phases. The first phase, with a total investment of USD 250 million, is expected to complete in 2006. The construction of Shang- hai Peninsular Hotel, the first item in the Waitanyuan project, also begun on the day the agreement was sign- ed. Developed by the joint venture between HK and Shanghai Ho- tels Ltd. and Australia

SPG (group) Co., Ltd., Peninsular Hotel hopes to open for business in 2008 as a five-star luxury hotel.

BANKING & FINANCE

Introduction

China's WTO agreements with the United States and the European Union opened the door, for the very first time, to many possibilities and opportunities for foreign investors who wish to gain a foothold in China's financial industry.

Under the WTO accession agreement, China will completely open its financial market to foreign competition in five years' time. It will thus be a hotly contested arena in the world of finance in the next few years. The world-class challenge requires a world-class solution, and certainly deserves the attention of top-notch international financial institutions and professionals.

As the de facto financial capital of the country, Shanghai will be at the frontier of all these developments. In 2002, the Financial Service Office was established to strengthen the service function of local government. The financial market in Shanghai includes securities, inter-bank offerings, bonds, futures, foreign currency and gold, etc. Among them, there are 730 companies and 914 stocks listed on the Shanghai stock market. The total transaction value on Shanghai stock market in 2003 accounted for 60% of China's total, with an amount up to RMB 8,280 billion (USD 1,000 billion) up 70.6%. Shanghai Gold Exchange opened in 2002, which indicated China has established all the Exchange Markets for main financial products and made Shanghai the domestic financial center of China.

Source: www.smert.gov.cn

Since acquiring WTO membership in December 2001, China has issued a number of new regulations and detailed measures that translate its WTO commitments into specific rules governing foreign participation in the financial market. For foreign financial companies eager to gain access to the China market, it is crucial to understand these regulatory changes.

BANKING

The Banking Industry and China's WTO Commitment

Currently, foreign banks' major business remains in foreign currency business with foreign-funded enterprises and a limited number of Chinese enterprises.

According to the WTO agreement, China will gradually lift, region by region, restrictions imposed on foreign banks on handling local currency business. By 11 December 2006, all geographic restrictions will be removed.

Upon China's accession to the WTO	Shanghai, Shenzhen, Dalian and Tianjin
11 December 2002	Guangzhou, Zhuhai, Qingdao, Nanjing, and Wuhan
11 December 2003	Jinan, Fuzhou, Chengdu and Chongqing
11 December 2004	Kunming, Beijing and Xiamen
11 December 2005	Shantou, Ningbo, Shenyang and Xi'an

In addition, China will also gradually abolish client restrictions on foreign banks in local currency business.

11 December 2003	China will allow foreign banks to handle local currency business for Chinese enterprises.
11 December 2006	China will permit foreign banks to provide services for all Chinese clients. It will also allow them to set up business outlets in the same region. The requirements of examination and approval are the same as those for the domestic banks.
	China will abolish all other restrictions imposed on foreign banks on ownership, forms of operation and establishment, including branches, representative offices and the issuance of licenses.

Banking Services – Entry Requirements

The State Council approved the Regulations of the People's Republic of China on Administration of Foreign-Invested Financial Institutions on 12 December 2001. They were promulgated on 20 December 2001 and came into effect on 1 February 2002. The Regulations cover wholly owned foreign banks, branches of foreign banks, JV banks, wholly owned foreign financial companies and JV financial companies in China.

The Regulations pertaining to minimum registered capital (in a freely convertible currency) are as follows:

- For wholly-owned foreign banks and JV banks – RMB 300 million (USD 36.25 million)
- For wholly-owned foreign financial companies and JV financial companies – RMB 200 million (USD 24.16 million)

In both cases, the actual paid-up capital should be 50% of the minimum registered capital. In addition, parent companies should allocate at least (freely convertible currency) the equivalent of RMB 100 million (USD 12.08 million) to their branches in China as operating funds.

The Regulations pertaining to total assets owned are as follows:

- The total assets of a party intending to establish a wholly-owned foreign bank or wholly-owned foreign non-bank finance company must not be less than USD 10 billion at the end of the year preceding the application.
- The total assets of a party intending to establish a foreign bank branch must be at least USD 20 billion at the end of the year preceding the application.
- The total assets of a foreign joint venture partner applying to establish a joint venture bank or joint venture finance company must be USD 10 billion at the end of the year preceding the application.

The Regulations provide that a foreign-invested financial institution must meet the following requirements in order to carry out Chinese currency business:

- It must have conducted business in China for at least three years before the application.
- It must have made a profit in the two successive years preceding the application.
- It must meet other requirements stipulated by the People's Bank of China.

Wholly foreign-owned banks, branches of foreign banks and JV banks may:

- Issue short-term, medium-term and long-term loans;
- Bill acceptance and discount;
- Purchase and sell government and financial bonds and securities in foreign currencies other than shares;
- Engage in credit and guarantee services;
- Handle domestic and foreign account settlements;
- Purchase and sell foreign exchange;
- Engage in foreign currency conversion;
- Execute inter-bank call loans;
- Engage in bankcard services;
- Handle safe keeping services;
- Offer credit investigation and consulting services; or
- Other operations approved by People's Bank of China (PBC).

INSURANCE

The Insurance Industry and China's WTO Commitment

The main commitments of the Chinese government in opening up the insurance business industry are as follows.

In terms of business type:

- Immediately upon China's entry to the WTO, foreign non-life insurance companies are allowed to set up branches or joint ventures in China. Foreign firms will be allowed to hold as much as 51% stake in the joint ventures.
- Immediately upon entry to the WTO, foreign life insurance

companies are allowed to set up joint ventures in China, and hold no more than 50% stake in the joint ventures. They will also be allowed to choose their partners independently.

- Immediately upon China's WTO accession, the foreign stake in Sino-foreign joint venture insurance brokerage companies may reach 50%, and the proportion may not exceed 51% within three years after the accession.
- Two years after entry, foreign non-life insurance firms will be allowed to set up wholly owned branches in China, i.e. there will be no restriction regarding the form of enterprise established.
- Five years after WTO entry, foreign insurance brokerage companies will be permitted to set up wholly owned sub-firms. With gradual cancellation of geographical limitations, foreign insurance companies will, after approval, be permitted to set up branches. The qualification conditions for initial establishment do not apply to the establishment of internal branches.

In terms of geographical restriction:

- Immediately upon WTO entry, foreign life and non-life insurance firms are permitted to offer services in Shanghai, Guangzhou, Dalian, Shenzhen and Foshan.
- Two years after entry, foreign insurance companies' business can be extended to Beijing, Chengdu, Chongqing, Fuzhou, Suzhou, Xiamen, Ningbo, Shenyang, Wuhan and Tianjin. All geographical restrictions will be lifted three years after entry.

In terms of business scope:

- Immediately upon entry, foreign non-life insurance companies from abroad are permitted to engage in general insurance and large-scale commercial insurance without any geographical limitation, and offer non-life services to overseas enterprises, property insurance to foreign-funded enterprises in China, and related liability insurance and credit insurance services.
- Immediately upon entry, foreign life insurance companies are permitted to provide individual (non-group) life insurance services to foreign citizens and Chinese citizens.
- Immediately upon entry, foreign reinsurance companies are

LUJIAZUI – THE RISING STAR

The dramatic development of the Lujiazui Finance and Trade Zone (LFTZ) has attracted the attention of the global business community. Its transition from a huge farmland to a bustling financial hub within a short span of time is indeed amazing. With its brilliant success, it is all set to be the international financial and trading center in the Asia-Pacific region by 2015.

The zone occupies a total land area of 28 km² in the midwestern part of Pudong New District, facing the Bund, and overlooking Huangpu River. In 2003, the Zone had attracted total foreign banking assets exceeding USD 20 billion to become the "Capital-pole" of the Asian-Pacific region.

More than 156 financial institutions are located or have relocated here, including 62 foreign banks and securities firms or their representative offices. So far, 32 banks have been approved to deal in RMB; 32 securities firms and 12 foreign banks are permitted to deal in foreign exchange. Financial trading houses like the Shanghai Stock Exchange and Shanghai Futures Exchange have also moved here. More than 300 famous corporations including Siemens, Alcatel, Thomson and Baosteel have now set up bases in Lujiazui.

permitted to provide life and non-life reinsurance services in the form of branch company, joint venture company or wholly owned sub-firm. There are no geographical restrictions or quantity limits in license granting.

- Two years after entry, non-life insurance companies from abroad will be able to offer all kinds of non-life insurance services to Chinese and foreign customers.

- Two years after entry, they will be permitted to provide health insurance, group insurance, pension insurance and annual pay insurance services to Chinese and foreign citizens.

In terms of business license issuance, immediately upon WTO entry, China is committed to abolishing the restrictions on the number of licenses issued to foreign insurance companies. Foreign insurance companies must satisfy the following conditions before applying for licenses in China: a business history of more than 30 years in a

WTO member country, operating a representative office in China for two consecutive years and holding no less than USD 5 billion in total assets by the end of the year prior to the application.

In terms of legal insurance scope, the regulated 20% proportion provided by Sino-foreign direct insurance companies to Chinese reinsurance companies will not be changed immediately upon entry to the WTO. It will be lowered to 15% one year after entry, to 10% the following year, and finally, to 5% in the third year after entry to WTO. Eventually all rates will be cancelled in the fourth year after WTO entry. However, foreign insurance companies will not be permitted to engage in third-party liability insurance of motor vehicles, liability insurance for public transport vehicles, commercial vehicle drivers and carriers, and other legal insurance services.

In terms of general insurance policy brokerage services, national treatment will be granted. However, the geographical scope for opening up to foreign insurance brokerage companies will follow that of foreign insurance companies, i.e., they will be allowed to do business in Shanghai, Guangzhou, Dalian, Shenzhen and Foshan immediately upon WTO entry, in 10 more cities two years after entry, and in all cities three years after entry.

Besides, the Chinese government has, in accordance with the General Agreement on Service Trade, made commitments with regard to the trans-territory delivery, for example, in international marine shipping, aviation and freight transport insurance and reinsurance and large-scale commercial insurance and reinsurance brokerage services.

Insurance Services – Entry Requirements

The conditions for establishing a foreign-funded insurance company in China are as follows:

- a proven track record of having operated the insurance business for more than 30 years;
- a representative office in China for more than two years; and,
- total assets of no less than USD 5 billion in the immediately preceding year prior to the submission of the application.

The financial center of the zone was originally designed by a group of world-renowned urban planners and architects. The world's third tallest building, the 88-storey Jinmao Tower and the 468-meter Oriental Pearl TV Tower have already become the landmarks of Pudong and Shanghai. Century Avenue, Riverside Avenue, a 10-ha central greenery area, and a sightseeing tunnel connected to the old town are the new attractions for tourists who are constantly curious about the fast-changing urban landscape in Pudong.

Important Financial Hub

With Lujiazui playing a pivotal role, Shanghai's capital market expanded further in 2003. The total value of shares, bonds and other securities reached more than USD 1,000 billion, an increase of 71%, representing 87% of the national total. Globally, it ranked 13 in size, and was one of the five biggest in Asia, overtaking Singapore and Kuala Lumpur.

The Shanghai Futures Exchange too, had made great strides in 2003. From a total transaction value of USD 198 billion, the figure jumped to USD 731 billion in 2003, constituting more than 60% of the national total. As for the imports and exports trade, the volume handled by Lujiazui was worth more than USD 16.5 billion, making it one of the most important trading platforms in the whole of China.

Source: www.shld.com

For insurance brokers, the asset requirement is USD 500 million. Within two years it will be reduced to USD 300 million, and finally to USD 200 million within three years after China's accession to WTO.

The minimum registered capital for a joint venture insurance company or a wholly owned insurance company should not be less than RMB 200 million or equivalent in foreign exchange. The registered capital should be paid up.

A branch is not deemed as a separate legal entity in China. Therefore, the concept of limited liability does not apply. The parent company is required to allocate a minimum of RMB 200 million or equivalent in foreign exchange as the branch's operating capital.

A foreign-funded insurance company, in accordance with its business scope verified by China Insurance Regulatory Commission (CIRC), is permitted to carry out either of the following categories of business, but not both:

- Property insurance, including property loss insurance, liability insurance, credit insurance and other insurance; and,
- Personal insurance including life insurance, health insurance, accident insurance and so on.

SECURITIES

The Securities Industry and China's WTO Commitment

At the end of 2001, the China Securities Regulatory Commission (CSRC) announced the contents of an open securities market upon China's WTO entry:

- Within three years after accession, foreign securities firms will be permitted to establish joint ventures, with foreign minority ownership not lower than 25% but not exceeding 33%.
- Securities joint ventures (or JVs) may engage in underwriting A-shares; underwriting and trading of B and H shares; and underwriting and trading of government and corporate debts.
- More competent domestic enterprises are encouraged to list overseas. While still encouraging them to list in Hong Kong market, global securities markets are to be tapped into such as New York, London, Tokyo, Singapore and Australia.
- Qualified foreign-funded enterprises are to be gradually permitted to issue stocks and get listed in China when conditions are mature.

Securities – Entry Requirements

According to the legislation on Sino-Foreign joint venture securities companies ("Securities JV Rule"), the conditions on a securities JV are as follows:

- it must have registered capital of not less than RMB 500 million;
- the Chinese and foreign parties as well as the proportion and methods of their capital contributions must comply with the provisions of the "Securities JV Rule";
- it must have no less than 50 practitioners with professional qualifications for securities business, as well as the necessary accounting, legal and IT professionals;
- it must have a sound international management and risk control system and a standardized system for the separate management of

personnel, finance and information for underwriting, brokerage and proprietary trading businesses, and have an appropriate technical system for internal control;

- it must have the required business premises and proper trading facilities; and
- other conditions specified by the China Securities Regulatory Commission (CSRC).

Conditions to be satisfied by a foreign party in order to set up a Securities JV:

- it must be located in a country with sound securities laws and regulatory systems, and the relevant securities regulatory authority must have concluded a memorandum of understanding on securities regulatory cooperation with CSRC;
- it must possess the legal qualification to conduct securities business in its home country, operated financial business for more than 10 years, and received no material punishment from the securities regulatory authority or judicial bodies in the last three years;
- every risk monitoring ration in the past three years must be in compliance with the provisions of laws and the requirements of the securities regulatory authority of its home country;
- it must have a sound internal control system; and
- it must have a satisfactory reputation and performance in the international securities market.

OTHERS

Fund Management

Upon accession to WTO, foreign investors are allowed to either invest in an existing fund management company or jointly establish a new enterprise. Initially, their share can be more than 25% but less than 33%; in three years that percentage of ownership may grow to 49%.

Other Financial Services

Upon entry to WTO, foreign non-bank financial institutions are allowed to set up wholly foreign-owned or joint venture automobile financing service companies. Within five years after WTO entry, Sino-foreign-funded banks can provide automobile credit service for individual Chinese clients. Foreign-funded financial leasing companies are permitted to provide financial leasing services within the same period of time as that of Chinese firms.

OPPORTUNITIES AND CHALLENGES

Shanghai places high priority on the financial industry in line with the support from the central government. In the early 1990s, the late paramount leader Deng Xiaoping made the call for re-establishing Shanghai as a financial center, which he stressed could help China integrate into the world economy. The blueprint of building Shanghai into a financial center was designed on the basis of the prosperous areas along the banks of the Huangpu River.

Among the 160 financial institutions located on both sides of the river are the People's Bank of China (Shanghai), the Industrial and Commercial Bank of China, China Construction Bank, Agricultural Bank of China, China Bank of Communications, Shanghai Stock Exchange (SSE), Shanghai Futures Exchange, Citibank, Bank of America, Bank of Tokyo-Mitsubishi, Mizuho Bank and Bank of Bangkok etc.

Since 1990, Shanghai's financial sector has recorded a rapid growth. Today, Shanghai has become the national center of fund management, and leads the formation of a healthy national capital market, including the inter-bank loans market, the bond market, and the foreign exchange market. Many Chinese banks, securities companies and fund management companies have set up their headquarters in Shanghai. Chinese-funded banks in Shanghai make up 6% of the country's total in terms of deposits, loans and assets. Overseas-funded banks in the city account for over 50% of the foreign banks' total deposits, loans and assets in China. This is a clear sign of the predominance of foreign banks in Shanghai, compared to any other Chinese city.

Shanghai's Financial Market 2003

BANKING	RMB billion	USD billion
Total Deposits	**1,731.8**	**209.14**
Total Loans	**1,316.8**	**159**
Personal Loans	193	23.32
Housing Loans	170.9	20.65
SECURITIES		
Total trading value (securities)	**8,280**	**1,000**
Shares	2,080	251.31
Bonds	6,160	744.26
Funds	36.2	4.37
INSURANCE		
No. of Insurance Companies	41	41
No. of Reinsurance Companies	59	59
Total Premium Revenue	28.9	3.49
Property Insurance	5.7	0.69
Personal Insurance	23.2	2.8
Revenue of Chinese-funded insurance companies	25.2	3.04
Revenue of foreign-funded insurance companies	3.8	0.46
Total insurance compensation	**6.2**	**0.75**
Property insurance compensation	2.7	0.33
Personal insurance compensation	3.5	0.42

Source: http://www.stats-sh.gov.cn

With better and more varied services and an expanded market size, the opening-up of Shanghai's financial industry in 2003 continued to proceed rapidly. At year end, there were 89 foreign-invested financial institutions in operation, of which 62 are banks and financial service providers, 19 are insurance companies, and 8 companies dealing in securities. Of these 62 banks and financial service providers, 47 are permitted to offer services to all Chinese clients. Four foreign banks have in fact set up their Chinese headquarters in Shanghai – Citibank, HSBC, Standard Chartered and Overseas Chinese bank. Total assets of the 62 banks and financial service providers amounted to USD 27.4 billion.

Due to previous restrictions on market entry and business scope, foreign financial institutions as a whole have acquired only a small share of Shanghai's banking, insurance, securities and fund management businesses. It is fair to say that until recently, the potentially lucrative China market was beyond the reach of most foreign financial institutions and that domestic players were enjoying a virtual monopoly.

Responding to China's inclusion into the WTO, and hence, its substantial market-opening commitment, financial institutions from all over the world have in the past two to three years begun to take more determined and concrete steps to explore or expand in China.

Shanghai is keen to leverage on foreign capital and expertise in order to bring greater sophistication to its financial market. Domestic financial institutions are to be put under more stringent and prudent supervision, in the face of foreign competition. The actual pace of the market's opening may therefore go beyond what China has envisioned.

At present, the partially open mainland financial market may bring greater opportunities to global giants than smaller-scale financial institutions. In particular, the asset/capital requirement stipulated for the foreign partner in a joint venture in many financial businesses virtually block the entry of smaller players. A lowering of the thresholds would therefore facilitate market access for many small foreign financial institutions.

Banking Services

China's banking services are in fact dominated by the big-four state commercial banks – Construction Bank, Industrial and Commercial Bank, Bank of China and Agricultural Bank – which, together, control 80% of the market. However, all of them suffer from problems like huge non-performing loans, lack of modern banking products, uncreditworthy customers (most are state-owned enterprises), and overstaffing and over-branching.

The government is using asset management companies to purchase the banks' bad loans at apparently full book value by converting to bonds guaranteed by the State. Despite the advantages of very large deposit bases, branch networks and government support, these problem-ridden banks remain unattractive for any large international institution to consider a serious tie-up with.

As a result, most of the foreign banks that wish to enter the China market are eyeing small and medium-sized banks. As these Chinese banks have a big share in niche markets, they are convenient vehicles for foreign banks to obtain relevant market demand information. For the Chinese banks, alliances with big foreign players provide a useful channel to quickly expand their capital and strengthen their capacity.

A key distinction here is whether the operating bank will be a "foreign-invested enterprise" (FIE) or a domestic bank under Chinese law. During the WTO transition period, FIEs are still subject to many of the prior limitations on foreign banking activities, which will be lifted gradually in the course of a five-year period. In contrast, a foreign investment in a Chinese bank with less than 25% stake means the Chinese bank in practice is not treated as an FIE. It can thus continue to conduct full local currency and other business permitted to domestic banks. However, the lack of control associated with this structure will not appeal to many international banks.

Compared to mainland banks, foreign banks may be more interested in corporate and investment banking. Foreign banks are thus in an advantageous position to capture a significant share of the market once it opens. Limited by their branch network, foreign banks may have difficulties competing with mainland banks in the mass market. However, they may be more successful in providing customized services to higher-income customers.

Source: www.smert.gov.cn

Insurance Services

The great potential and liberalization of China's insurance market makes the insurance industry a new focal area for foreign investment. Compared with 11% in Japan and 8% in the United States, the insurance industry only represents less than 2% of China's GDP. By 2005, the total value of insurance premiums in China is expected to reach USD 33.82 billion, constituting 2.3% of the total GDP; the average premium per person will be USD 27.78, still at a considerably low level. With 16 million people and GDP per capita over USD 4,500, Shanghai holds great promise for foreign players such as AIG, AXA and Allianz. Currently, Shanghai takes up 13.6% of foreign insurance companies' market share in China.

A few state-owned companies, in particular the People's Insurance Company of China (PICC), monopolized insurance services till the late 1986. Shanghai opened to foreign insurance companies in 1992. So far, there are 8 foreign-controlled and 6 Sino-foreign JV insurance companies operating in Shanghai. Several foreign insurance companies have already taken minority stakes in Chinese domestic insurance companies, pursuant to an insurance regulation specifically authorizing foreign minority investments of less than 25%.

Similar to the banking area, such a structure preserves the domestic character of the insurer and exempts it from restrictions on foreign insurance companies. Alternatively, establishing an FIE insurance company with a 25% or greater foreign interest is also possible, but the scope of business will be limited to that permitted to foreign insurance companies, bearing in mind this scope expands during the course of the following three years.

STOCK EXCHANGE

Shanghai Stock Exchange Performance 2003, in billion

	RMB	USD	Increase
Total value of transaction	8,208	991.7	+70.6%
Total capital raised	68.9	8.32	+10.2%
Total no. of securities listed	914	914	+88
Total value raised through IPOs	45.35	5.48	-
Total value of newly issued shares	10.74	1.3	+10.4%
Total value of convertible loan stocks	12.89	1.56	(Increased tenfolds)

Source:www.stats-sh.gov.cn

Securities

The Shanghai Stock Exchange recorded a total securities transaction value of RMB 8,208 billion(USD 991.7 billion), an increase of 70.6% from the preceding year. Different types of securities were listed on the market, and at end-2003, there were 914 listed securities, 88 more than the preceding year. Of the 914 securities, there were 824 company shares, compared to 759 the preceding year. Total capital raised for the year was RMB 68.9 billion (USD 8.32 billion), an increase of 10.2% from the first half of 2003. Initial public offerings (IPOs) raised a total of RMB 45.35 billion (USD 5.48 billion). Newly issued shares raised a sum of RMB 10.74 billion (USD 1.3 billion), an increase of 10.4% over the preceding year. Convertible loan stocks had a tenfold increase in value, constituting a sum of RMB 12.89 billion (USD 1.56 billion).

From the beginning, the SSE possesses its own distinctive personalities different from the Shenzhen Stock Exchange. In Shanghai, the listed companies are mainly large state-owned enterprises; the Shanghai market's performance is therefore sometimes seen as an indicator of China's domestic economy. On the other hand, the manufacturing and export companies doing business with nearby Hong Kong dominate the Shenzhen Stock Exchange, so the Shenzhen Stock Exchange is sometimes a barometer of that sector.

Of this group, the first two, with huge volume held by government or state-owned enterprises, remain largely non-circulating, though occasionally the central government intends to sell into the open stock. Due to strong market resistance, in June 2002 the State Council decided to suspend its previous plan of reducing state-owned shares by trading in the stock market, which was interpreted as a positive signal in both stock markets of Shanghai and Shenzhen. For foreign portfolio investment, the last four are the major ways to invest in Chinese stocks. To date, no foreign-funded companies has been approved to be listed on SSE and no foreign stockbrokers have been allowed to buy seats in the exchange.

PROFESSIONAL SERVICES

Introduction

China's service industries, especially professional services, are among the most heavily regulated and protected sectors of the national economy. However, for sustainable economic growth, effective and efficient measures to open its service sector to foreign competition will have to be adopted. A strong service sector will help improve economic productivity along the value chain of all industries, be it Chinese or foreign-dominant.

China has made WTO commitments to gradually phase out most restrictions in a broad range of services, including accounting and auditing, legal and advisory, advertising, management consulting, IT and engineering consulting services. Shanghai, being a pioneer in the modernization of China, has once again caught global attention with the opening of these service sectors following the country's accession to the WTO.

China's WTO Commitments

Under the WTO agreements, China is obliged to permit foreign enterprises greater access to its service sector. Services such as telecommunications, insurance, banking and professional services are gradually opening to foreign participation.

China has made commitments in all major service categories and will eventually eliminate most foreign equity restrictions. It is also committed to opening up other services auxiliary to distribution including rental and leasing, air courier, freight forwarding, storage and warehousing, advertising, technical testing and analysis, and packaging services. All restrictions will be gradually phased out in 3 to 4 years' time, at which time, foreign investors will be able to establish wholly-owned subsidiaries.

Distribution of CPA Firms by Province, by 1 Jan, 2002

Source: China Knowledge Press

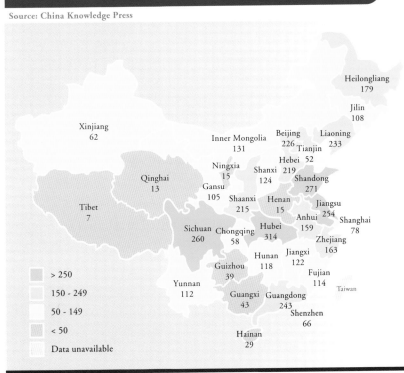

Heilongliang 179

Jilin 108

Xinjiang 62

Inner Mongolia 131

Beijing 226

Liaoning 233

Tianjin

Hebei 52

Ningxia 15

Shanxi 124

Shandong 271

Qinghai 13

Gansu 105

Shaanxi 215

Henan 15

Jiangsu 254

Tibet 7

Anhui 159

Shanghai 78

Sichuan 260

Chongqing 58

Hubei 314

Zhejiang 163

Hunan 118

Jiangxi 122

Guizhou 39

Fujian 114

Taiwan

Yunnan 112

Guangxi 43

Guangdong 243

Shenzhen 66

Hainan 29

> 250

150 - 249

50 - 149

< 50

Data unavailable

In relation to professional services, China currently tightly restricts operation of foreign law firms and accounting firms. In the WTO agreement, China has provided a broad range of commitments, including legal, accountancy, taxation, management consultancy, architecture, engineering, urban planning, medical and dental, and computer and related services.

China will permit foreign majority control except for practicing law (an exception common to many WTO members). For accountancy, China has agreed to eliminate a mandatory localization requirement. It will now allow licensed professionals unrestricted access to its market.

Accounting Services

Introduction

The accounting services sector has grown by leaps and bounds in the period since economic liberalization began in earnest. As China moved toward a market economy, it had to reinvent this key sector after long neglect. In fact, under the command economy, accounting and auditing professionals were mainly confined to working in state-owned enterprises or public sector budgeting. There is a need now to change the mentality to fit the rapidly-growing new economy, and to train new staff to fill the gaps as privatization takes place and private sector companies move to the forefront as employers and agents of growth and change.

Accounting was one of the first service sectors to open up. Even in the 1980s, foreign accounting firms were permitted to set up representative offices and to provide audit, tax and consulting services to both local and foreign clients.

Compared to highly monopolized and closed industries like telecommunications, the accounting sector is in a better position to adapt and develop in the WTO period. With investors' rising expectations for publicly-listed companies, demand for high-quality auditing is increasing.

The Certified Public Accountants industry has undergone rapid development since 1980. It established a regulations system, implemented an examination system, developed training and follow-up education, opened up the accounting market, and increased international cooperation. Overall, the new development of CPA firms has played an active and important role in economic reforms, the development of security markets, reforms of state-owned enterprises, and national development.

As well-known foreign CPA firms enter the country, the standards of local firms are expected to rise to approach international standards. Rules and regulations concerning foreign-invested CPA firms are expected to be improved and perfected.

The development trend is encouraging. With an increasing number of accounting service enterprises, the sector has already achieved a much larger scale. To enhance professionalism and standardization, industry groups in major cities founded the Institute of Certified Public Accountants.

China's WTO membership and the Industry

In accordance with agreed terms in China's WTO accession agreements, China will give market access and national treatment to accounting, auditing and bookkeeping services.

- Foreign accounting firms can be affiliated to Chinese firms and enter into contractual agreements with other affiliated firms in WTO member countries;
- Foreign accounting firms must be represented by Certified Public Accountants (CPA) licensed by Chinese authorities, but existing accounting firms are exempted from this requirement;
- Foreigners who have passed the CPA examination will receive national treatment (i.e. they can form partnerships or incorporated accounting firms);
- CPA certifications are issued on a national treatment basis. Applicants will be informed of results in writing no later than 30 days after submission of their application;
- Accounting firms can provide taxation and management consulting services that are subject to Joint-Venture (JV) restriction (see *Forms of Foreign Investment*);
- There is no mandatory localization requirement.

Opportunities

In China, the accounting market is growing at an average of 20-30% annually. The growth of foreign accounting firms in China is remarkable.

Traditionally, foreign accounting firms only provided services for multinational clients operating in China and working on projects of the World Bank and other international organizations. However, the growing ambition of China's leading companies to make initial public offerings (IPOs) abroad helps to expand the business activities of foreign accounting firms because hardly any Chinese accounting firm is internationally recognized. Domestic firms, such as Unicom and Sinopec, have no choice but to hire foreign accounting firms if they plan to launch IPOs in New York and other major international stock exchanges. Reportedly, over 95% of Chinese companies that have sold shares to foreign investors use international accounting firms with operations in China. In addition, China's determination to integrate its economy into the global system provides a promising future for foreign accounting companies.

Recent developments in Shanghai's accounting sector demonstrate that demand for quality accounting services is growing. First, as part of a broader program to separate business from government, accounting firms have become independent from government-related entities. The fundamental economic restructuring that aims to separate ownership from management will create opportunities for international accounting firms.

Second, China's accounting industry "clean-up" and revision of its Accountancy Law paved the way for the development of China's capital market to which the growth of the accounting sector is largely tied. International accounting firms may benefit in two ways. On one hand, the expanding market and demand for quality services require the expertise and other resources that domestic accounting firms do not yet possess. On the other hand, international firms are expected to play a role in the process of regulation drafting.

Finally, with China's entry into the WTO, more areas are to be liberalized, restrictions to be loosened, national treatment to be applied, and procedures to be followed with more transparency. These will work together to the advantage of foreign accounting firms in developing their capacities and delivering quality services in China.

It can surely be expected that accounting professionals who are proficient in international accounting and auditing standards will be much needed in post-WTO China. According to a survey conducted

The "Big Four" Accounting Firms

PricewaterhouseCoopers

PricewaterhouseCoopers is the world's largest professional services provider with more than 120,000 professionals in 142 countries. In China it has 6000 staff and offices in Beijing, Chongqing, Dalian, Guangzhou, Shanghai, Shenzhen, Suzhou, Tianjin, and Xi'an. After acquiring AA (China) in 2001, it took a leading position in China.

KPMG

KPMG has 85,300 staff in 155 countries around the world. KPMG provides services for half of the top 500 banks and 100 insurance companies in the world. KPMG (China) was founded in 1992 in Beijing and later established offices in Shanghai, Guangzhou and Shenzhen. Now it has 700 staff in China.

Deloitte Touche Tohmatsu

One of the world's leading professional services organizations, Deloitte Touche Tohmatsu opened an office in Shanghai in 1917. It now provides services to large state-owned enterprises MNCs, and new enterprises. In 1997, Deloitte merged with Kwan Wong Tan & Fong (KWTF), the largest Hong Kong CPA firm. Deloitte has 90,000 staff and claims 20% of the auditing and consulting business for the world's top companies. In China, it provides services in accounting, audit, tax and commercial consulting.

Ernst & Young

Ernst & Young is the world's fourth-largest CPA firm and the second in the US. In 1998, Ernst & Young had 675 offices in 132 countries with 82,000 staff. Its services include insurance, tax, corporate finance, and management consulting.

by Britain's ACCA, China's market would soon demand over 300,000 accounting professionals, especially those with eight or more years of working experience in multinational companies.

Foreign Firms

The Big Four – Pricewaterhouse Coopers, KPMG, Deloitte Touche Tohmatsu and Ernst

and Young – earn 20% of total sector revenues and 30% of total sector profit. They provide audit services for listed companies with B and H shares and undertake most of the business for MNCs in China. The China Securities Regulatory Commission requires companies making IPOs or refinancing in equity markets to be audited by international and local CPA firms.

Domestic Firms

Although there are many domestic CPA firms in China, their size is small compared to international CPA firms.

In addition, Chinese accounting practitioners, on average, are less qualified, less familiar with international rules, and less experienced compared to their counterparts overseas.

Because of shortcomings both in facilities and human resources, many local CPA firms are also somewhat informal in their audit procedures, methods, and tools. Auditing is mostly manual work and computerized operations are not yet widespread.

Finally, many accounting firms are still partially or completely attached to government departments or organizations. A fair competition system is not yet well-established. Under international rules, accounting firms compete with each other in an open market. However some accounting services in China, especially for audit, are arranged by the government instead of the market.

With the opening of the market, Chinese companies are facing competition from foreign MNCs. There is a need to increase capital, to improve internal organizational structure, and to apply modern management methods like capital restructuring within or between large enterprises. CPA firms would play an important role in this restructuring process.

Future Development

Small and Medium Enterprises

There are large regional differences in economic development in China. In underdeveloped regions, there are many small to medium enterprises. Targeting these companies, small CPA firms can start businesses in auditing, capital assessment, assets evaluation, tax and legal consulting, management consulting, company registration services, and accounting services.

Such services are characterized by high quantity, low price, low risk, and a small size requirement for CPA firms. This is an important target market for small to medium sole proprietorship or partnership CPA firms.

Foreign investment in small and medium enterprises is also expected to increase. The entry of these new small- or medium-sized foreign projects should also provide opportunities for small- and medium-sized CPA firms.

Mergers and Acquisitions

The China market increasingly shows a trend for CPA firms to merge. There are several reasons for this. To surmount competition from foreign and local accounting companies, firms are merging in order to strengthen their overall capabilities. There are increasing requirements for the application of practice licenses. Mergers may be a way to more easily obtain and keep various licenses. Finally, successful local and international mergers suggest that bigger firms are more likely to attract clients.

Rapid Development of Partnership CPA Firms

Partnership is the general organizational form in the global CPA industry. To ensure consistency with the international system, national laws and administrative actions are being formulated. For firms that cannot fulfill the requirements for limited liability, partnership is a good choice in a market seeing increasing demand from private enterprises.

New Emphasis on Consulting Services

Currently most revenues derive from auditing, with consulting still relatively underdeveloped. Effective demand is presently low, though there is a big potential market and marketing remains inadequate. After WTO entry, CPA firms are getting new businesses from tax and management consulting. With increasing market pressure, companies are seeking more management consulting. These trends are helpful for the development of new accounting-related services.

Multinational Practices

After WTO entry, large local CPA firms may undertake overseas projects, bringing China's CPA services to the international market. Some of the more competitive local CPA firms have the chance to attract foreign clients. Overseas subsidiaries of Chinese companies may choose Chinese CPA firms for services.

Standardization and globalization

Learning from successful experiences in foreign and international audit organizations, China has been building up its independent audit capacity since the early 1990s. An audit principle system has begun to take shape, basically consistent with international norms.

With further development and opening, the new system will be more standardized and globalized. As globalization of the economy proceeds, China will soon be more and more integrated with world markets.

Accounting is the world's "business language". There is significant potential for further developing accounting services as China's professionals learn advanced skills and build up sector experience.

Organizations and Authorities

Administrative organizations and authorities include:

- Ministry of Finance (MoF)
- People's Bank of China (PBC)
- China Institute of Certified Public Accountants (CICPA)
- China Securities Regulatory Commission (CSRC)
- China National Audit Office (CNAO)
- Chinese Institute of Internal Auditing (CIIA)

The Ministry of Finance (MoF) reports directly to the State Council and is responsible for supervising:

- Drafting of strategies, plans, laws, regulations, and reforms on finance, taxation, tariffs, state capital funds, and debt;
- Verification of assets, defining ownership of capital funds, and directing property appraisal;
- implementation of accounting regulations by SOEs and government organs; and,
- CPAs and their offices
- directing auditing

The People's Bank of China (PBC) is the central bank. Its chief mandate is to formulate and implement monetary policy and to supervise and regulate the financial industry. PBC's main functions include: formulating and implementing monetary policy;

- issuing and administering currency circulation;
- licensing and supervising financial institutions;
- regulating financial markets; managing official foreign exchange and gold reserves;
- acting as fiscal agent;
- maintaining the national payments and settlement system;
- collecting and analyzing financial statistics;
- participating in international financial activities in the capacity of the central bank; and,
- overseeing the State Administration of Foreign Exchange.

The China Institute of Certified Public Accountants (CICPA) is the national CPA organization. Established in 1988, it is now one of the world's largest professional accounting bodies, with around 135,000 individual members and 4,800 group members (CPA firms). While the Institute is nominally an independent organization, it is under the direct supervision and direction of MoF.

Legal services

Introduction

In accordance with agreed terms in China's WTO accession agreements, China's commitment related to foreign law firms are as follows:

- Foreign law firms can provide legal services in the form of profit-making Representative Offices (ROs);
- Within one year of China's accession to the WTO (i.e. by 11 December 2002), all geographic and quantitative restrictions will be phased out, which means that foreign firms can open more than one office anywhere in China.

On 1 January 2002, the "Regulations on the Administration of Foreign Law Firms' Representative Offices in China"—which the representative offices of foreign law firms in China are required to abide by—came into force. Under the regulations, the ROs of foreign law firms may be set up, if they meet the following requirements:

- Such a representative office must be affiliated with a foreign law firm that has been legally registered in its home country;
- The representative thereof must be a legally registered attorney, having been qualified as a member of the bar association in the country where his/her license is issued, and exercising his/her license for no less than two years outside China. All representatives must reside in China no less than six months each year;
- The chief representative is required to have been practicing as a registered attorney for no less than three years outside China, being a partner of the firm or holding an equivalent position.

Any representative office of foreign law firms that are legally established in China cannot be involved in any Chinese legal business, but they can:

- provide clients with legal consultation with regards to the laws and regulations of the country, where its attorneys have been licensed to practice legal business and consultation on any relevant international conventions and treaties or common practice;
- handle the legal affairs in the country, where its attorneys have been licensed to practice legal business, as entrusted by the relevant parties or Chinese law firms;
- entrust Chinese attorneys to handle Chinese legal affairs, on behalf of foreign clients;
- maintain long-term cooperative relationship with Chinese law firms by entering into contracts;
- provide information on the Chinese legal environment.

Such an RO of a foreign law firm should be named as "Representative Office in (city name in Chinese) of the (Chinese translation of its foreign name) Law Firm". Foreign law firms or organizations of any kind are not allowed to be involved in legal services in China in the name of a consulting company or others.

The RO of a foreign law firm in China may not employ any Chinese attorney, and the assistants hired are not allowed to provide legal services to the clients. All of the service charges must be settled in China. To set up such an RO, a foreign law firm shall file an application to the local judicial department at the relevant provincial level.

While the foreign firm cannot employ Chinese nationals as lawyers for the practice of Chinese law, it can enter into long-term "entrustment" contracts providing for close working relationships, including the right to provide instructions, with firms practicing Chinese law.

Opportunities

In Shanghai, there are now over 4,700 lawyers (0.036% of the local population) and over 477 law firms. Due to the growing business in the legal sector, some firms have undergone mergers and restructuring to form large-scale ones – usually with over 100 employees. In recent years, many law firms in big cities, such as Beijing, Shanghai and Guangzhou, have adopted the business form of partnerships.

China allows three types of law firms: state-invested, cooperative and partnership. A law firm established with the assistance of government capital shall be independent in its practice and shall undertake liability for its debts with its total assets. Cooperative law firms can also be established, and will also be liable for their debts. For a partnership law firm, all partners shall undertake unlimited and joint liability for all debts. The only difference between a cooperative and a partnership law firm in China is the scope of liability.

China's accession to WTO has brought changes to its law service industry. All state-invested law firms and cooperative law firms are being transformed into partnership law firms. In Shanghai, almost all law firms are partnership law firms.

Since the restoration of the legal professions, the number of lawyers has risen and the quality of legal services has improved significantly. However, few lawyers in China specialize in dealing with foreign-related issues and litigations and even fewer are able to provide legal services in a foreign language.

With China's accession to the WTO, overseas law firms are now able to set up multiple offices. Its bilateral agreement with the United States and the European Union led to the lifting of quantitative and geographical restrictions on the establishment of ROs by foreign law firms in the year following China's accession to WTO.

China's agreement with the EU also allows foreign law firm ROs to provide information on the impact of the Chinese legal environment. This provision acknowledges the role of foreign law firms in providing their understanding of the Chinese legal system with respect to foreign investment and trade

without disturbing the prohibitions on the issuance of legal opinions on Chinese law or representing clients in Chinese courts.

Following WTO entry, the foreseeable rapid economic development and increase in number of Chinese companies venturing abroad will fuel greater demand for legal services. As a result, more large foreign law firms armed with financial and human resources will enter to explore the tremendous opportunities and to exert great influence on China's legal service market.

However, the WTO accords did not lift other fundamental barriers to the operation of foreign law firms in China. Foreign law firms mainly offer legal consultation to clients with investments in China. They are not permitted to interpret the Chinese law, appoint Chinese lawyers or represent their clients in court. They can only act as legal consultants. Legal services relating to litigation, public listing, loans, real estate and intellectual property rights must be offered by mainland Chinese lawyers.

Furthermore, unlike their counterparts in other service industries including accounting, architecture and insurance, foreign law firms are not permitted to establish joint ventures with Chinese law firms. Lesser relationships will be permissible but these are unlikely to be sufficient.

In a certain sense, the WTO accession agreements have actually caused a tightening of restrictions on foreign law firms in some areas. China's bilateral agreement with the United States and European Union provide that the chief representative of a foreign law firm representative office must be a partner or equivalent, which is more stringent than under current requirements. All attorneys or representatives under the EU agreement must be members of the bar of a WTO member and also have practiced for no less than two years (which need not be consecutive). These conditions limit the ability of foreign law firms to assign junior attorneys to their offices in China. The experience requirement for representatives also seems restrictive as the resident partner or equivalent can supervise and train junior attorneys on-the-job as is done in the United States.

CONSTRUCTION

Introduction

Shanghai has been one of the world's fastest growing economies since the last decade. It has undergone continuous development in urban construction and infrastructure. The city's landscape is constantly changing. Infrastructure development has been an important growth engine for Shanghai's economy. Over RMB 360 billion (USD 43.5 billion) has been injected into these infrastructure projects. Average annual growth stands as high as 30.7%.

Major functional and hub infrastructure projects include the Inner Ring Road, Metro Line 1, the North-South Viaduct, Yan'an Road Viaduct, Metro Lines 2 and 3, and the Pudong International Airport.

A three-dimensional express transportation network has taken shape in Shanghai. It is formed by the Inner and Outer Ring roads, viaducts, Humin Elevated Road, Yanggao Road, highways to Jiading, Xinzhuang and Songjiang, Shanghai-Nanjing and Shanghai-Hangzhou expressways, Huqingping Expressway, Metro lines, the Longhua-Jiangwan light railroad, Phase I Project of Pudong International Airport (already in operation) and suburban ring roads (presently under active construction).

Apart from Songpu Bridge built in 1970s, four grander bridges spanning the Huangpu River have been built since the development of Pudong in the early 1990s, namely, Nanpu, Yangpu, Fengpu and Xupu Bridges.

Impact of WTO Agreements

Contract Construction

Within three years of WTO accession, wholly-owned foreign enterprises (WOFEs) will be allowed. They are, however, still restricted to undertaking

only the following contract construction projects:

- Projects solely funded by foreign investment or foreign donation;
- Projects financed by international financial institutions' loan through international tendering;
- Joint projects undertaken by Chinese and foreign enterprises with the latter's share over 50%;
- Joint venture projects and special domestic projects that are technically difficult for a domestic enterprise to undertake by itself; relevant government bodies have agreed to their engaging foreign contractors.

At the moment, a joint venture contractor is, in theory, capable of undertaking all construction projects in China.

Within three years of WTO accession, Sino-foreign joint ventures can enjoy national treatment. Within five years of WTO accession, WOFEs are allowed without projects restriction.

Survey and Consulting

- Equity joint ventures or cooperative joint ventures are allowed;
- Architects, engineers or enterprises who wish to undertake survey or consulting businesses in China must be licensed architects, engineers, or enterprises in their home country;
- Within five years of WTO accession, WOFEs will be allowed in this area.

Real Estate

- WOFEs are allowed to undertake most real estate development projects with

Shanghai is one of the fastest growing construction markets in the world with great potential of growth over the coming years. According to the 10th Five Year Plan (2001-2005), investments in residential housing in Shanghai will reach RMB 250 billion (USD 30.2 billion), which will account for 8-9% of the city's GDP and about 25% of the total fixed assets; the total housing floor area to be built will reach 75-80 million m^2, after 750,000 new home units are built; per capita residential space will increase to 19 m^2; and green land coverage will be increased to 2,200 ha.

the exception of high-grade projects (star hotels, condominiums, golf courses etc);

• Sino-foreign joint ventures are allowed to provide real estate agency services (real estate valuation and management etc.);

• Within five years of WTO accession, WOFEs are allowed to operate without restrictions.

Urban Planning

• Sino-foreign joint ventures are allowed in urban planning and design with the exception of master urban planning;

• Foreign individuals or enterprises who undertake businesses in this area must be licensed planners or enterprises in their home country.

Construction Projects

In 2002, the Shanghai municipal government announced a mega plan to spend a record RMB 50 billion (USD 6 billion) on major construction

projects. These include another elevated road, an underground tunnel across the Huangpu River, a light railroad, a 98-km ring road and three expressways. Phase 1 of Metro Line 2, a 16.3-km line running from Zhongshan Park in Puxi to Longdong Road in Pudong, may be completed ahead of schedule.

In the first half of 2002, over RMB 5.56 billion (USD 670 million) had already been invested in the city's construction projects. This figure constitutes 60% of Shanghai's total fixed assets investment in the same period. A total of 22 major construction projects were launched, among which the most remarkable include the first phase of the Yangshan Deepwater Port, Shanghai Railway South Station and the public transportation interchange at People's Square.

Another 23 major projects including the Gonghexin Viaduct will be completed in the second half of 2002. Construction has already started for nine projects, including the extension of Metro line No.2. The first phase of the Suzhou Creek dredging project will be completed soon and the city's greenery coverage will be increased to over 25%, or 6.5 m² per capita.

New houses are to be distributed as follows:

Distribution of New Houses 2001 - 2005

Area	million m²
Within the Inner Ring	19.5 – 20.8
Between the Inner and Outer Ring	32.2 – 34.4
Beyond the Outer Ring	23.3 – 34.8

Construction Companies

Currently, in Shanghai's construction market, most of the large players are state-owned and medium-sized ones are often collectively owned. Private or quasi-private enterprises also exist but of less influence.

China's entry to the WTO creates many opportunities for foreign construction companies. A more open, regulated, and transparent market

Total Output Value of Construction

Year	RMB billion	USD billion
1997	55.24	6.67
1998	58.6	7.08
1999	56.83	6.87
2000	62.24	7.52
2001	72.16	8.72
2002	82.23	9.94
2003	105.59	12.8

Source: China Statistical Yearbook 2003

Value-added of Construction

Year	RMB billion	USD billion
1997	12.1	1.46
1998	13.1	1.58
1999	12.25	1.48
2000	13.81	1.67
2001	14.33	1.73
2002	18.46	2.23
2003	26.49	3.21

Source: China Statistical Yearbook 2003

Total Profit of Construction Enterprises

Year	RMB billion	USD million
1997	1.26	150
1998	1.31	160
1999	1.42	170
2000	1.84	220
2001	1.92	230
2002	2.35	280

Source: China Statistical Yearbook 2003

for foreign players can be expected. In addition, reduction in import duties will lower the market threshold and improve market access.

Entry Requirements for Foreign Construction Company

Foreign-invested construction enterprises shall be established in accordance to the 'Law on Sino-foreign Equity Joint Ventures of PRC', the 'Law on Sino-Foreign Cooperative Enterprises of PRC', and the 'Regulation on the Control of the Qualifications of Construction Enterprises' and other related laws, decrees and regulations.

In addition, the establishment of a foreign-funded construction enterprise shall meet the following conditions:

- The Chinese partner to a foreign-funded construction enterprise shall be a construction enterprise holding at least a second-grade qualification certificate; the foreign partner shall be a construction enterprise with the status of a legal person that possesses advanced technology, efficient management practices and a good reputation.
- Foreign construction enterprises can import from overseas advanced technology and equipment for construction and can train Chinese staff in engineering and management expertise.
- The minimum registered capital of a foreign applicant is USD 10 million for first-grade construction-engineering enterprises, USD 5 million for second-grade construction-engineering enterprises, and USD 1.6 million for third-grade construction-engineering enterprises.
- The minimum registered capital is USD 2 million for first-grade construction-decoration and fitting enterprises, USD 1.5 million for second-grade decoration and fitting enterprises, and USD 600,000 for third-grade decoration and fittings enterprises.

Relevant Rules and Regulations

According to the Regulations of Shanghai Municipality on the Administration of Construction Market, Shanghai Municipal Construction Commission (SMCC) is the major government authority responsible for the municipality's construction market. The district/county construction bureaus or committees, within its scope of authority, are responsible for relevant affairs in their areas.

Industry Performance 2003

Value-Added	USD 26.48 billion	+1.3%
Value of Work Performed	USD 105.59	+28.4%
Total Area of Land		
• Under Construction	85.47 million m²	+37.0%
• Completed Construction	28 million m²	+15.5%
Construction workers per capita productivity	USD 18,600	+15.1%

It is necessary for individuals or organizations to register at local industrial and commercial administration and obtain certificates of professional qualifications issued by the government authorities before they can undertake the following:

- survey, design and construction for construction projects;
- contracting-out agency, supervision and cost consultation for construction projects.

For individuals or organizations from Hong Kong, Macau, Taiwan or other countries to engage in construction activities, they have to obtain the business contracting permit approved by both Shanghai Municipal Foreign Economic Relations and Trade Commission (SMERT) and SMCC, and register at Shanghai Industrial and Commercial Administration (SICA) before they are allowed to commence operations in Shanghai.

The project proposal and feasibility study for establishing foreign-funded construction enterprises shall be examined and approved by the relevant authorities. The examination and approval will be carried out at different levels based on the size of the business.

Applications for first-grade construction enterprises will be examined and determined by the Ministry of Construction (MOC) and approved by the Ministry of Foreign Trade and Economic Cooperation (MOFTEC); applications for second-grade and lower level foreign-funded construction enterprises will be examined and determined by SMCC and approved by SMERT.

If the Chinese partners are enterprises directly affiliated to State Council departments, the applications shall be examined by MOC and approved by MOFTEC.

The application for establishing a foreign-funded construction JV involves the following steps:

- The Chinese partner shall submit the project proposal, feasibility study report and related documents of the proposed foreign-funded construction enterprises to the government authorities. If all the requirements are met, a 'Recommendation for the Examination of Foreign-Funded Construction Enterprises' shall be issued.

- The Chinese partner shall, on the effect of the 'Recommendation for the Examination of Foreign-Funded Construction Enterprises', submit the contract and articles of association and related documents for examination and approval by SMERT. If all the requirements are met, a 'Certificate of Approval for the Establishment of Foreign-Funded Enterprises' shall be issued.

- The Chinese partner shall go through the legal person registration procedures with SICA upon the effect of the 'Recommendation for the Examination of Foreign-Funded Construction Enterprises', the 'Certificate of Approval for the Establishment of Foreign-Funded Enterprises' and other related documents.

- After obtaining the business license, the foreign-funded construction enterprise shall go through the qualification examination and approval procedures with the construction authorities.

In applying for a foreign-funded construction enterprise, the Chinese partner shall submit the following documents:

- Application letter for the establishment of foreign-funded construction enterprises;

- Qualification certificates of the Chinese partner;

- Document of examination by relevant departments;

- Project proposal for establishing foreign-funded construction enterprises;

- Feasibility study jointly compiled by all partners of the joint venture;

- Certificates of all partners for the registration with SICA; and

- Credit rating certificates of all partners and other relevant documents.

LOGISTICS

Introduction

Logistics services has become one of the most important industries and a new growth factor for China's national economy in the 21st century. China's logistics service as a newly emerging economic sector is now on a path of rapid progress, backed up by the development in this sector around the world. According to official statistics, China's logistics industry will be worth USD 114.8 billion by 2010, of which Shanghai will contribute about USD 21.7 billion. It is predicted that the third-party logistics market in Shanghai could reach 25% in the years 2004 and 2005.

By the end of 2001, the logistics industry had employed 452,400 people, and generated a revenue of RMB 66.35 billion (USD 8.02 billion) – 13.4% of the GDP and 6 times more than that of 1990. In 2002, total logistic capacity exceeded 500 million tons. The number of containers handled by Shanghai Port totaled over 8.6 million TEUs. This figure led the Shanghai Port to rank 4th in the world, one position forward compared to previous year.

WTO Agreements

Under the rules of the World Trade Organization (WTO), China is expected to open its service sector and logistics market within three years. By December 2004, foreign companies will be able to operate wholly-owned logistic units in China to provide a wide range of services ranging from inventory management, sorting and grading, to light assembly.

In most logistics sub-sectors, foreign-majority owned joint ventures are allowed within one to two years after China's entry to the WTO, and WOFEs in three to six years.

Foreign-invested freight forwarders are no longer restricted to international freight forwarding; domestic freight forwarding and other logistics services are open to foreign participation after WTO accession.

On the whole, new opportunities for foreign logistics service providers arise not only because of the relaxation of regulatory constraints, but also in the face of fast growing domestic and global demands.

Freight Forwarding
- Foreign majority ownership in JVs allowed the year after accession;
- Wholly owned subsidiaries allowed four years after accession;
- JVs not confined to international freight forwarding business only.
- Foreign service suppliers allowed to establish as minority-owned JVs upon accession and allowed to hold a majority equity share within one year;
- Restrictions to be phased out within three years.

Courier Services
- Commitments cover land-based international courier services and all services related to an international shipment handled by an express carrier;
- Foreign majority ownership in JVs allowed within one year. Wholly owned subsidiary allowed four years after accession.

Land Transportation
- For road transport, foreign service suppliers will be able to establish JV upon accession, hold majority equity share within one year, and be free of ownership restrictions within three years;
- For railroad transport, foreign service suppliers will be able to establish JV upon accession, hold majority

equity share within two years, and be free of ownership restrictions within six years.

Current situation

Shanghai's logistics industry has developed rapidly since the start of the economic reforms. In May 2002, Shanghai Logistics Center (SLC) announced that, in its first phase of operation in Waigaoqiao the country's first and largest free trade zone – it had begun to provide services for both resident and non-resident companies.

Being the only one of its kind in Shanghai, the Waigaoqiao Free Trade Zone will significantly contribute to the development of Shanghai's logistics industry. According to Administrative Committee of WFTZ, more than 70 Fortune 500 multinationals, 3,000 trading companies and 500 logistics specialists have made their presence in the zone. More than RMB 10 billion (USD 1.23 billion) will be invested over the next five to 10 years in the Waigaoqiao Logistics Park. It is estimated that cargo flows at WFTZ will amount to 20 million tons, annual foreign trade will hit USD 40 billion, and the value added of the logistics industry will account for 50% of WFTZ's total. By then, Waigaoqiao will be established as a procurement, distribution and transhipment center in the Asia-Pacific region.

Apart from the WFTZ, Shanghai also enjoys the highest level of logistics infrastructure compared to other cities in China. Located at the midpoint of China's coastline and the start of the Yangtze River waterway, Shanghai thus has a locational advantage. It is easy to access other cities located in the Yangtze River Delta areas such as Hangzhou, Nanjing, Suzhou and Chongqing. In addition, Shanghai's railway network such as the Beijing-Shanghai and Shanghai-Guangzhou railway lines also link Shanghai to the whole country. Moreover, the highway network of Shanghai also provides convenient land transportation for domestic logistics.

In order to become the largest logistics center in China, Shanghai has developed its harbor into the largest harbor in China. 11.28 million TEUs containers were handled in 2003. As we can see from the chart on the next page, container handling has increased to 31%, compared with the figure for 2002. The Shanghai Harbors Authority also expect that the number of container handling will exceed 13 million TEUs in 2004. Therefore, Shanghai Harbor is expected to become the world's second largest harbor after Singapore with its annually increasing container handling capacity.

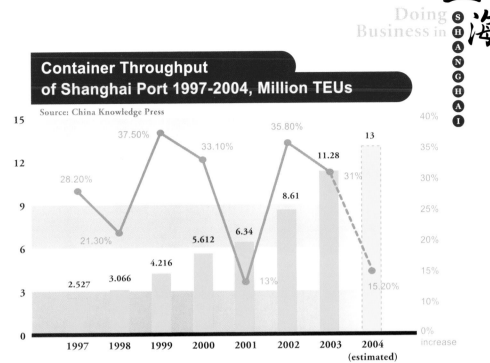

Container Throughput of Shanghai Port 1997-2004, Million TEUs

Source: China Knowledge Press

- 1997: 2.527 — 28.20%
- 1998: 3.066 — 21.30%
- 1999: 4.216 — 37.50%
- 2000: 5.612 — 33.10%
- 2001: 6.34 — 13%
- 2002: 8.61 — 35.80%
- 2003: 11.28 — 31%
- 2004 (estimated): 13 — 15.20% increase

Developments in the Industry

One of the four main new industries in Shanghai's 10th Five-Year Plan, the logistics industry is becoming an important pivot in the metropolis' efforts to develop into an economic center, financial center, trading center, and shipping center. Shanghai is dedicated to becoming a key supply chain node in the global logistics arena by the end of the 10th Five-Year Plan.

In order to accomplish the goal, Shanghai has designed three main platforms.

• **Facility Platform** – to develop into a modern transportation network that integrates port, air, highway, and railway. This includes:

Port Logistics Pivot

Based on the development of Shanghai international shipping center and construction of Yangshan Port, and with a focus on containers transport, Shanghai strives to establish the largest logistics industrial park in China, and make it one of the most important in the Asia Pacific region.

Aviation Logistics Pivot

Focused on international cargo transport and air express service. With Pudong Aviation Logistics Park as the major base, the plan is to establish an international and domestic aviation logistics network.

Railway Logistics Pivot

To streamline the railway transport system, and to establish the express railway transport network.

Highway Logistics Pivot

To construct the basic framework of the expressway system and establish a comprehensive highway network across the inland.

• **Information Platform** - to develop into the largest and most completed EDI-based logistics public information platform within the country and probably in the Asia Pacific region. This includes: region-wide united logistic information platform within Yangtze River area, nationwide integrated transportation information platform, industrial goods trading information platform, and worldwide port logistic public information platform.

• **Policy Platform** - to implement policies that facilitate the development of logistics industrial parks, introduction of international corporations, and restructuring of domestic logistics companies.

As a prominent distribution center for the prosperous East China region as well as for the rest of China, Shanghai clearly needs to develop its strength in logistics-related areas. Three major logistics industrial parks have been launched.

> • Waigaoqiao Logistics Park – Port-based Logistics Park focusing on entrepot trade. Over 3000 trading firms and 600 warehousing logistics companies, such as APL, Maersk, Sumitomo and Marubeni have operations in the park. During the 10th Five-Year Plan,

development of logistics parks will focus on two international districts, North District of size 1.01 km² and South District of 1.6 km², to build up a 2 million m² warehouse that can handle logistic capacity up to 10 million tons.

- Pudong Aviation Logistics Park – Aviation-based industrial park focusing on express service. With 220, 000 m² freight area (phase one) and 385, 000 m² custom warehouse, the park has attracted four global logistic enterprises, namely UPS, Fedex, TNT and DHL, and some 17 agents to set up their express service centers in the park.
- Northwest Logistics Park – Land-based industrial park. With 936 logistics companies and 600, 000 m² warehouse, the park handles 60% of the city's total highway freighting. To name a few major logistics enterprises, US APW, France's Schneider, Japan's Marubeni, Taiwan's T-Join Transportation, Dazhong Communication Groups.

Industry Outlook

Sound government policies

The operation of logistics involves various government sectors, such as communications, industries and commerce, taxation and information, etc. The rules and regulations from the different government sectors could be outdated and may not meet the requirements of current logistics development. Therefore a complete government policy is necessary to create an environment for logistics development in Shanghai.

Regulate the Market

Many logistic sectors are affiliated to the enterprises themselves. From manufacture to distribution, these logistics sectors are separate. Third Party Logistics (TPL) is not fully developed and widely adopted. The few large specialized logistics companies are serving only the big corporations. Most of the SMEs are still basically in the self-supplying stage. Therefore, low efficiency, high costs, and small sizes are common among these logistics sectors. Contemporary logistics requires an interdependent relationship between these different companies. Moreover, these companies can manage those processes cooperatively, to eliminate waste and to create greater value for all partners.

Application of Information Technologies

Currently, many logistics companies are still adopting the traditional methods of operation. The complete logistics information management system EDI and GPS system are still not in place. For example, most companies are still doing manual data input. And information sharing and updating are mainly through telephone and fax.

As a result, this kind of information exchange leads to high-cost logistics and outdated real-time information in the current logistics market. Hence, information transfer speed and accuracy are barely improved; and, operational cost is not effectively under control. Unique in the international logistics sector, information technologies can help to circumvent and resolve some challenges such as extended lead time of supply, unreliable transit times etc. Therefore, improving the infrastructure of information technology in Shanghai is significant to increasing the standards of competition for the status of largest logistics center in the world.

Training Logistics Specialists

Modern logistics requires not only the employees involved in traditional transportation and distribution, but more importantly a group of specialists who are:

- Familiar with customer's manufacturing, marketing and operation processes;
- Trained with professional expertise in logistics and transportation management;
- Equipped with marketing skills and information technologies.

IT AND COMMUNICATIONS

Introduction

The information industry has become one of the fastest-growing industries in Shanghai, and has contributed significantly to the economy. The total output value of the information industry has increased annually by 49%, a rate far higher than other industries.

In 2003, the city's information industry reported a total added value of RMB 62.2 billion (USD 7.54 billion), up 17% from the previous year and accounting for 10% of the city's GDP, up 0.9 percentage point. The added value of the IT products manufacturing sector reached RMB 35 billion (USD 4.24 billion), representing a year-on-year growth of 12.5%. The figures for IT product sales and IT services stood at RMB 1.98 billion (USD 2.49 million), up 21.7% and RMB 25.2 billion (USD 3.05 billion), up 24% respectively.

With an output expected to reach RMB 400 billion (USD 48.33 billion) by 2005, and the information industry now plays a strategically important role in both social and economic development of Shanghai. As targeted in the city's planning outline, an IT-based economy and society will be in place in Shanghai by 2010, and the overall level of informatization is expected to approach that of developed nations.

Currently one of six pillar industries in Shanghai – the other five being automobile, petrochemical, iron and steel, set equipment manufacturing and pharmaceutical – the development of the information technology and communications industry in Shanghai is paving the way for the establishment of Shanghai as an "information harbor". In the next few years, Shanghai will keep abreast with Hong Kong and Singapore in terms of IT application and infrastructure. It is set to become an important communications hub in the Asia Pacific region.

Shanghai has established five major information networks over the last few years, including a foreign trade data network, a social security network and a community service network. It has also set up 20 key information systems in such areas as urban planning, finance, employment, and industrial and commercial administration. Shanghai has placed high priority on the development of the high-tech communications sector. Over the past few years, the industry has churned out integrated circuits, computers, mobile telecommunications facilities and a series of other profitable IT products. Today, Shanghai produces one-fifth of China's integrated circuits and one-third of telecommunications equipment.

The 10th Five-year Plan for Informatization in Shanghai

In the 10th Five-year development period, the blueprint of Shanghai's informatization is to include the following tasks:

- pushing forward the information industry based on information service and the production of integrated circuits, software, communication equipment, digital audio video frequency products;
- furthering the innovation of information technology;
- promoting industrial restructuring based on informatization;
- improving the informatization in terms of government service, public service, city construction and administration;
- facilitating the construction of information infrastructure such as the installation of wide band equipment;
- ensuring information security, and so on.

Integrated circuits

The manufacturing industry of integrated circuits produced 2.25 billion pieces of integrated circuits in 2001, of which, 1.07 billion are LSIs (large-scale integrated circuits). IC-related industries in Shanghai have a total investment of USD 8 billion. Six 8-inch-chip production lines are scheduled to be built, or are currently being built. A batch of accessory and service enterprises engaging in packaging, testing, equipment accessories photomasks, materials, lead frames and gases etc. is expected

to be produced.

Software

The software industry has been developing at a rapid pace. There are 7 bases of software industry in Shanghai, including the Pudong Software Park. A USD 12 million software company was also set up. The Fudan Grandorizon Information Technology Co., Ltd., the largest of its kind in the metropolis, is funded by the Shanghai Post and Telecommunications Administration, and is designed to develop information technology and various software products. The industry has developed a wide array of software products for use in banking, futures, negotiable securities, business management, finance, securities etc.

Digital electronic products

Digital electronics products achieved an output value of RMB 42 billion (USD 5.07 billion), an increment of 20% from the preceding year. Shanghai has successfully developed 16:9 color CRT and set top boxes used by digital TV receivers. The city also produced four million DVD machines, most of which were exported. The export quantity ranked in the top flight nationwide.

Communications

Siemens mobile phones, Bell program-controlled switches, Ricoh fax machines, fiber-optical communications products and network products have become leading products in Shanghai's communications industry, enjoying high exposure and maintaining a market share of 20% to 50%. As communication products have begun to have an edge in the high-end product market, a comparatively comprehensive range of leading products is being produced. These products include those from the fields of mobile networking, fixed networks and optical networks.

Total number of fixed-line telephone users	7.33 million	-
Total number of fixed-line telephone users (residential)	5.28 million	-
Total number of mobile phone users	10.97 million	Increase: 1.85 million
Total duration of international calls	2.56 billion mins	Increase: 14.3%
Total duration of international calls (from mobile lines)	1.98 billion mins	Increase: 46.7%
IP phone usage	3.52 billion mins	Increase: 75.1%
Number of Internet subscribers	4.316 million	Increase: 120,000
Number of broadband users	924, 900	Increase: 577,000
Number of cable TV subscribers	3.67 million	Increase: 400,000

Source: www.stats-sh.gov.cn 2003

Information services

With the quickened pace of construction of information infrastructure, the information service industry, an integration of digital information and communication technology, continued to develop in 2003. Its annual operating income reached RMB 62.2 billion (USD 7.54 billion), increasing by 17% over 2002. Digital and multimedia communication, IP phones, mobile SMS and other technologies will further the development of the information service industry. In addition, the digitization of Shanghai's broadcasting industry will quicken its pace and become an important driving force to boost the development of the information service industry.

Source: www.shanghaiit.gov.cn

New Technologies

With an R & D expenditure estimated at 2.06% of China's GDP, Shanghai took on a total of 1508 technological projects in 2003. Of these, 71 projects led international standards, while 532 projects attained "advanced" standards, when compared in the international arena. Major projects involving fuel batteries, information security, the magnetic levitation rail system and digital signal processing chips had made excellent progress.

In 2003, Shanghai reported a record number of patent applications. Shanghai saw a total of 22,374 patent applications - of which 5936 items were inventions - and 16,671 patent certificates were awarded.

As a member of Shanghai's science and technology committee hadsaid, in an interview, the increase in patent applications may be attributed to the establishment of a mechanism that encourages inventions and protection of intellectual property rights and patented products research achievements has been set up in local enterprises, schools of higher learning and research institutes. Legal advisors have also been invited to guide people in the application for the protection of patents.

Source: www.chinaview.cn

The transformation of high-tech research results and technological innovations into commercial and industrial products has made new progress. By year end, Shanghai had established 25 national-level technological centers, and 103 city-level technological centers. Newly developed products from these centers bring opportunities for profit. For example, between January and September 2002, Shanghai Bao Steel Group achieved a profit of RMB 2.6 billion (USD 310 million), a 5.5-fold increase on the year-to-year basis, thanks to a computerized online control system on its modern production line.

In addition, 543 technological innovations have found their way to the commercial market. 71% of these technological innovations are in the areas of electronic information, biopharmaceuticals and new materials. 84.3% of these new products have been awarded patent rights and software copyright.

It is no surprise that by end-2003, the commercialization of high-tech innovations in Shanghai recorded a new high. A total number of 27, 300 contracts were signed in technological transfer, up 4.9% from the preceding year, with a total value of RMB 14.28 billion (USD 1.73 billion), up 18.8% from the preceding year.

Adopting New Technologies

Shanghai has adopted various forms of new technology in the city. A good example is the new airport departure controlling system installed at Shanghai Pudong International Airport. This system adopts IBM hardware and services plus SITA's CUTE (common use terminal equipment) system expertise to handle and manage the passenger departure process, from assignment of seats through to passenger boarding.

The proliferation of new technologies has also motivated the establishment of a new data sub-center in Shanghai. The sub-center integrates import and export business information, capital flow data and cargo distribution information, which is a new breakthrough in the electronic port regulation system. The data center allows different departments, different industries and different regions to share information online. It also offers companies comprehensive online services related to customs clearance.

Also, the opening of the Cadence High-Speed Technology Center in Shanghai by Cadence Design Systems, Inc. – the world's leading supplier of electronic design products and services, suggests a recognition of Shanghai's value in the area of new technologies. The Center is the first of its kind in the Asia Pacific region and will serve a growing customer base in the region with training, education programs, as well as methodology and consultancy services. Initially, the Center will serve three markets: wireless communication, wired communication and computing applications. Over the next two years, the scope of service will expand to include advanced packaging design and digital consumer applications.

INTERNATIONAL EXHIBITIONS AND CONFERENCES

Shanghai's numerous exhibitions and conferences greatly promote the formation of an international market and indicate Shanghai's rapid rise in international standing.

The area of exhibition industry increases at the rate of 30%. Many world-famous conferences have been held in Shanghai, such as Fortune forum, APEC, Shanghai 5 States Summit, ADB annual meeting, and the 32nd ICC. Shanghai International mould expo has been listed in UFI. World Expo 2010, which will be held in Shanghai, will set several records. It will be the largest in terms of area and number of visitors, and it is the first time the World Expo is held in a developing nation. Shanghai will invest over USD 3 billion in the event.

Source: http://www.smert.gov.cn

Shanghai New International Expo Center

SNIEC currently has seven halls with one-storey and column-free exhibition space. Each hall is 11,500m² big, thus amounting to a total of 92,000m² exhibition space. Halls one to four, and six to seven, are 11-17m tall, whereas hall five is 17-23m tall. SNIEC is being expanded. Upon full completion, the centre will have 18 halls and an integrated hotel and conference centre complex. The total exhibition area is estimated to be 250,000m² (200,000m² of indoor and 50,000m² of outdoor).

Contact Information

Venue booking hotline:

86 21 2890 6856 (for overseas organizers)
86 21 2890 6854 (for domestic organizers)
2345 Longyang Road, Pudong New District, Shanghai 201204
Tel: 86 21 2890 6666   Fax: 86 21 2890 6777
Email: info@sniec.net; marketing@sniec.net (Venue Booking)

www.sniec.net

Shanghai Mart

Shanghai Mart, located in the major financial trade centre in China, is one of the largest exhibition and trade centers in Asia. Comprising an international Trade Mart with 200,000m², an office tower of 42,000m², exhibition halls of more than 37,000m², a Sky Lobby of 2,000m² and several conference rooms of various sizes, Shanghai Mart houses a trade information centre, business centre, post office, bank, customs office, courier and catering services all under one roof.

Contact Information

2299 West Yan'an Road, Shanghai 200336
Tel: 86) 21 6236 6888 ext 6368
Fax: 86 21 6236 0181
Email: sam.fang@shanghaimart.com.cn
www.shangmart.com.cn

INTEX Shanghai

Covering 12,000m², Intex Shanghai provides both domestic and foreign exhibitors a perfect exhibiting place with all kinds of well-equipped facilities. The ground floor of 8.1 metres in height, can accommodate all kinds of special designs. Since its establishment in 1992, Intex Shanghai has undertaken more than 180 large-scale exhibitions, over 150 of which were international ones. Apart from that there have been more than 560 seminars held in INTEX.The annual occupancy has reached 49.2%.It has received more than 132,000 exhibitors and over 6 million visitors. All this made INTEX Shanghai is indeed an ideal exhibition venue.

Contact Information

88 Loushanguan Rd, Shanghai 200336
Tel: 86 21 6275 5800   Fax: 86 21 6275 7210
Email: intex@public.sta.net.cn
www.intex-sh.com

SHANGHAI EXHIBITION CALENDAR 2004

Date	Exhibition	Location
Feb 11 - 12	7th Shanghai Int'l Spare Parts & Materials Purchase Fair	INTEX Shanghai
Feb 16 - 20	China Logistics 2004 Conference	Shangri-La Pudong Hotel
Feb 17 - 20	FurniTek China 2004	Shanghai Mart
Feb 17 - 21	WoodBuild China 2005	Shanghai Mart
Feb 18 - 20	ChemSpec China 2004	Shanghai Mart
Feb 19 - 22	World Travel Fair	Shanghai New International Expo Center
Feb 25 -28	The 5th China (Shanghai) International Wedding & Photographic Equipment Exhibition	Shanghai Everbright Convention & Exhibition Center
Mar 1 - 2	Embedded System Conferences	Shanghai Mart
Mar 1 - 2	The 9th Annual International IC-China Conference & Exhibition	Shanghai Mart
Mar 1 - 7	East China Fair	Shanghai New International Expo Center
Mar 9 - 12	Electronic China	Shanghai New International Expo Center
Mar 10 - 12	CPCA 2004	INTEX Shanghai
Mar 11 - 13	China National Hardware Fair (Spring) 2004	Shanghai New International Expo Center
Mar 17 - 20	Garment Expo 2004	Shanghai New International Expo Center
Mar 17 - 24	electronicChina	Shanghai New International Expo Center
Mar 24 - 26	Biotech and Pharma	INTEX Shanghai
Mar 25 - 27	DESSOUS CHINA	Shanghai Mart
Mar 30 - Apr 2	HOTELEX SHANGHAI 2004	Shanghai New International Expo Center
Mar 31 - Apr 2	GAS EXPO SHANGHAI 2004	INTEX Shanghai
Mar 31 - Apr 3	Expo Shanghai 2004	INTEX Shanghai
Apr 12 - Apr 16	CCMT 2004 (China CNC Machine Tool Fair)	Shanghai Everbright Convention & Exhibition Center
Apr 13 - 15	China Sourcing Fair: Electronics & Components	Shanghai Mart
Apr 14 - 16	CHINA CYCLE 2004	Shanghai New International Expo Center
Apr 15 -17	China International Bicycle & Motor Cycle Fair	Shanghai New International Expo Center
Apr 20 - 22	China Sourcing Fair: DIY & Home Improvement	Shanghai New International Expo Center

Apr 20 - 24	National Electronic Fair	Shanghai Everbright Convention & Exhibition Center
Apr 21 - 23	Expo Real China	Shanghai New International Expo Center
Apr 26 - 29	CeBIT Asia 2004	Shanghai New International Expo Center
Apr 26 - 29	NEPCON MICROELECTRONICS SHANGAI	Shanghai Everbright Convention & Exhibition Center
Apr 27 - 29	Opto CHINA 2004	INTEX Shanghai
May 11 - 24	Transport Logistic China 2004	Shanghai New International Expo Center
May 12 -14	INFOCOMM CHINA	Shanghai Everbright Convention & Exhibition Center
May 12 -16	DIE & MOULD China 2004	Shanghai New International Expo Center
May 21 - 24	International Building & Construction Trade Fair 2004	Shanghai New International Expo Center
May 28 - 30	Bakery China	Shanghai Everbright Convention & Exhibition Center
May 28 - 31	China International Sporting Goods Fair Exhibition	Shanghai New International Expo Center
May 31 - Jun 2	2004 Shanghai Int'l Water Supply, Drainage and Treatment Equipment Fair	Shanghai Everbright Convention & Exhibition Center
Jun 5 - 9	The 10th Shanghai TV Festival	Shanghai New International Expo Center
Jun 5 - 13	The 7th Shanghai International Film Festival-International Film and TV Market	Shanghai New International Expo Center
Jun 5 - 7	China Int'l Exhibition on Cable & Wire Industry	Shanghai Everbright Convention & Exhibition Center
Jun 8 - 10	CRC	Shanghai Exhibition Center (SEC)
Jun 15 - 17	CPHI CHINA	Shanghai Everbright Convention & Exhibition Center
Jun 16 - 18	METRO CHINA 2004	INTEX Shanghai
June 16 - 19	Advertise, Print, Pack & Paper Exhibition 2004	Shanghai New International Expo Center
Jun 29 - Jul 2	International Trade Fair for Environmental Protection	Shanghai New International Expo Center
Jul 9 - 11	CiEX: 2nd China Interactive Entertainment Expo	Shanghai Exhibition Center
July 09 - 11	China Interactive Entertainment Expo (CIEX)	Shanghai Exhibition Center

July 13 - 16	The 10th International Processing, Packaging and Printing Exhibition (PROPAK CHINA BEIJING)	SNIEC Shanghai Pudong
Jul 13 - 16	ProPak China	Shanghai New International Expo Center
Jul 22 - 25	Shanghai Int'l Diamond Jewellery Fair '04	Shanghai International Convention Center
Jun 23 - 26	CIT Shanghai 2004/ China ELECOMM 2004	INTEX Shanghai
Sep 1-3	Intertextile Shanghai Autumn (Home Textiles)	Shanghai New International Expo Center
Sep 1-3	Cinte Techtextil China 2004	Shanghai Int'l Exhibition Center
Sep 1 - 9	All China Leather Exhibition	Convention & Exhibition Center
Sep 7 - 9	China Paper-Shanghai	INTEX Shanghai
Sep 9 -10	AnalyticaChina 2004	Shanghai New International Expo Center
Sep 11 - 14	The 8th China International Furniture Expo	Shanghai New International Expo Center & Shanghai Everbright Convention & Exhibition Center
Sep 11 - 14	The 8th China International Furniture Manufacturing Expo	Shanghai New International Expo Center & Shanghai Everbright Convention & Exhibition Center
Sep 14 - 19	FHC - Food and Drink	INTEX Shanghai
Sep 15 - 18	Furniture China 2004	Shanghai New International Expo Center
Sep 25 - 27	Fashion China	Shanghai New International Expo Center
Oct 8 -11	China International Building & Housing Expo 2004	Shanghai New International Expo Center
Oct 11 - 13	China Sourcing Fair: Electronics & Components	Shanghai Mart
Oct 12 - 15	PTC (Power Transimission and Control	Shanghai New International Expo Center
Oct 12 - 15	INTERFOOD SHANGHAI 2004	INTEX Shanghai
Oct 12 - 15	Factory Automation	Shanghai New International Expo Center
Oct 12 - 15	Metal Working China	Shanghai New International Expo Center
Oct 19 - 22	Auto Parts & Equip Shanghai 2004	INTEX Shanghai
Oct 26 - 29	Shanghai International Plastics & Rubber Industry Exhibition	Shanghai New International Expo Center
Nov 10 -12	Tubetec China	INTEX Shanghai
Nov 10 -12	Wire Asia	INTEX Shanghai

Nov 14 -19	The 6th Int'l Welding & Cutting Fair (Beijing Essen Welding 2004)	Shanghai Everbright Convention & Exhibition Center
Nov 15 -18	The 64th National Electronic Fair	Shanghai New International Expo Center
Nov 16 -19	Bauma China	Shanghai New International Expo Center
Nov 25 - 28	China tourism Fair	Shanghai New International Expo Center
Nov 26 - 28	SuperStore China 2004	Shanghai Exhibition Center (SEC)
Nov 29 - Dec 2	Shanghai Int'l Advertising Printing Industrial Exhibition (Autumn)	INTEX Shanghai
Dec 11-13	China National Medicine Trade Fair	Shanghai New International Expo Center

SHANGHAI EXHIBITION CALENDAR   2005

Date	Exhibition	Location
Mar 8-11	WOODMAC CHINA 2005 Forestry and Woodworking Machinery and Supplies	INTEX & Shanghai Mart
Mar 8-11	FURNITEK CHINA 2005 Machinery and Accessories for Furniture Production, Upholstery and Furnishings	INTEX & Shanghai Mart
Mar 8-11	WOODBUILD CHINA 2005 Machinery & Supplies for Timber Construction	INTEX & Shanghai Mart
Jul 13 –16	PSC 2005 (Shanghai): The 6th International Exhibition on Rotating Equipment, Fluid, Gas & Air Handling Systems, Fluid Power and Control Systems & Instrumentation in China	Shanghai New International Expo Center
Jul 13-16	PUMPS & SYSTEMS CHINA 2005	Shanghai New International Expo Center
Jul 13-16	VALVES & PIPING CHINA 2005	Shanghai New International Expo Center
Jul 13-16	COMPRESSORS & SYSTEMS CHINA 2005	Shanghai New International Expo Center
Jul 13-16	FLUID POWER CHINA 2005	Shanghai New International Expo Center
Jul 13-16	CONTROL & INSTRUMENTATION CHINA 2005	Shanghai New International Expo Center
Jul 13-16	CHEMTEC CHINA 2005	Shanghai New International Expo Center
Jul 13-16	WATERTECH CHINA 2005	Shanghai New International Expo Center
Jul 13-16	ENVIROTEC CHINA 2005	Shanghai New International Expo Center

USEFUL HOTLINES

SERVICE	CONTACT NUMBER
Police	110
Local Telephone Number Enquiry	114
Domestic Long Distance Enquiry	116
Time Enquiry	117
Fire	119
Ambulance	120
Weather Forecast	121
Traffic Police	122
Post Code Enquiry	184
Emergency Mail	185

GOVERNMENT AGENCIES

MINISTRIES	CONTACT NUMBER
Foreign Economic Commission of Huangpu District, Shanghai	(86 21) 3313 4800
Shanghai Administration of Culture and Radio Broadcasting	(86 21) 6361 2556
Shanghai Administration of Labor and Social Insurance	(86 21) 6367 7216
Shanghai Agriculture Administration	(86 21) 6321 2810
Shanghai Audit Administration	(86 21) 6378 7200
Shanghai Civil Defense Commission	(86 21) 2402 8888
Shanghai Construction and Administration Committee	(86 21) 6443 1576
Shanghai Customs	(86 21) 6323 2410
Shanghai Development Planning Commission	(86 21) 6321 2810
Shanghai Development Research Center	(86 21) 6321 2810
Shanghai Economic Commission	(86 21) 6358 6666
Shanghai Economic Cooperation Office	(86 21) 6246 3539
Shanghai Education Commission	(86 21) 6256 3010
Shanghai Ethnic and Religion Commission	(86 21) 5289 1653
Shanghai Environmental Protection Administration	(86 21) 6226 0296
Shanghai Finance Administration	(86 21) 6271 6004
Shanghai Foreign Affairs General Office	(86 21) 6256 5900
Shanghai Foreign Economic Relations & Trade Commission	(86 21) 6275 2200
Shanghai Foreign Investment Board	(86 21) 6236 8800
Shanghai Forestry Administration	(86 21) 6485 5090
Shanghai Housing Development Board	(86 21) 6319 3188
Shanghai Health Administration	(86 21) 6275 8710
Shanghai Industrial & Commercial Administration (SICA)	(86 21) 6422 0000
Shanghai Informationalization General Office	(86 21) 6282 2266
Shanghai Intellectual Property Administration	(86 21) 5298 1809
Shanghai Medical Insurance Administration	(86 21) 6255 8001
Shanghai Municipal Engineering Administration Bureau	(86 21) 6507 9898
Shanghai News and Publication Administration	(86 21) 6437 0176
Shanghai Overseas Chinese Administration	(86 21) 6249 0880
Shanghai Personnel Administration	(86 21) 6404 5566
Shanghai Port Authority	(86 21) 6329 0660
Shanghai Public Safety Administration	(86 21) 2402 3456
Shanghai Science & Technology Commission	(86 21) 6439 3089
Shanghai Sports Administration	(86 21) 6327 5330
Shanghai Statistics Bureau	(86 21) 3511 0517
Shanghai Tourism Board	(86 21) 6439 0793
Shanghai Transportation Administration	(86 21) 5382 0733
Shanghai Urban Environment Administration	(86 21) 6247 3288
Shanghai Urban Planning Administration	(86 21) 6427 6246

Doing
Business in

FOREIGN EMBASSIES & CONSULATES

EMBASSY / CONSULATE	CONTACT NUMBER
Australia	(86 21) 6279 8098
Austria	(86 21) 6474 0268
Belgium	(86 21) 6437 6579
Brazil	(86 21) 6437 0110
Canada	(86 21) 6279 8400
Chile	(86 21) 6249 8000
Cuba	(86 21) 6275 3078
Czech Republic	(86 21) 6471 2410
Denmark	(86 21) 6209 0500
Finland	(86 21) 6474 0068
France	(86 21) 6437 7414
Germany	(86 21) 6433 6951
India	(86 21) 6275 8885
Iran	(86 21) 6281 4666
Israel	(86 21) 6209 8008
Italy	(86 21) 6471 6980
Japan	(86 21) 6278 0788
Korea	(86 21) 6219 6420
Mexico	(86 21) 6437 9585
Netherlands	(86 21) 6209 9076
New Zealand	(86 21) 6471 1127
Norway	(86 21) 6323 9988
Poland	(86 21) 6433 9228
Russia	(86 21) 6324 2682
Singapore	(86 21) 6437 0776
Sweden	(86 21) 6474 1311
Swiss	(86 21) 6270 0519
Thailand	(86 21) 6321 9371
Turkey	(86 21) 6474 6838
United Kingdom and Northern Ireland	(86 21) 6279 7650
United States of America	(86 21) 6433 6880
Yugoslavia	(86 21) 6208 1388

FOREIGN-CHINA BUSINESS ASSOCIATIONS

ASSOCIATION	CONTACT NUMBER
American Chamber of Commerce	(86 21) 6279 7119
AustCham Shanghai	(86 21) 6248 8301
Belgian Business Association	(86 21) 5879 1599
Benelux Business Association	(86 21) 3423 0084
British Chamber of Commerce	(86 21) 6219 8185
Canada China Business Council	(86 21) 6390 6790
Canadian Business Forum	(86 21) 6279 8400
China Australia Chamber of Commerce	(86 21) 6248 8301
China Britain Business Council	(86 21) 6218 5183
China-Italy Chamber of Commerce, Shanghai	(86 21) 3222 0891
ChinaLink Liverpool Chamber of Commerce	(86 21) 6323 7703
Danish Business Association	(86 21) 6219 2711
Delegation of German Industry & Commerce	(86 21) 6330 9791
Dutch Business Association	(86 21) 6437 6598
Finland Trade Centre	(86 21) 6471 0388
French Chamber of Commerce	(86 21) 6281 3618
French Trade Commission	(86 21) 5306 1100
German Centre of Industry & Trade	(86 21) 6501 5100
Hong Kong Chamber of Commerce	(86 21) 5306 9533
Hong Kong Trade Development Council	(86 21) 6352 3453
Italian Institute for Foreign Trade Shanghai	(86 21) 6248 8600
Japanese Chamber of Commerce	(86 21) 6275 2001
Russian Federation Chamber of Commerce	(86 21) 6228 1304
Shanghai-Japan Club for Commerce & Industry	(86 21) 6278 0416
Shanghai Singapore Business Association	(86 21) 6437 0511
Swedish Trade Council	(86 21) 6474 3533
US-China Business Council	(86 21) 6415 2579

AIRLINE OFFICES

FOREIGN AIRLINES IN CHINA

AIR CANADA   **CONTACT NUMBER**

Beijing	(86 10)	6468 2001
Shanghai	(86 21)	6279 2999
Hong Kong	(852)	2867 8111

AIR FRANCE

Beijing	(86 10)	6588 1388
Shanghai	(86 21)	6360 6688

AIR NEW ZEALAND

Hong Kong	(852)	2524 9041

ALITALIA

Beijing	(86 10)	6567 2299

ASIANA AIRWAYS

Beijing	(86 10)	6468 4000
Changchun	(86 431)	894 8948
Chengdu	(86 28)	8676 7518
Chongqing	(86 23)	6383 3908
Hangzhou	(86 571)	8577 3699
Harbin	(86 451)	234 4000
Hong Kong	(852)	2523 8585
Guangzhou	(86 20)	8760 9037
Guilin	(86 773)	588 4000
Nanjing	(86 25)	8689 3141
Shanghai	(86 21)	6219 4000
Shenyang	(86 10)	6468 4000
Tingji	(86 431)	894 8948
Xi'an	(86 29)	8879 3405
Yantai	(86 535)	662 8000

BRITISH AIRWAYS

Beijing	(86 10)	8511 6699

FINNAIR

Beijing	(86 10)	6512 7180
Shanghai	(86 21)	5292 9400
Hong Kong	(852)	2117 1238

GARUDA AIRLINES

Hong Kong	(852)	2840 0000
Shanghai	(86 21)	5385 5398

IRAN AIR

Beijing	(86 10)	6512 0047

JAPAN AIRLINES

Beijing	(86 10)	6513 0888
Guangzhou	(86 20)	8669 6688
Hong Kong	(852)	2523 0081
Kunming	(86 871)	315 8000
Qingdao	(86 532)	571 0088
Shanghai	(86 21)	6288 3000
Tianjin	(86 22)	2313 9766
Xiamen	(86 592)	268 7777
Xi'an	(86 800)	810 6663

LUFTHANSA

Beijing	(86 10)	6465 4488
Shanghai	(86 21)	5830 4400

MALAYSIA AIRLINES

Beijing	(86 10)	6505 2681
Guangzhou	(86 20)	8335 8828
Hong Kong	(852)	2521 8181
Shanghai	(86 21)	6279 8607
Xiamen	(86 592)	210 8388

PAKISTAN INTERNATIONAL

Beijing	(86 10)	6505 1681

PHILIPPINES AIRLINES

Hong Kong	(852)	2301 9300
Xiamen	(86 592)	239 4729

QANTAS

Beijing	(86 10)	6467 3337
Shanghai	(86 21)	6279 8660

ROYAL BRUNEI AIRLINES

Beijing	(86 10)	6465 1625
	(86 10)	6465 1576
Guangzhou	(86 20)	8612 3962
Shanghai	(86 21)	5298 6688

SINGAPORE AIRLINES

Beijing	(86 10)	6505 2233
Guangzhou	(86 20)	8732 0600
Shanghai	(86 21)	6289 1000

THAI AIRLINES

Shanghai	(86 21)	5298 5555

VIRGIN ATLANTIC AIRWAYS

Shanghai	(86 21)	5353 4600

CHINESE AIRLINES OFFICES

AIR CHINA — CONTACT NUMBER

Beihai	(86 779)	305 3468
Beijing	(86 10)	6601 6667
Changsha	(86 731)	225 3354
Chengdu	(86 28)	8665 6317
Dalian	(86 411)	480 1159
Fuzhou	(86 591)	760 4867
Guangzhou	(86 20)	8363 7523
Guilin	(86 773)	281 2789
Haikou	(86 898)	6672 5086
Harbin	(86 451)	233 4603
Kunming	(86 871)	315 9165
Nanjing	(86 25)	481 8747
Qingdao	(86 532)	388 3650
Shanghai	(86 21)	5239 7227
Shenyang	(86 24)	2318 0409
Shenzhen	(86 755)	8377 9948
Urumqi	(86 991)	588 1775
Wuhan	(86 27)	8361 8666
Xiamen	(86 592)	508 4377
Xi'an	(86 29)	870 9689
Yantai	(860 535)	628 5744

AIR MACAU

Beijing	(86 10)	6515 8988
Guilin	(86 773)	286 5400
Haikou	(86 898)	6853 3269
Kunming	(86 871)	716 7378
Nanjing	(86 25)	679 9127
Shanghai	(86 21)	6248 1110
Xiamen	(86 592)	222 9260

CHINA NORTHERN AIRLINES

Anshan	(86 412)	223 5817
Changchun	(86 431)	272 5001
Dalian	(86 411)	761 9290
Harbin	(86 451)	362 5521
Sanya	(86 898)	8827 7580

Shenyang   (86 24)   2324 4137

CHINA SOUTHERN AIRLINES

Beijing	(86 10)	6459 0539
Chengdu	(86 28)	671 2777
Guangzhou	(86 20)	8613 0870
Hainan	(86 898)	6671 9742
Hubei	(86 27)	8530 0477
Hunan	(86 731)	455 7095
Shanghai	(86 21)	6211 3604
Shenzhen	(86 755)	605 6081

CHINA YUNNAN AIRLINES

Yunnan   (86 871)   711 2638

NORTHWEST CHINA AIRLINES

Shaanxi   (86 29)   8879 2299

SHANGHAI AIRLINES

Beijing	(86 10)	6606 1260
Chengdu	(86 28)	8612 7000
Chongqing	(86 23)	6362 8000
Fuzhou	(86 591)	330 0721
Guangzhou	(86 20)	8666 8800
Guilin	(86 773)	282 7046
Haikou	(86 898)	6679 1927
Hangzhou	(86 571)	8511 9528
Harbin	(86 451)	8263 7953
Kunming	(86 871)	313 8502
Nanjing	(86 25)	8449 9757
Macau	(86 853)	787 877
Qingdao	(86 532)	572 5519
Sanya	(86 898)	8826 5322
Shanghai		
• No. 212 Jiangning Road	(86 21)	6255 0550
• No. 90 South Shanxi Road	(86 21)	5403 0954
• No. 88 Bing Lanxi Road	(86 21)	6216 3557
• No. 1465 South Pudong Road	(86 21)	5831 9090
Shenyang	(86 24)	2323 5858

Shenzhen	(86 755)	8324 1431
Taiyuan	(86 351)	413 9910
Wuhan	(86 27)	8224 1008
Xiamen	(86 592)	221 0600
Xi'an	(86 29)	426 1630

SHANDONG AIRLINES

Jinan	(86 531)	691 6737
Shandong	(86 531)	873 0777
Qingdao	(86 532)	575 5658

SOUTHWEST CHINA AIRLINE

| Chengdu | (86 28) | 8666 8080 |

XIAMEN AIRLINES

| Xiamen | (86 592) | 573 9888 |

HOTELS

NAME OF HOTEL	ADDRESS	TELEPHONE
Sheraton Grand Tai Ping Yang Hotel Shanghai	5 Zunyi South Road Shanghai 200336	(86 21) 6275 8888 (86 21) 6275 5420
Crowne Plaza Shanghai	400 Panyu Road	(86 21) 6280 8888
Shanghai Jinjiang Tower	161 Changle Road	(86 21) 6415 1188
Portman Ritz Carlton Shanghai	Shanghai Center, 1376 Nanjing West Road, Shanghai 200040	(86 21) 6279 8888 (86 21) 6279 8800
Pudong Shangri-La	33, Fu Cheng Road, Pudong New Area	(86 21) 6322 3855
Hilton Shanghai	250 Huashan Road Shanghai 200040	(86 21) 6248 0000
Huating Sheraton Hotel Shanghai	1200 Caoxi North Road	(86 21) 6439 1000
Okura Garden Hotel Shanghai	58 South Maoming Road, Shanghai	(86 21) 6415 1111
Xinya Tangchen Hotel Shanghai	777 Zhangyang Road, Pudong New District, Shanghai	(86 21) 5831 8888
Shanghai JC Mandarin	1225 Nanjing West Road, Shanghai	(86 21) 6279 1888
Howard Johnson Plaza Hotel	595 Jiu Jiang Road Shanghai 200001	(86 21) 3314 4888
Regal International East Asia Hotel	516 Hengshan Road, Shanghai 200030	(86 21) 6415 5588
The St. Regis Shanghai	889 Dongfang Road, Pudong District, Shanghai 200122 China	(86 21) 6322 3855
Sofitel Jinjiang Oriental	889 Yanggao South Road, Pudong, Shanghai	(86 21) 5050 4888
Purple Mountain Hotel	778 Dongfang Road, Pudong Shanghai	(86 21) 6322 3855

★★★★

NAME OF HOTEL	ADDRESS	TELEPHONE
Galaxy Hotel	888 West Zhongshan Road	(86 21) 6275 5888
Jianguo Hotel Shanghai	North Caoxi Road, Xuhui District	(86 21) 6439 9299
Rainbow Hotel Shanghai	2000 West Yan'an Road	(86 21) 6275 3388
Jinjiang Hotel	59 South Mao Ming Road	(86 21) 6258 2582
Courtyard Shanghai	838 Dongfang Road Pudong	(86 21) 6886 7886
Jing'an Hotel	370 Huashan Road, Jing'an District	(86 21) 6248 1888
Yangtze Hotel	740 Hankou Road	(86 21) 6351 7880
Peace Hotel	20 East Nanjing Road	(86 21) 6321 6888
Hotel Sofitel Hyland Shanghai	505 East Nanjing Road	(86 21) 6351 5888
Shanghai Mansion	20 North Suzhou Road	(86 21) 6324 6260
Shanghai Worldfield Convention Hotel	2106 Hong Qiao Road, Shanghai	(86 21) 6270 3388
Park Hotel	170 West Nanjing Road, Huangpu District, Shanghai	(86 21) 6327 5225
Shanghai International Equatorial Hotel	65 West Yan'an Road, Jing'an District, Shanghai	(86 21) 6248 1688
Radisson SAS Lansheng Hotel Shanghai	1000 Quyang Road, Shanghai	(86 21) 6542 8000
Ocean Hotel Shanghai	370 Huashan Road, Shanghai	(86 21) 6248 1888
Hotel Nikko, Pudong Shanghai	969 Dongfang Road, Pudong	(86 21) 6322 3855
Bao Steel Group Baoshan Hotel	1813 Mudanjiang Road, Shanghai	(86 21) 5669 8888
Ramada Pudong Airport Shanghai	1100 Qihang Road, Pudong Shanghai	(86 21) 6322 3855
Renaissance Yangtze Shanghai Hotel	2099 Yan An West Road, Shanghai	(86 21) 6322 3855

NAME OF HOTEL	ADDRESS	TELEPHONE
City Hotel Shanghai	5-7 South Shaanxi Road, Luwan District Shanghai	(86 21) 6255 1133
Donghu Hotel	70 Donghu Road	(86 21) 6415 8158
Huaxia Hotel	38 Caobin Road	(86 21) 6436 0100

★★★

Shanghai Hengshan Hotel	534 Hengshan Road	(86 21) 6437 7050
Longhua Hotel Shanghai	2787 Longhua Road	(86 21) 6457 0570
Shanghai Pacific Hotel	108 Nanjing Road West, Shanghai	(86 21) 6327 6226
Novotel Hotel Yuanlin	201 Bai Se Road, Shanghai	(86 21) 6470 1688
Pine City Hotel	777 Zha Jia Bang Road, Shanghai	(86 21) 6443 3888

BANKS

ABN AMRO BANK
20 Zhongshan Dongyi Lu, Shanghai 200002, China
Tel: (86 21) 6329 9303   Fax: (86 21) 6329 5199

AMERICAN EXPRESS
Shanghai Rep Office Room 206, Retail Plaza, Shanghai Centre, 1376 Nanjing Xi Lu,Shanghai 200040, China
Tel: (86 21) 6279 8082   Fax: (86 21) 6279 7183

AUSTRALIA & NEW ZEALAND BANKING GROUP LTD
10/F, Novel Plaza, 116-128 Nanjing Xi Lu Shanghai 200003, China
Tel: (86 21) 6350 9599   Fax: (86 21) 6350 9590

BANGKOK BANK
7 Zhongshan Dong Yi Lu, Shanghai 200002, China
Tel: (86 21) 6323 3788   Fax: (86 21) 6323 5400

BANK OF AMERICA NT & SA
Room 104-107A, Union Bldg,100 Yanan Dong Lu,Shanghai 200002, China
Tel: (86 21) 6329 2828   Fax: (86 21) 6320 1297

BANK OF CHINA
23 Zhongshan Dong Yi Lu,Shanghai 200002, China
Tel: (86 21) 6472 9268   Fax: (86 21) 6472 9384

BANK OF CHINA SHANGHAI TRUST & CONSULTANCY CO.
10, Lane 18, Gaoan Lu, Shanghai 200030, China
Tel: (86 21) 6433 3088   Fax: (86 21) 6474 6278

BANK OF EAST ASIA LTD
299 Sichuan Zhong Lu,Shanghai 200002, China
Tel: (86 21) 6329 7338   Fax: (86 21) 6329 1813

BANK OF COMMUNICATIONS
200 Jiangxi Zhong Lu,Shanghai 200002, China
Tel: (86 21) 6321 3400   Fax: (86 21) 6321 9823

BANK OF NEW YORK
Room 503, Dynasty Business Centre, 457 Wulumuqi Bei Lu,Shanghai 200040, China
Tel: (86 21) 6249 4110   Fax: (86 21) 6249 4112

BANK OF TOKYO LTD
Room 1207, Ruijin Bldg,205 Maoming Nan Lu,Shanghai 200020, China
Tel: (86 21) 6472 3166   Fax: (86 21) 6472 7540

CITIC INDUSTRIAL BANK

16/F, Union Bldg,100 Yanan Dong Lu,Shanghai 200002, China
Tel: (86 21) 6320 3089   Fax: (86 21) 6320 1728

CHEMICAL BANK

Shanghai Rep Ofc Suite 700A, Shanghai Centre,1376 Nanjing Xi Lu,
Shanghai 200040, China
Tel: (86 21) 6279 7288   Fax: (86 21) 6279 8101

CHINA INVESTMENT BANK

200 Huaihai Zhong Lu,Shanghai 200021, China
Tel: (86 21) 6318 1818   Fax: (86 21) 6327 1460

CITIBANK

NA 5/F, Union Bldg,100 Yanan Dong Lu,Shanghai 200002, China
Tel: (86 21) 6328 9661   Fax: (86 21) 6373 1317

COMMONWEALTH BANK OF AUSTRALIA

Shanghai Rep Ofc Room 805, Shanghai Union Bldg,100 Yanan Dong
Lu,Shanghai 200002, China
Tel: (86 21) 6355 3939   Fax: (86 21) 6373 5066

CREDIT LYONNAIS

6/F, Central Place, 16 Henan Nan Lu,Shanghai 200002, China
Tel: (86 21) 6355 0070   Fax: (86 21) 6355 0071

CREDIT SUISSE FIRST BOSTON 1

1/F, Shartex Plaza,88 Zunyi Nan Lu,Shanghai 200335, China
Tel: (86 21) 6219 0808   Fax: (86 21) 6219 0454

HANG SENG BANK LTD

Room 1301, Ruijin Bldg,205 Maoming Nan Lu,Shanghai 200020, China
Tel: (86 21) 6472 8781   Fax: (86 21) 6472 8776

HANIL BANK

Room 2302, Shanghai Int'l Trade Centre,2200 Yanan Xi Lu,Shanghai 200335,
China
Tel: (86 21) 6219 0606   Fax: (86 21) 6219 5543

HYPO-BANK

Shanghai Rep Ofc Suite 356, Shanghai Centre,1376 Nanjing Xi Lu,
Shanghai 200040, China
Tel: (86 21) 6279 8549   Fax: (86 21) 6279 7268

ING BANK

2/F, Central Place,16 Henan Nan Lu,Shanghai 200002, China
Tel: (86 21) 6355 6006   Fax: (86 21) 6355 7005

INDUSTRIAL & COMMERCIAL BANK OF CHINA PUDONG BRANCH
2024 Pudong Nan Lu, Pudong,Shanghai 200122, China
Tel: (86 21) 5878 8280   Fax: (86 21) 5884 0579

METROBANK SHANGHAI
3/F, Shenmao Bldg,3-3900 Lane, Hongmei Lu,Shanghai 200335, China
Tel: (86 21) 6219 2020   Fax: (86 21) 6219 5208

MITSUBISHI BANK LTD
Room 2107, Ruijin Bldg,205 Maoming Nan Lu,Shanghai 200020, China
Tel: (86 21) 6472 0882

MITSUBISHI TRUST & BANKING CORP.
Shanghai Rep Ofc Room 2404, Ruijin Bldg,205 Maoming Nan Lu,
Shanghai 200020, China
Tel: (86 21) 6472 3963   Fax: (86 21) 6472 3965

NATIONAL WESTMINSTER BANK
Room 708, Shanghai Centre,1367 Nanjing Xi Lu,Shanghai 200040, China
Tel: (86 21) 6279 8804   Fax: (86 21) 6279 8491

OVERSEAS-CHINESE BANKING CORP. LTD
120 Jiujiang Lu,Shanghai 200002, China
Tel: (86 21) 6323 3888   Fax: (86 21) 6329 0888

PEOPLE'S BANK OF CHINA
18 Lujiazui Lu,Shanghai 200120, China
Tel: (86 21) 5884 5015   Fax: (86 21) 5884 5066

ROYAL BANK OF CANADA
Room 403,100 Yanan Dong Lu,Shanghai 200002, China
Tel: (86 21) 6320 2823   Fax: (86 21) 6320 0417

SAKURA BANK LTD
5/F, Ruijin Bldg,205 Maoming Nan Lu,Shanghai 200020, China
Tel: (86 21) 6472 3656   Fax: (86 21) 6472 0867

STANDARD CHARTERED BANK
Level 7, Shanghai Centre,1376 Nanjing Xi Lu,Shanghai 200040, China
Tel: (86 21) 6326 4820   Fax: (86 21) 6279 8813

SWISS BANK CORP.
Shanghai Rep Ofc 812-813, Shanghai ITC,2200 Yanan Dong Lu,
Shanghai 200335, China
Tel: (86 21) 6219 9208   Fax: (86 21) 6219 9188

THE HONG KONG & SHANGHAI BANKING CORP. LTD

6/F, Fu Tai Mansion,104 Huqiu Lu,Shanghai 200002, China
Tel: (86 21) 6321 8383   Fax: (86 21) 6329 1659

TOKAI BANK LTD

Room 750, Shanghai Centre,1376 Nanjing Xi Lu, Shanghai 200040, China
Tel: (86 21) 6279 8811   Fax: (86 21) 6279 8833

TOYO TRUST & BANKING CO.

Room 1901,205 Maoming Nan Lu, Shanghai 200020, China
Tel: (86 21) 6472 9554   Fax: (86 21) 6472 9554

UNION BANK OF SWITZERLAND

Room 1904, Union Bldg,100 Yanan Dong Lu, Shanghai 200002, China
Tel: (86 21) 6329 1438   Fax: (86 21) 6329 4422

WESTDEUTSCHE LANDESBANK

Shanghai Rep Ofc Room 2301, Rui Jin Bldg,205 Maoming Nan Lu,
Shanghai 200020, China
Tel: (86 21) 6472 1380

RESTAURANTS

THE TANDOOR-SHANGHAI
Food Street, Jin Jiang Hotel, 59 Mao Ming Road (S).   Tel: (86 21) 6472 5494
Shanghai

THE TANDOOR-BEIJING
1st Floor, Great Dragon (Zhaolong) Hotel, 2 Workers'   Tel: (86 10) 6597 2211
Stadium Road (N), Beijing

THE TANDOOR-CHENGDU
Sunjoy Inn, No.34, Section 4, Ren Ming Nan Lu,   Tel: (86 28) 8555 1958
Chengdu

THE SPICE MARKET
West Building, Somerset Grand Shanghai,   Tel: (86 21) 6384 6838
8 Ji Nan Road, Shanghai

SAN FRANCISCO STEAKHOUSE
Unit 8, 7/F, Super Brand Mall, 168 Lujiazui Xi Lu,   Tel: (86 21) 5047 3377
by Yin Cheng Xi Lu, Pudong, Shanghai

M ON THE BUND
7/F, 20 Guangdong Lu, by Zhongshan Dong Yi Lu,   Tel: (86 21) 6249 3195
Huangpu District, Shanghai

DA MARCO
62 Yan dang Lu, by Huai Hai Zhong Lu, Luwan District,   Tel: (86 21) 6385 5998
Shanghai

LA SEINE
8 Ji Nan Lu, by Taicang Lu, Luwan District, Shanghai   Tel: (86 21) 6384 3722

SHINTORI NULL II
803 Ju Lu Lu, By Fu Min Lu, Jing'an District, Shanghai   Tel: (86 21) 5404 5252

ELEMENT FRESH
Rm 112, Shanghai Center, 1376 Nanjing Xi Lu, Jing'an   Tel: (86 21) 6279 8682
District, Shanghai

EDUCATION

DULWICH COLLEGE INTERNATIONAL SCHOOL
425 Lan An Rd, Jin Qiao, Pudong, Shanghai 201206   Tel: (86 21) 5899 3785

SHANGHAI COMMUNITY INTERNATIONAL SCHOOLS (SCIS)
No.79, Lane 261, Jiangsu Road, Changning, Shanghai   Tel: (86 21) 6252 3688

CONCORDIA INTERNATIONAL SCHOOL SHANGHAI
999 Mingyue Road., Pudong, Shanghai   Tel: (86 21) 5899 0380

L'ECOLE FRANCAISE DE SHANGHAI
New Rainbow Asia Garden A8, 1655 Hu Qing Ping   Tel: (86 21) 5976 3431
Gong Lu, Shanghai

SIS - SHANGHAI INTERNATIONAL SCHOOL
11 Shuicheng Road, Shanghai   Tel: (86 21) 6242 3243

THE JAPANESE SCHOOL IN HONGQIAO
3185 Hongmei Lu, Shanghai   Tel: (86 21) 6401 2747

SHANGHAI SINGAPORE INTERNATIONAL SCHOOL
288 Jidi Road, Zhu Di Town, Minhang District, Shanghai   Tel: (86 21) 6221 9288

THE BRITISH INTERNATIONAL SCHOOL SHANGHAI
600 Cambridge Forest New Town, 2729 Hunan Road,   Tel: (86 21) 5812 7455
Shanghai

MEDICAL/ DENTAL

CIDI DENTAL CLINIC
西　典　齒　科

Professional Dental Care

Business Hours: Mon - Sun
9:30AM - 5:30PM
Evening service 6247-0709
to make a reservation during daytime
#495, Jiang Ning Lu, 200041

江宁路495号

tel: 86-21 6247-0709　fax: 86-21 6247-0757
http: www.cididental.com　email: dentist@cididental.com

HUASHAN WORLDWIDE MEDICAL CENTER (HWMC)

No.12 Wulumuqi Zhong Lu, Shanghai

Tel: (86 21) 6248 3986

**INTERNATIONAL MEDICAL CARE CENTER SHANGHAI JIAOTONG UNIVERSITY
AFFILIATED FIRST PEOPLE'S HOSPITAL (IMCG)**

585, Jiulong Lu, Shanghai

Tel: (86 21) 6324 3852

SHANGHAI GUANGCI HOSPITAL

197 Ruijin Er Lu, Shanghai

Tel: (86 21) 6466 4483

SHANGHAI CONCORD MEDICAL SPECIALISTS CLINIC

6/F, Jin Tai Office Building, 58 Mao Ming Nan Lu, Shanghai

Tel: (86 21) 5465 5001

WORLD LINK MEDICAL CENTER

Room 203, West Tower, Shanghai Center   Tel: (86 21) 6279 7688
(Portman Hotel), 1376 Nanjing Xi Lu, Shanghai

NEW PIONEER INTERNATIONAL MEDICAL CENTER (NPIMC)

2/F, Geru Building, 910 Hengshan Lu,   Tel: (86 21) 6407 0434
Xujiahui District, Shanghai

HUADONG HOSPITAL

221 Yan An Xi Road, Pudong, Shanghai   Tel: (86 21) 6248 4867

REAL ESTATE/ DEVELOPERS

SHANGHAI HENGHE REAL ESTATE CO., LTD

11th F, No. 339, Le du Road, Songjiang District, Tel: (86 21) 6781 2500
Shanghai

NINGBO HENGLONG REAL ESTATE

Room H 5th Floor, Construction Building, 212 Tel: (86 21) 6781 2500
Jie Fang South Road, Ningbo, Zhejiang

HANGZHOU SHENG SHI YI CAI ENTERTAINMENT CO., LTD (GOLF PROJECT)

1st floor, Farm Building, Pingshan Farm, Changle town, Tel: (86 21) 6781 2500
Yuhang District, Hangzhou, Zhejiang

DTZ DEBENHAM TIE LEUNG SHANGHAI

27th Floor, South Tower, Hong Kong Plaza, 283 Tel: (86 21) 5306 1383
Huaihai Zhong Road, Shanghai 200021, China

COLLIERS INTERNATIONAL SHANGHAI

1881 City Center Tower B100 Zun Yi Road Tel: (86 21) 6237 0088
Shanghai 200051

LUJIAZUI REAL ESTATE

No.818, Dongfang Rd., 13/F Zhongcheng Building, Tel: (86 21) 5820 0880
Pudong Shanghai

SIIC DEVELOPMENT LTD. (SHANGHAI)

1c, 38 Caoxi North Road, Shanghai 200030, China Tel: (86 21) 6487 9077

SHANGHAI FORTUNE WORLD DEVELOPMENT CO., LTD

Shanghai Pudong New District Dongfang Rd. Tel: (86 21) 5886 2888
No. 1369

SHANGHAI FORTUNE WORLD DEVELOPMENT CO., LTD

Shanghai Pudong New District Dongfang Rd. No. 1369 Tel: (86 21) 5886 2888

SHANGHAI JIA XIN REAL ESTATEDEVELOPMENT CO., LTD.

Rm. 504-507, Zhong Nan Building, 158 Puhuitang Rd., Tel: (86 21) 6468 8809
Shanghai

SHANGHAI BAILAOHUI PROPERTY DEVELOPMENT CO., LTD

7F/617 Zhongshan North Rd, Tel: (86 21) 6318 7728

SHANGHAI SANBAO REAL ESTATE CO., LTD
B, No 627, Yongjia Rd, Shanghai 200031, China   Tel: (86 21) 6433 0565
Shanghai 200010, China

FULLHOME REAL ESTATE (SHANGHAI OFFICE)
Unit 902, Huaxia Bank Tower, No. 256 Pudong Road South, Shanghai 200120
Tel: (86 21) 5115 0666   Fax: (86 21) 6886 5060

FULLHOME REAL ESTATE (BEIJING OFFICE)
Unit 1500, China Travel Service Tower, No.2 Beisanhuan East Road,
Beijing 100028
Tel: (86 10) 8448 0157   Fax: (86 10) 6462 4510

COURIER SERVICES

NAME	CONTACT NUMBER
DHL-Sinotrans Int'l Air Courier	(86 21) 6536 2900
DZL	(86 21) 6256 9636
FedEx Shanghai	(86 21) 6275 0808
Global Express Service	(86 21) 6355 1915
Shanghai Hengda Air Cargo Group	(86 21) 5270 5555
Sunsir Express Co Ltd	(86 21) 6240 5511
TNT Skypack-Sinotrans Ltd	(86 21) 6421 1111
Shanghai Express	(86 21) 6459 1777
Shanghai Aviation Express	(86 21) 6268 8657
Post Express	(86 21) 6540 0000
COSCO Express	(86 21) 6268 4288
Mitex International	(86 21) 6294 8835

EXECUTIVE SEARCH

NAME	CONTACT NUMBER
Andersen Consulting	(86 21) 6391 5588
Asia Pacific Management Institute	(86 21) 3878 4882
Bo Le Associates Ltd	(86 21) 5396 6686
China Human Resources Group	(86 21) 6317 9979
Dayu Job Consulting	(86 21) 6428 5063
EMDS Shanghai Office	(86 21) 5257 4104
Eve Business Consulting	(86 21) 6876 6568
Gainful Consulting	(86 21) 6270 0400
Hewitt Consulting Co. Ltd.	(86 21) 6451 5230
Join – Link Consulting Ltd	(86 21) 6322 3767
LEK Consulting LLC	(86 21) 6272 8200
Manpower Business Consulting	(86 21) 6875 2897
Nicholson International	(86 21) 6364 8895
Norman Broadbent International	(86 21) 6279 8575
Oasis Executive Searching Group	(86 21) 6286 1992
Pudong Human Resource	(86 21) 6854 1246
Russell Reynolds Services	(86 21) 6445 0955
Shanghai China Human Resources Market	(86 21) 5887 6116
Shanghai Director & Manager Resources Company	(86 21) 6233 8413
Shanghai Fortune Consultant	(86 21) 6240 2111
Shanghai Human Resources Co. Ltd.	(86 21) 6277 4770
Shanghai Int'l Multisearch Company	(86 21) 5215 0010
Shanghai Zhiying Commercial Consulting Co., Ltd.	(86 21) 5404 3205
TMP Worldwide eResourcing	(86 21) 2890 3230
Wang & Li Asia Resources Online	(86 21) 6217 5626
Watson Wyatt Consultancy	(86 21) 5298 6888

INDUSTRIAL PARKS IN SHANGHAI

Caohejing High Tech Park

Caohejing High Tech Park, established in 1991, is a state-level economic & technological development zone as well as a high-tech park. It is the only development zone in China to enjoy the preferential policy of being both an economic & technological zone, and a high-tech park. Currently, the main industries in the park are namely microelectronics, photoelectronics, computer software and new materials, forming the four centres: Research & Development, Network Operations, Financial Data and Technology & Innovation.

Address: 17F Technology Building, 900 Yishan Road, Shanghai, China
Post Code: 200233
Tel: (86 21) 485 0000
Fax: (86 21) 485 0523
E-mail: webmaster@caohejing.com
Website: www.caohejing.com

Minhang Economic & Technological Development Zone

Established in 1983, Minhang Economic & Technological Development Zone was among the first 14 state-level development zones in China designated by the State Council in 1986. Topping the list among other development zones in six major economic indices, the Minhang Development Zone has set a successful example of mature development zones in China.

Address: 1251 Jiangchuan Road, Minhang Development Zone, Shanghai, China
Post Code: 200245
Tel: (86 21) 6430 0888
Fax: (86 21) 6430 0789
E-mail: smudc@online.sh.cn
Website: www.smudc.com

Jinqiao Export Processing Zone

Jinqiao Export Processing Zone, located in the centre of Pudong New District, was approved in 1990 and enjoys the same preferential policies as those state-level economic and technological zones. The four pillar industries in the JEPZ include information electronics, automobile and its components, modern household electric appliances and biological medicines.

Address: 28 Jinqiao Road, Pudong New District, Shanghai, China
Post Code: 201206
Tel: (86 21) 5899 1818/ 1951
Fax: (86 21) 5899 1812
Website: www.pdjq.com/introduce/introg.htm

Waigaoqiao Free Trade Zone

Waigaoqiao Free Trade Zone is the country's biggest and oldest free trade zone approved by the State Council in June 1990. It incorporates various functions including free trade, export processing, and logistic warehousing and bonded commodities displaying.

Address: 2 Huajing Road, Waigaoqiao, Pudong New District, Shanghai, China
Post Code: 201204
Tel: (86 21) 5046 1100
Fax: (86 21) 5046 1441
Website: www.china-ftz.com

Zhangjiang High-Tech Park

The Zhangjiang High Tech Park was established in July of 1992 as a state-level park designated for the development of new and high technology. The Park's two leading industries are information technology and modern biotechnology and pharmaceuticals, and its principal focus is to develop innovation and entrepreneurship.

Address: 200 Longdong Avenue, Pudong New District, Shanghai, China
Post Code: 201204
Tel: (86 21) 5080 1818
Fax: (86 21) 5080 0686
E-mail: zjpark@zjpark.com
Website: www.zjpark.com

Songjiang State-Level Export Processing Zone

Songjiang State-level Export Processing Zone SJEPZ was approved on 27 April 2000 by the State Council for its establishment. It is the very first state-level export processing zones in China and presently is the only one in Shanghai area.

Address: 81 Rongle East Road, Songjiang, Shanghai, China
Post Code: 201613
Tel: (86 21) 5774 1102
Fax: (86 21) 5774 3188
E-mail: sjiz@public.sta.net.cn
Website: www.sjepz.com

Shanghai Chemical Industrial Park

Shanghai Chemical Industrial Park SCIP is one of four key industrial bases designated by the municipal government to develop petrochemical industries. With registered capital of RMB 2.16 billion USD 260 million, the SCIP Development Corporation is the sole developer of this mega project.

Shanghai Chemical Industrial Park Development Co. Ltd.
Address: 10, Lane 18, Goaan Road, Shanghai, P.R. China 200030
Tel: (86 21) 64713298
Fax: (86 21) 64713301
Email: webmaster@scip-cn.com
Website: www.scip-cn.com

Hongqiao Economic and Technological Development Zone

Initially established in 1983, the Hongqiao Economic and Technological Development Zone HQETDZ is a new commercial and business zone in Shanghai that combines office and exhibition facilities, residential area, restaurants and shopping centers.

Shanghai Hongqiao Economic and Technological Development Zone United Development Co., Ltd

Address: 34-35th Flr, New Town Center, 83 Loushanguan Road, Shanghai, P. R. China 200336
Tel: (86 21) 62756888
Fax: (86 21) 62194505
Website: www.shudc.com

Qingpu Industrial Zone

The Qingpu Industrial Zone QPIZ is divided into five industrial clusters, namely, IT, biopharmaceuticals, high-tech materials, precision machinery, green food and packaging. The QPIZ is one of only two incubation bases for high-tech achievements in Shanghai; the other being Zhangjiang in Pudong New District.

The Development Corporation of Qingpu Industrial Zone

Address: 5500 Waiqingsong Highway, Qingpu District, Shanghai, P.R. China 201700
Tel: (86 21) 59724619
Fax: (86 21) 59722856
Email: sqpiz@sqpiz.com
Website: www.greenin.com.cn

Shanghai Software Development Park

The Shanghai Software Development Park SHSDP comprises three parks – Pudong Software Park located in Zhangjiang High-Tech Park, Fudan Software Development Center, and SJTU Shanghai Jiaotong University Caohejing Software Park. The establishing of the SHSDP is aimed at boosting Shanghai's Capacity in software development. It is estimated that by 2005, the turnover of the industry in Shanghai will be at least RMB 50 billion USD 6.04 billion and exports will reach USD 400 million.

Shanghai Pudong Software Development Park Co. Ltd.

Address: Zhangjiang High-Tech Park, Pudong New District, Shanghai, P.R. China 201203
Tel: (86 21) 38954510
Email: spsp@public.sta.net.cn
Website: www.spsp.com.cn

Shanghai Jiaotong University Scientific Development and Cooperation Park

Haoran Scientific Building, Shanghai Joatong University

上
海

S
H
A
N
G
H
A
I

Address: 1954 Huashan Road, Xuhui District, Shanghai, P.R. China 200030
Tel: (86 21) 62932047, 62932048
Fax: (86 21) 62932451
Email: kaifa@mail.sjtu.edu.cn
Website: www.kejichu.sjtu.edu.cn

Fudan University Science Park

Address: Fudan University Science Park Investment Service Center, 139 Handan
Road, Shanghai, P.R. China 200437
Tel: (86 21) 65311017
Fax: (86 21) 65448060
Email: xcqian@fudan.edu.cn
Website: 202.120.224.90/xiaochan/web/kejiyuan.htm

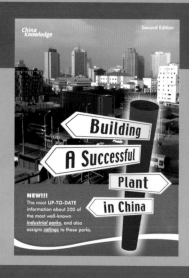
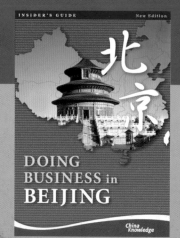